Islam and the Challenge of Human Rights

Islam and the Challenge of Human Rights

ABDULAZIZ SACHEDINA

OXFORD
UNIVERSITY PRESS
2009

OXFORD
UNIVERSITY PRESS

Oxford University Press, Inc., publishes works that further
Oxford University's objective of excellence
in research, scholarship, and education.

Oxford New York
Auckland Cape Town Dar es Salaam Hong Kong Karachi
Kuala Lumpur Madrid Melbourne Mexico City Nairobi
New Delhi Shanghai Taipei Toronto

With offices in
Argentina Austria Brazil Chile Czech Republic France Greece
Guatemala Hungary Italy Japan Poland Portugal Singapore
South Korea Switzerland Thailand Turkey Ukraine Vietnam

Published by Oxford University Press, Inc.
198 Madison Avenue, New York, New York 10016

www.oup.com

Library of Congress Cataloging-in-Publication Data

Sachedina, Abdulaziz Abdulhussein, 1942–
Islam and human rights / Abdulaziz Sachedina.
p. cm.
Includes bibliographical references.
ISBN 978-0-19-538842-8
1. Human rights—Religious aspects—Islam. 2. Islam and humanism.
I. Title. BP173.44.S235 2009
297.2′72—dc22 2009007220

The Edward Cadbury Lectures, 2005
University of Birmingham, U.K.

Project funded by
Carnegie Corporation of New York

9 8 7 6 5 4 3 2 1

Printed in the United States of America
on acid-free paper

To Farid Ud-din Akanni-Batts (d. 1995)

My student and friend, a conscientious African American student leader who inspired me and others at the University of Virginia with his exemplary demonstration of what it means to have a dignity and spirituality that leads one to stand firm against all odds to make a difference in the world of discrimination and violation of human rights.

Foreword

David Little, Harvard Divinity School

The human rights revolution, prompted by the devastating effects of fascism and inaugurated by the adoption of the Universal Declaration of Human Rights after World War II, represented, then and now, a challenge not only to the international political and legal order but also to many philosophical and theological assumptions. The idea, clearly espoused in the declaration, that "all peoples and all nations" and "every individual and every organ of society" would be held morally and legally accountable to a set of "fundamental rights and freedoms," "without distinction of any kind, such as race, color, sex, language, religion, political or other opinion [or] national or social origin," bore radical implications. Just as governments might no longer treat their citizens in any way they saw fit, so, according to a subsequent covenant, any pronouncement in the name of one or another religion, philosophy, or ideology that "constitutes incitement" to acts of discrimination or violence, understood as violations of said rights and freedoms, "shall be prohibited by law."

As such, the subject of human rights has been the source of continuing disagreement and debate among religious and nonreligious advocates of one kind or another. One reason is because the fundamental rights and freedoms enumerated in the Universal Declaration and its progeny constrain action on grounds that need not depend for their authority on "comprehensive doctrines," religious or otherwise. A comprehensive doctrine is a religious or philosophical system encompassing major aspects of human aspiration and behavior under a conception of ultimate values and ideals. While human rights language provides, within limits, ample protection for the free exercise of beliefs and prescriptions associated with such doctrines, it neither endorses nor requires for its authority one or more of these doctrines. Rather, its authority is located in what the preamble to the declaration calls "the conscience of mankind." That reference, also identified in other authoritative international documents as "the elementary considerations of humanity" or "the dictates of the public conscience," is assumed to consist of a set of limited, relatively free-standing, universally binding, moral and legal norms taken to constitute an understanding of minimal human decency. According to the preamble, it is that minimal understanding that was "outraged" by the "barbarous acts" perpetrated in the mid-twentieth century, effects that consequently awakened the human rights revolution.

The fundamental challenge, over which widespread controversy continues to rage, is what religiously or philosophically minded people are to make of this understanding. Do they embrace it and thereby acknowledge its authority to define and impose outside constraints on the behavior of their followers and the followers of others? If so, on what grounds do they do that? Do they find within their tradition a basis for affirming the existence of a public conscience, a "conscience of mankind," capable under certain circumstances of yielding judgments that may overrule solemn beliefs and actions concerning, say, the treatment of citizens, criminals, women, or minorities? Moreover, is there a basis for legitimately holding "all peoples and all nations" accountable and even justly punishing them, regardless of creed, opinion, or identity?

Or do the religiously or philosophically minded oppose such an understanding? Do they regard it as a threat to the overriding authority of their own tradition and, accordingly, reserve for themselves the last word on right action and belief, even if it means defying existing human rights standards?

Working out consistent and convincing responses to these questions is not an easy task. The issues are complicated and demanding, requiring theoretical sophistication, a command of human rights standards and ideals, deep knowledge of the comprehensive doctrines in question, a subtle practical grasp of points of tension and convergence, and a certain amount of courage, particularly in some cases. Conscientious responses are devoutly to be welcomed.

Such a response we most certainly have in this volume on Islam and human rights by Professor Sachedina. Although all major religions exhibit disagreement and dissension over the subject of human rights, Muslims have been especially prominent recently in addressing the issues involved. Because of the visibility and contentiousness of current Islamic discussions, it is particularly valuable to have a book like Sachedina's. Unlike most examinations I have seen,

Sachedina directly considers the worries and concerns over human rights that exist among traditionalists in regard to the interpretation of the Qur'an and the history of doctrine based on that interpretation, though he does not leave it at that. He also confronts with care and persistence urgent practical problems like religious freedom and the treatment of women and minorities. Though an outsider and nonexpert (like me) is not qualified to pass final judgment on the substance of the arguments concerning Islamic history, scripture, doctrine, and practice, Sachedina provides arresting evidence and argumentation that will, undoubtedly, need to be considered very seriously by all observers.

In respect to the central question of whether human rights rests on an understanding of minimum human decency, a notion of public conscience, that need not depend for its authority on any comprehensive doctrine, Sachedina presents a complex argument. In much of the book, he strongly defends such a conviction. He contends that there exists deep in Islamic scripture and theology the idea of *fiṭra*, meaning intuitive reasoning, close to the concept of conscience, which implies "universal ethical cognition." It points to an inherent moral capacity assumed to be available to and incumbent upon all human beings prior to any particular commitments they may undertake, religious or otherwise, or to any special social, political, or cultural identity they may come to acquire. Although this sort of ethical knowledge is divinely inspired, it "does not require," states Sachedina, "any justification independent of the naturally endowed innate measure" (Chapter 2, p. 50). This idea provides, on Sachedina's account, an analogue in Islam to the concept of natural law and natural rights in Western Christianity. As in the Western example, it is this inherent moral capacity, with its accompanying "natural" standards for judging right from wrong, that becomes the basis for universal moral and legal accountability, regardless of creed, opinion, or identity.

It is also this idea that provides the grounds for affirming the fundamental ideals of equal dignity and equal protection enshrined in human rights language. The argument is that since every human being is assumed to possess the same inherent status as a moral agent, everyone is therefore equally entitled to have a say in religious matters ("no compulsion in religion") and in regard to how one is treated, particularly as to the threat or use of force and the allocation of benefits and burdens (provisions against arbitrary legal and political abuse and against discrimination on the basis of gender, religion, or identity). Sachedina compellingly turns this line of argument against what he considers to be extensive human rights abuses in parts of the Muslim world (and, no doubt, elsewhere), especially against citizens, women, and minorities.

One forceful illustration of just how seriously Sachedina takes this position is his sharp critique of the Cairo Declaration of Human Rights in Islam

(1990), which affirms "freedom" and the "right to a dignified life" for all humanity, but only insofar as those ideals are defined "in accordance with the Islamic Shari'ah." He objects that because the document "fails to articulate universal appeal... beyond the boundaries of the faith community to include all human beings," it "could hardly convince the international community about the universal intent of Islamic revelation," much less provide grounds for "the drafters' commitment to protect the human rights of all humans as humans."

Beyond the Qur'anic warrants, Sachedina supplies additional Islamic evidence in support of a set of limited, relatively free-standing, universally binding moral and legal norms taken to constitute an understanding of minimal human decency. That evidence draws on the Mu'tazilite tradition, which, in contrast to the Ash'arites, emphasizes the human capacity for rational judgment in morality and other matters, prior to and independent of revelation. Sachedina has relied on this tradition in earlier works, and he here carries the discussion forward in a way that is (to the outsider) illuminating and plausible. One aspect of the analysis that might invite further reflection is an explanation as to how it was that the Mu'tazilites themselves failed to draw the practical implications for politics and social life that Sachedina infers from their thought. Such failures are not, of course, without precedent, but they do call for an account.

Sachedina's additional appeals to the principle of plural interpretation in the Islamic tradition and to the need for understanding the Qur'an and Shari'a in their historical setting contribute further support to the idea of functional secularity of the public sphere, which implies a distinction between religious reflection and practice, characterized by freedom to dissent and differ, to reexamine and reinterpret, from the function of government, which ultimately rests not on persuasion but compulsion. As such, functional secularity compares to a similar distinction presupposed in human rights language between the exercise of religion or other expressions of conscience and the coercive role of the state.

However, while Sachedina wants to make room for an independent secular public sphere in his thought, in order to protect public life from domination by one or another comprehensive doctrine and provide secure protection for equal freedom and dignity, he also has some persistent doubts about how that sphere is currently understood, especially by Western-oriented human rights advocates. Indeed, much of his argument is addressed to inadequacies he perceives in the outlook of such people, and he is at pains to suggest what he believes is a superior approach in the form of a reconstructed version of Islam, an approach he takes to be necessary if the cause of human rights is truly to be sustained and advanced.

One major problem with Western-oriented human rights interpreters is that they assume that the public sphere, once secularized, once liberated from the domination of religion or other comprehensive doctrines, has nothing more of consequence to do with such doctrines. In regard to the central concerns of the society, matters of religion and conscience become marginal by being individualized and privatized, by being relegated to the crevices of society, and thus cut off from the essential character of these doctrines, namely, to comprehend all aspects of human experience, including public life, under some overarching concept of purpose and value. If in trying to protect freedom of religion and conscience, human rights policy does not in some way permit practitioners to express themselves in their own comprehensive idiom, human rights policy will not have safeguarded religion and conscience, but will have caused their demise. Sachedina contends that Islam by its very nature, and perhaps more than other religions, requires some form of public expression.

A second major problem is that by isolating comprehensive doctrines and thereby minimizing their influence, Western-oriented advocates have lost sight altogether of the importance of the justification of human rights. They have failed to address the subject in the belief that it is somehow unimportant. Sachedina claims, however, that human rights language itself requires defense, and it is here, he thinks, that a reconstructed theory of Islam can be of considerable help. On the one hand, his interpretation of Islam provides for an independent, functionally secular public sphere, thoroughly compatible with human rights standards enumerated in the international instruments, and self-consciously justified in reference to a natural human moral capacity called *fiṭra*.

On the other hand, his version of Islam also answers a question that, he believes, can never entirely be silenced in raising these issues, the question of the "ultimate" grounds of justification. While the idea of *fiṭra* is understood as independent and self-sufficient, it is also linked in important ways in the Islamic system to the need for revelation to "complete" human understanding. In its nature, *fiṭra* calls out, so to speak, to revelation for fulfillment. As Sachedina himself puts it, "the Qur'an lays down the foundation of theological pluralism that takes the equivalence and equal rights of human beings as a divinely ordained system." Accordingly, the basic doctrines of revealed Islam provide a final grounding for the human rights beliefs Sachedina espouses.

Whether one finally accepts Sachedina's approach or solutions to the two problems he raises in his conversation with Western-oriented human rights advocates, it is instructive to watch him work. He is undoubtedly struggling with deep and challenging questions in the interaction between religion and human rights in general and Islam and human rights in particular. His effort to account for and connect the tangle of features and issues that must be handled in such an undertaking is illuminating and identifies a set of concerns for further investigation and reflection that will be with us for a long time.

My own view is that the problems Sachedina detects among Western-oriented advocates, including his concern about the marginalization of comprehensive doctrines, are to a degree accurate and need to be attended to. Some Western-oriented advocates have come close to excluding matters of religion and conscience unduly from the public sphere by supporting their marginalization and thereby denaturing them. Similarly, some advocates have, it is true, ignored the questions surrounding the justification of human rights, both the obviously normative notions contained in the documents themselves, like "the conscience of mankind" or "the dictates of public conscience," or the relation of those ideas to broader questions of philosophical and theological justification. Sachedina is surely right to raise these matters, and thereby to stimulate further reflection on them.

At the same time, some of the considerations Sachedina introduces in his response to Western-oriented human rights advocates about the need for religions like Islam to implement their comprehensive teachings in public, and for human rights to have some sort of ultimate comprehensive justification, seem to me to threaten somewhat the force of his argument, outlined above, in favor of a set of limited, relatively free-standing, universally binding moral and legal norms taken to constitute an understanding of minimal human decency, a set of norms justified independently on the basis of a conception of "the conscience of mankind."

Still, Sachedina is to be congratulated for raising fundamental questions and for posing challenging answers in such a thought-provoking way.

Acknowledgments

The research for this book would not have materialized without the affiliation granted by the Ferdowsi University of Mashhad in 2005 and 2007, which enabled me to use the libraries in Mashhad, especially the Astāne Quds-i Raḍawī library. In this connection Professor Abdolreza Bagheri, the chancellor of the Ferdowsi University, and Professor Muhammad Reza Hashemi, the dean of the Faculty of Letters and Humanities, were extremely helpful. My research assistants 'Ali Shokohi and 'Abbas Shari'ati in Mashhad, and Betsy Mesard and Omar Shaukat at the University of Virginia, worked long hours to collect the materials, scan them, and make them available to me while in Iran.

As for the contents of the book, my friend and colleague, Professor Charles Mathewes, read the entire manuscript, offering detailed comments to improve it in many places. In my course on "Human Rights and Islam" taught at the Ferdowsi University in 2005, and "Islam, Democracy and Human Rights" at Virginia, graduate and undergraduate students have from time to time inspired me to formulate and discuss, with clarity and accuracy, issues related to the basic freedoms in Islam.

At Oxford University Press, Cynthia Read, as always, gave enormous support, and Justin Tackett and Paul Hobson provided expert advice on many occasions to enable smooth publication of the book.

Finally, I am grateful to the University of Birmingham for providing me the opportunity to present the Edward Cadbury Lectures in the spring of 2005, which, through the generous grant received from the Carnegie Foundation of New York, made it possible for me to spend the spring and summer of 2007 in Iran to complete the book.

Contents

Islam and the Challenge of Human Rights

I

The Clash of Universalisms

Religious and Secular in Human Rights

In 2004 I was overseeing the Persian translation of my book *The Islamic Roots of Democratic Pluralism* (2001) in Iran when I had a rare opportunity to experience the difficulty of translating and conveying Western political culture into an Islamic Iranian one. The translation of my book into Persian posed severe conceptual and cultural problems. The idea of democratic pluralism not only reflected Western influences in my rendering of Islamic-Arabic idiom into English; it also underscored the importance of taking contextual historical perspective seriously in efforts to transmit ideas from one culture into another. Writing in English, I had assumed the inclusiveness and universality of secular political language that dealt with human dignity and human agency, not realizing that for my Persian readers I could not rely solely on usages and political nuances in English.

In order to render the key ideas and concepts into idiomatic Persian, I had retained the services of an excellent translation professor who spent long hours mastering the terminology in Persian-language books on modern political thought and culture. The goal was to make the translation accessible to educated Iranian readers. However, as soon as I began to circulate the early drafts of the translation among my colleagues in the seminaries, with whom I freely discussed the ideas of the book, I was faced with severe criticism from traditionalist scholars for having compromised the cultural legitimacy of my book. The core of my thesis that democratic governance and pluralism had roots in Islamic revelation and, hence, were not peculiar to Western cultural and philosophical assumptions was difficult to sustain, for the terminology in the translation appeared to be informed by secular presumptions of modern Iranian social scientists. Not only were my choices like *democracy* and *pluralism* critically evaluated for intellectual and cultural legitimacy, but the rendering of these concepts into Persian, and my claim that they were "Islamic," were challenged as lacking authenticity in Islamic political-religious thought. The entire exercise of translating *The Islamic Roots of Democratic Pluralism* into Persian underscored the ongoing problems in cross-cultural communication and legitimization, and the domination of certain secular claims of inclusiveness and universalism of the language of modern international public order.[1]

This translation project dealing with universal themes like democratic pluralism or human rights made me reflect upon my claim to authenticity as a native interpreter and "expert" representative of the Islamic tradition. My thesis about the inclusive and universal language of democracy and pluralism for the new world order and the search for these in Islamic tradition through an interpretive project engaging original Arabic texts became more difficult to maintain, because both secular and religious documents revealed the problem of ethnocentrism. They both smacked of claims of superiority of one over the other. The subtlety of this ethnocentric facet of the language that I had assumed to be inclusive and had used so confidently to argue about the moral comprehensiveness characteristic of Islamic revelation shook my confidence in the universality of any idiom that claimed cross-cultural applicability, regardless of whether that idiom was secular or religious. If the Persians could not think like the Arabs, and vice versa, how could one assume that the secular presumptions about a tradition-free and foundationless universal morality could be acceptable to the religious-minded peoples of the world without any conversation to placate their fears and suspicions? The most revealing part of the translation project was the realization that, although I am a staunch supporter of the Universal Declaration of Human Rights and its enforcement through constitutional democracy in the Muslim world, it was impossible to formulate postulates about so-called universal notions of democracy, pluralism, and human rights without taking into consideration contextual and communitarian interpretations imposed upon the inclusive language of secular and religious texts. This is the crux of the problem in the political development of Muslim societies. The moment one admits cultural relativism in the application of universal moral values, one is face to face with the flouting of all those concerns that we have about the violation of human rights of individuals and, more particularly, the most vulnerable in the autocratic and totalitarian political systems that crowd the political landscape of the Muslim world (not to mention in other regions of the world).

What is the remedy then? If what I have observed about the problematic of translation of secular political-cultural idiom into an Islamic one were impossible to overcome through cross-cultural communication, then the entire project of demonstrating that Islam was compatible with democracy, or that Islam legitimized the Universal Declaration of Human Rights as a valid source of directives to protect human agency and human dignity, would have to be abandoned as impracticable. Understandably, a religious idiom like the secular one that enunciated universal and cross-cultural themes like the nature of the just, the public good, or human dignity, and yet responded to the political and social needs of a different period and a different audience, had to be taken seriously. Was it epistemically or ontologically possible to stimulate a conversation with different cultures and peoples about universal human values and aspirations without seeking to discover the philosophical and metaphysical origins and legitimizing sources of such values? In other words, whether in the context of constitutional democracy or the Universal Declaration of Human Rights, is it possible to proceed without examining the moral or metaphysical foundations of these universal values?

Epistemological and ontological discussions about the foundations of human rights are divisive and controversial. Arguments for avoiding such controversial conversations, simply because they are unimportant for the development of human rights regimes, are defeatist. Without engaging those Muslim scholars and intellectuals who deny these universal principles and their cross-cultural application, these important values—which underlie the protection of human dignity and human agency in the context of universal human rights—will lack the necessary legitimacy and enforcement in the Muslim world. As long as the moral and metaphysical foundations of human rights norms remain unarticulated, they will be easily dismissed as yet another ploy to dominate Muslim societies by undermining their religiously based culture and value system. Moreover, since the rise of Islamic political consciousness in the postcolonial age, Muslim authorities, for various reasons, have found it legitimate to dismiss compliance with some articles in the Universal Declaration of Human Rights by labeling them as imperialistic or culturally Eurocentric, parallel with the "Asian values" argument by Singapore's Lee Kwan Yoo. As it stands, the Declaration is viewed as insensitive to particular Muslim cultural values, especially when it comes to speaking about individual rights in the context of collective and family values in Muslim society.

The Moral Foundations of Human Rights

In the last three decades, especially since the early 1970s—the date that marks social and political upheavals in the Muslim world and the rise of militant religiosity among some Muslim groups—there has been sustained interest in the foundations of the Universal Declaration of Human Rights and its compatibility with Islam. A number of books and articles in Arabic and Persian written by some prominent traditionalist interpreters of the Islamic revealed texts, like Muḥammad al-Ghazālī among Egyptians and ʻAllāma Muḥammad Taqī Jaʻfarī Tabrīzī among Iranians to mention only a few, underscore the attention and interest the international document has attracted among the champions of Islamic tradition as an independent and universal metaphysical source for human rights. The major thrust of Islamic critique of the Declaration is its secularism and its implied hostility to divergent philosophical or religious ideas. Although there are no discussions about natural rights and natural law in classical Muslim theology or philosophy that could serve as a springboard for international conventions about common moral standards for the entire human race, the very secular foundation of the Declaration is deemed epistemologically insufficient to account for the derivation of inherent and inalienable human rights. Perhaps the sore point in the secular human rights discourse, as far as Muslim theoreticians of rights language are concerned, is the total dismissal of anything religious as an impediment to the modern development of a human rights regime. It is worth reminding ourselves that Christian assessments of the Declaration are founded upon entirely different kinds of concerns, ones that arose from its reaction to the liberal paradigm based on radical individualism that was derived from historically situated political and social discourse of eighteenth-century philosophical thought.[2]

It will be a mistake to think that even the most traditionalist Muslim thinkers are against the need for universal human rights to protect human dignity and human agency in the context of a nation-state today. There are some people who reject the idea of human rights as philosophically untenable. Nevertheless, even the staunchest opponents of the Universal Declaration of Human Rights, who regard the document as being morally imperialistic and culturally ethnocentric, concede the fact that human beings have rights that accrue to them as humans.[3] Human rights language is modern, firmly rooted in a secular liberalism that safeguards and promotes citizens' rights and that demands privatization of religion from the public sphere to allow the development of a politics independent of religion. This secularization of the public sphere is absent in Islamic juridical and theological anthropology. There, the human being is not conceived of as a compartmentalized individual who can separate the spiritual from the temporal in his person and keep the former from interfering with his everyday life lived with others. Consequently, the secularism that undergirds the Declaration does not translate into Islamic idiom without raising serious questions about the relationship of religion to state. More important, the overriding emphasis on the autonomy of the individual with an independent moral standard that transcends religious and cultural differences to claim rights without considering the bonds of reciprocity runs contrary to the Islamic tradition's emphasis on the community and relational aspects of human existence.

These concerns notwithstanding, the universal appeal of protecting human agents against abuse and oppression is being heeded even in those regions of the Muslim world where human rights violations occur more frequently. For Muslim scholars, the idea of human rights cannot be new because protecting human beings from cruel, inhuman, or degrading treatment has been recorded in major religious and nonreligious traditions throughout history. The Declaration of Article I of the international document that "all human beings, are born free and equal in dignity and rights" captures the essential characterization of human wisdom that has been transmitted under different historical circumstances when humans have fought and killed fellow humans, having denied them their dignity.

Foundationless Human Rights?

There is context to every text. The Universal Declaration of Human Rights provides a good example of this observation. The language that was constructed at the height of European colonialism over the ruins of the world wars and atrocities committed by humans against humans (under various pretexts of racial or religious claims of superiority of one people over another) could not have evolved without some kind of soul-searching into the depth of moral and spiritual heritage of the colonizers (the power wielders and political brokers of the 1940s). The historical backdrop of the period should make it possible for researchers of human rights debates and deliberations to indicate the moral and philosophical foundations that ultimately provided a language of international justice across cultures and peoples of the world. However modern the human rights idiom might be, it could not have emerged in a philosophical-theological vacuum without serious search for usages and ideas that lent themselves more readily to the universal language that was needed to bind the peoples of the world together in their commitment to redress the wrongs that were committed against civilians and innocent bystanders. The drafters of the Declaration were fully aware of traditional communities and their ability to live together with some kind of overlapping consensus that responded to the pragmatic need to avoid endless conflicts and destruction of human life and environment. The post–World War II nations were in search of even more exact universal language to capture the crisis that the world community was faced with and propose ways of protecting humans from indiscriminate violence and oppression resembling the anti-Semitism that led to the horrors of the Holocaust.

There are two studies affirming and denying any metaphysical or religious foundation undergirding the universal morality of human rights that I need to examine in order to make a case for an urgently needed dialogue between secularist and religious claimants of universal norms that attach to humans solely as humans. The first is Johannes Morsink's *The Universal Declaration of Human Rights: Origins, Drafting, and Intent* (1999), and the second is Michael Ignatieff's *Human Rights as Politics and Idolatry* (2001). Morsink and Ignatieff wrote their studies around the fiftieth anniversary of the Declaration and had the advantage of the hindsight with which they examined the document and its impact on the development of the human rights regime. More pertinently, they have raised the most intriguing question that continues to be debated even today, namely, whether there is a single moral foundation for human rights that spans many cultures, or whether there are many culturally specific moral foundations, or none.

In the present study my working assumption is that regardless of its secular or religious foundation, were the Declaration without universal morality that speaks to each and every person on this earth, it would lack moral enforcement in the world community. To ensure that the Declaration will continue to protect an individual's inalienable human rights, its advocates need to state time and again the unshakeable universal moral foundation of the Declaration and its ability to speak to peoples of different traditions and cultures without denying them an opportunity to affirm or deny that universalism in the name of some comprehensive religious doctrine. The ultimate support for the Declaration cannot simply come from its pragmatic purpose of protecting human agency; rather, it can come from the reasons as to why that personhood deserves to be protected from unjust conduct of those in power. Moral assessment of human action and its valuation as right or wrong is the only concrete source of its universal appeal and legitimacy to secure the support of the international community of nations.

Before assessing the two studies by Morsink and Ignatieff, it is necessary to once again open up the subject of the moral foundation of human rights that provides it with the fundamental argument to claim universal application, and examine and compare this secular universalism with the universalism that is claimed by the upholders of comprehensive religious doctrine. The ongoing Muslim criticisms of the Declaration as being prejudicially antireligious and politically hegemonic are founded upon rejection of a universal claim of secular morality. These criticisms can be best tackled by raising the kinds of philosophical and metaphysical issues that undergird the international document and that can find resonance in Islamic philosophical theology. However controversial, I believe that considerations about the foundations will lead to frank exchange about the sources of a universal moral foundation of human rights, providing a corrective to many Muslims' perceptions about the intended secularist bias of the Declaration. To forgo an opportunity to engage traditional Muslim scholars to rethink their anti-Declaration stance and challenge them on their own terms to recognize that Islamic revelation and the Declaration share the common moral terrain to protect individuals from oppression will be detrimental to the overall goal of the universality of the secular document in garnering support for its implementation in the Muslim world.

Johannes Morsink's valuable study of the history of the drafting of the Declaration, by affirming the ways in which metaphysical and philosophical issues connected with Christian experience of the Enlightenment provided the drafters a language that could claim universal application, affords the opportunity to engage Islamic universalism. In *The Universal Declaration of Human Rights,* Morsink has meticulously and sensitively traced the drafting of the Universal Declaration of Human Rights, stage by stage, showing in clear contours the thought process and the universal language that emerged to capture and express international concern for the oppressed, the poor, and the politically powerless of the world for which religious and humanitarian traditions had already established a vocabulary that could now be appropriated for the Declaration. At the same time, to underscore the drafters' good intentions, Morsink has also responded to the charge of ethnocentrism leveled against the Declaration by those who question its universal applicability to all human beings by tracing the complex and complicated negotiations that took place to avoid any ethnocentric or particularistic language that would have actually defeated the very purpose of universal human rights. More pertinently, in the last chapter he examines the language of the Declaration to investigate the presumption that there is a connection between the universal Declaration and Enlightenment ways of thinking about morality that is universal and at the same time secular. But this secularism is not totally nonreligious in the sense that nature and reason, "the two secular components of the triad—were still kept in close proximity to the God from which they flowed."[4] The Enlightenment view of humanity was derived from natural rights philosophies, which located human equality and inalienable rights in human beings simply by virtue of their own humanity and not because of some extraneous reason. However, in pursuit of universal morality to support human rights across traditions, the drafters pursued thorough-going secularism and kept the language of the Declaration free from any religious idiom. Most strikingly, they severed God from nature and reason. Paradoxically, while the search for universality through secularization of human rights norms also paved the way for pluralistic sources of morality, it also led to their inevitable relativity.

The problem of relativism in the context of human rights standards and values is an old one. Practical experience of life in societies with very different cultures has been at the root of relativism in international debates about standards of justice across state boundaries. It is accurate to say that despite all the intellectual efforts at thorough secularization of universal morality, it has been difficult, if not outright impossible, to build consensus over common standards for the entire human race in international conventions. Moreover, detaching universal morality from any foundational consideration in order to accommodate diverse cultures and national communities has, unfortunately, served as a pretext for ignoring the universal thrust of the human rights document across different Muslim countries where, time and again, political authorities have used cultural relativity to justify their lack of commitment to promoting certain freedoms for their Muslim as well as non-Muslim citizens. An immediate corrective to this persisting problem, as I shall argue, depends upon articulating the link between secular values expressed in the document and the philosophies of the eighteenth-century Enlightenment that influenced the conceptualization of inherent attributes of human persons. It is significant to note that such topics are also the focus of Muslim theological ethics (and not necessarily juridical studies) and acceptable to traditionalist Muslim authorities. To be sure, those who participated in the drafting of the Declaration were looking at the issue of protection of human rights from their particular historical experience and cultural context. They were responding to the carnage inflicted upon the victims of World War II and the Holocaust in the early 1940s. As Morsink has shown in admirable detail, each article of the Declaration was responding to the urgent need to protect human personhood in all its manifestations in the social and political contexts of nation-states. It is quite revealing that Muslim participation was minimalist in the sense that there was no real effort to expound comprehensive Islamic doctrines to get the sense of the tradition's stance on different articles. Further, as the profile of the different representatives from participating Muslim countries like Saudi Arabia, Pakistan, and Syria reveals, the representatives from Muslim countries were secularly educated individuals, who had little or no human rights training in the foundational sources of Islamic tradition to adequately articulate the universal impulse of Islamic comprehensive doctrines that would have enriched the debates that were being conducted, for instance, by Christian representatives from Lebanon, and contribute to debates that took place on important issues like freedom of religion and conscience. In fact, Jamil Baroody, the Saudi representative on the drafting committee, was a Lebanese Christian and lacked even the basic Islamic credentials to speak on any theological aspects of Islam authoritatively.

This lack of serious Muslim participation has continued to cast a long shadow of doubt over the cultural and political contours of the Declaration that reveal an indubitable secular-Western bias.[5] This bias continues in the second study that deals with Islamic encounters with Western human rights. In Michael Ignatieff's treatment of the Islamic challenge in *Human Rights as Politics and Idolatry*, one can observe the obverse of Morsink's treatment of the deliberations about the foundation of human rights norms. In these lectures Ignatieff argues for a pragmatic approach to human rights. His liberal secular stance relies on a presupposition that there is a common denominator of rationality that remains when the particularities of one's religious convictions are bracketed or suppressed. He treats human rights as "pragmatic political instruments" that should aspire to be effective before they aspire to be more comprehensive in their pronouncements. After all, there is a sense in which religious reasons, based on comprehensive doctrines in Ignatieff's secular evaluation, do not count as contributing to a proper human rights discourse. They can be added to whatever universal character is to be protected by a human rights regime. Protections against cruel, inhuman, and degrading treatment should constitute the purpose of human rights and the core of a human rights regime. Moreover, according to Ignatieff, to believe in human rights does not entail believing that they exist independently of human purpose. All that we need to believe is that human rights are important instruments for protecting human beings against cruelty, oppression, and degradation. Hence, there is no need to believe and insist on a divine or natural source of human rights. Ignatieff understandably denies human rights any creedal status, lest it become the source of a new humanist idolatry.

However, this denial of a single or multiple moral foundation for human rights that spans many cultures and traditions has led to the prevailing suspicion in traditionalist Muslim circles that the Declaration is nothing more than the continuation of colonialist, hegemonic discourse that imposes its will through a human rights regime.[6] There is no doubt that human rights can serve a multitude of purposes, and those purposes can be expressed in many ways, not only across different societies and cultures, but within them as expressions of plurality of moral assessment of human agency. In order to defend human rights in traditional and religious societies, it is imperative to establish the reason why human beings have rights in the first place. In Muslim culture the emphasis is on responsibilities without any mention of rights. Although there is a purpose to human life, the purposive agent simply fulfills his or her duties in society to make sure that justice prevails in all human undertakings. Claims about human dignity or respect owed to human beings are viewed strictly within the larger social good and not independent of it. At the same time, Islamic doctrines speak about equal creation of human beings, sharing the parentage and endowed with honor and dignity as the "children of Adam."

Ignatieff's prescription to forgo foundational arguments rooted in human dignity, divine purposes, natural law, and related philosophical and moral ideas would function as a conversation stopper in Muslim societies where human rights can be more readily defended by claims about human dignity and the equal creation of human beings by God. Human beings are created with intuitive reason and an innate capacity to know right from wrong. Yet they are in need of constant guidance from God to fulfill their true roles in society. The relationship between human agency and human dignity is the result of purposive creation of humanity, with a goal to guide it to create a just public order. By avoiding such foundational arguments because they happen to be unimportant as part of "pragmatic political instruments" to further a human rights regime, the Declaration exposes itself to an unintended relativism. Ignatieff's reason to avoid foundational arguments because the Declaration is compatible with "moral pluralism" is part of this unintended relativism that suggests that ultimately each culture and people will determine the valuation of human agency and protect what they believe to be in accord with their moral judgment. The referent in "moral" is necessarily human action and not human belief; and yet, that that hurts human dignity is the unacceptable behavior of another human agent which is irreconcilable with any human rights regime. Nevertheless, no one disputes the need to convince those who abuse the rights of the people in the name of some sacred authority to revisit their doctrines to realize the discrepancy between what they teach and their practice.

The drafting of the Declaration clearly shows that there were several key sources for the writing of the articles that are now enshrined in the document. What made it possible for this lingua franca of human rights to emerge was a convergence rather than an upholding of a single cultural or philosophical tradition, even though, as some Muslims have argued, modern, secular values formed the core of the norms that informed human rights. It is common to assume that arguments about human agency, dignity, and natural law tend to be quite philosophical and abstract, and it may therefore be tempting to assume that not much of practical importance is at stake. But such an assumption would be rash. What is at stake in determining the foundations of human rights is often the very legitimacy of human rights talk among Muslim religious scholars. A human rights regime that takes into consideration and promotes an overlapping consensus is more compatible with respect for many cultural and philosophical traditions that converge in support of a similar set of human rights. This convergence between, for instance, Islamic and secular humanist traditions is not complete or perfect, but neither is the convergence on human rights from within a modern, secular cultural or philosophical tradition.

Ignatieff's doubts about the need for a metaphysical foundation of human rights are built upon claims about such abstract ideas as that human beings have an innate or natural dignity, or that they have been endowed with natural and intrinsic self-worth and hence, they are inviolable. These abstract claims, as Ignatieff argues, are controversial and detrimental to advancing human rights. In his words, such propositions may weaken the reinforcement of human rights: "Far better, I would argue, to forgo these kinds of foundational arguments altogether and seek to build support for human rights on the basis of what such rights actually *do* for human beings."[7]

This is a fundamentally flawed argument at the international level when attempts must be made to resolve the controversial aspects of the Declaration's moral foundations in order to build overlapping consensus among different cultures and metaphysical positions to enroll the full cooperation of various peoples and governments to do something more than just pay lip service to human rights. Moreover, one of the major problems confronting the secular document from the Islamic point of view is the charge of relativity against the Eurocentric sources of the Declaration. This charge of relativism cannot be taken lightly, and the only way it could be overcome is by simply recognizing the need for dialogue with other claimants of comprehensive doctrines, whether religious or secular. The ultimate goal of this conversation is to reach a consensus about human agency linked to human dignity as a special mark of humanness that is entitled to inalienable human rights.

Further, Ignatieff believes that while foundations for human rights belief may be contestable and divisive, the pragmatic grounds for believing in human rights protections are much more secure. Foundational considerations, as I want to show in this study, are critical to building an overlapping consensus between secular and religious norms that support human rights. Moreover, it is actually in the area of "believing" in human rights protections that we have problems across cultures and traditions. Without securing theoretical agreements, it is hard to see how we can convince the Muslim world that the Declaration is not a "secular European religion."

In addition, Ignatieff's denial of the foundational sources for practical reasons to allow a universal regime of human rights to emerge fails to understand that different cultures and a wide variety of civilizations, despite their fundamental disagreements about such matters as what constitutes a good human life, have never denied the existence of injustices that are committed by the powerful against fellow humans. More important, as Jeffrey Stout has shown in his *Democracy and Tradition*, conflicting religious conceptions of good in the public sphere, however problematic, do not in any way diminish the role of public reason in building an overlapping consensus in pluralistic societies.[8] An appeal to metaphysical foundation of human nature that leads to recognizing common moral terrain among divergent cultural groups may actually enhance the validity of a minimum dignity to which all humans are entitled by a simple fact of being created equal. Hence, diverse and sometimes divisive religious validation of what is good is not detrimental or obstructive to the search for a shared belief in what it is to be a human being and what norms can be identified in each set of comprehensive doctrines maintained by different faith communities that are compatible with the stated purpose of human rights, namely, protection of human dignity and agency. However, Ignatieff maintains that the universal commitments implied in human rights can be compatible with other comprehensive doctrines only if the universalism implied in the Declaration is self-consciously "minimalist."

This is problematic in the international communities where there is no agreement about "thin" and "minimalist" descriptions that are dependent upon "thick" and "maximalist" descriptions of the comprehensive doctrines held by different communities. As a world community with much to say about its achievements (and failures), Muslim society has much to add to Eurocentric discussions of human rights to become full participant in the development of a human rights regime. More pertinently, to put its forces behind minimalist universalism, it needs to demonstrate both to its faith communities around the world and to the international community that for a human rights regime it is important to extract such "minimalist" universalism embedded in religious doctrines. It is unhelpful to dismiss Islamic or any other religious comprehensive doctrine as parochial or relativist with no impact whatsoever in the development of a human rights regime.

This study intends to do just that. It endeavors to go to the foundational sources of Islamic doctrines in the Qur'an and the Tradition[9] to demonstrate to its own membership as well as the international community that it shares the universal language of morality and human agency, including human dignity, to enhance its commitment to the protection of human rights. In the Muslim world, the legitimacy of the Declaration is being challenged as an affront to a God-centered worldview about the ends of human agency and dignity. Even if the bias of human rights advocacy can be directed toward the victim, and the test of legitimacy—and hence universality—is what might be termed the victim's consent, the tarnished image of selective Western advocacy of human rights in certain regions of the world to the exclusion of the others and endless institutionalized violence against certain groups, which have ended up devouring the minimal legitimacy that human rights had among Muslims, has not resulted in furthering the rights of minorities or women in the Muslim world. People cannot help themselves and protect their agency without the support of the traditional authorities that actually provide legitimacy to the state authorities who have constantly trampled upon the rights of their own people, while dismissing the universal claim of the international conventions. If it can be shown that Islamic doctrines share the universalism of human rights, however minimalist, then we will have opened a real conversation between the secularist and the Islamic notions of human agency and human dignity for the protection of abused individuals. Without this fundamental theoretical breakthrough in the foundational aspects of human rights, the credibility gap between the international document and the Muslim world will continue to widen, making it difficult to believe that individuals in traditional societies with strong communitarian ties could ever exercise the minimum understanding of their capacity to protect their rights against autocratic states and their agencies.

I agree with Ignatieff's statement that human rights matter because they help people to help themselves. Nevertheless, this statement is based on Western liberal confidence in the empowered individual who, having been brought up in a liberal political system, understands and undertakes to protect himself or herself. Without a constitutional democratic system in place, no individual has the minimalist understanding of what it means to fight for one's civil rights. While it is true that human rights are a language of individual empowerment, an empowerment by means of which people can protect themselves against injustices, Ignatieff is speaking in the context of political development of individuals in a liberal democratic society, where a concept such as injustice is understood relative to one's experience in a democratic system that guarantees certain basic rights to its citizens. How can people in Darfur, for instance, protect themselves with this kind of empowerment when they have had no experience of seeing their agency or their rational capacity as important instruments to assert their human rights and defend themselves?

Ignatieff's prescriptive avoidance of any foundational consideration at the international level, in my opinion, leads to an imposition of a Western conception of individualism even if one were to take it in the sense of moral individualism that protects cultural diversity. Moral individualism claims to be a sort of thinking that must respect the diverse ways individuals choose to live their lives. According to Ignatieff, in this way of thinking, human rights are only a systematic agenda of "negative liberty," a tool kit against oppression, a tool kit that individual agents must be free to use as they see fit within the broader frame of cultural and religious beliefs they live by. But in Muslim societies where traditionally people have conceived their individuality within the context of their communal and collective life, human rights will have to protect individuals as members of collective groups and require collective groups to work toward a just balance between individual and collective concerns.

The Present Study

I need to state in no uncertain terms where I come from in this research. As a Muslim I do not believe that the universal Declaration can be dismissed outright as merely a product of Western secular philosophy with deep roots in Enlightenment thought. Nor do I accept the charge of Eurocentric bias of the document as a valid one because, as I will demonstrate in this study, liberal views about human individuality, dignity, and agency are compatible with Islamic revelation as developed in Muslim philosophical theology and juridical methodology to understand human personhood. Thus far Muslim studies of the human rights document have concentrated on investigating its compatibility, or the lack of it, from the point of view of Sharī'a—the Sacred Law of Islam—without engaging the juridical system's theological-ethical foundations.[10] Given the Declaration's intellectual anchoring in the historically specific secular and Christian experience of the drafters, academically such an investigation of the Sharī'a's compatibility with the Declaration is unproductive for understanding the origins of the universal underpinnings of both the Islamic tradition and the secular international document. To get to the root of the Muslim traditionalists' arguments against the antireligion bias of the Declaration, this study will endeavor to undertake a critical analysis of Muslim theological resources to propose a fresh understanding of Muslim theology to support universal human rights that envision the derivation of human rights on the basis of the principle of inherency and inalienability of the rights that accrue to all humans as humans.[11]

Accordingly, my argument in this study is that in the postcolonial age, and more particularly in the age of economic and cultural globalization, it is important to dispel doubts about the universality of human rights by seriously engaging metaphysical and epistemic foundations of human rights norms to demonstrate that these norms can be essentially grounded in religious notions about human dignity and divinely ordained human freedom of will. Religious doctrines have the potential of working toward an overlapping consensus on important articles in the Declaration—a consensus that secular human rights theoreticians can ill afford to ignore. The Declaration's normative discourse must be critically reinvestigated for its universal presumptions about human inherency in the light of theological discourse whose universal language continues to guide ethical and jurisprudential values of common life. Whereas I do not share Alasdair MacIntyre's rejection of universal rights as fictitious,[12] I agree with him in insisting that traditional societies had universal notions of justice and had worked toward principles of coexistence among themselves and others long before secular modernists spoke about a contractarian theory of corporate life that shaped modern politics.[13] The founder of Islam, for instance, not only recognized temporal existence as part and parcel of one's faith commitment; he also created stable and universal institutional structures to further the vision of a just public order under God's guidance. Islam's experience with the temporal world was sociologically and linguistically inclusive and universalistic. As a world-embracing tradition, Islamic ethical and jurisprudential guidance set out to provide fixed norms for building a multifaith, multiethnic, and multicultural society that spoke to the vision of universal community founded upon justice. Since this moral context was potentially inclusive, the need to compromise its faith-based vision of the public order to accommodate other communities actually never arose. As a matter of fact, it had no problem in endorsing a common moral stance that was founded upon a universally recognizable account of individual autonomy, common good, and a divinely endowed self-subsisting moral standard that transcends religious and cultural differences.[14]

Having argued for the inclusion of conversation about the foundations that undergird the Declaration, let me also hasten to add that in principle I agree with the secularist theoreticians of human rights who actively advocate in international and intertraditional documents, avoiding entanglement with particular metaphysical and religious notions like human dignity, natural law, and divine purposes for humanity so that the true purpose of the international document, namely, protection of human beings from abuse, oppression, and cruelty, is not in any way diminished. It is a truism to reiterate the secularist concern that when human dignity itself is in danger, all the academic controversy about the foundations of universal morality intensifies moral complacency in protecting individual human rights. Nonetheless, ignoring Muslim criticisms about ethnocentric and hegemonic goals of the Declaration, however unfounded, has the danger of further marginalization of human rights in the Muslim world.

Although in this study I would have liked to limit myself to the theological and juridical problems connected with one major article of the Declaration that speaks about the freedom of religion and to investigate that freedom in Islamic tradition, the more I tried to understand the culture of human rights that predominates in the present discourse on the subject, the more I was convinced to expand my inquiry into wider topics that seemed to separate the secular context of the Declaration and Islamic tradition as represented by both traditionalist scholars and Muslim secular intellectuals. The reason for pursuing this line of inquiry is quite personal and yet sufficiently academic to allow me to explore the idea of rights and their ethical and political dimensions. As I investigated the relevant literature in Islam, I found that the literature on human rights produced by Muslim traditionalists lacked the necessary rigor and candid analysis of the problem of violation of human rights on the ground. In contrast, even when secular Muslim scholarship on the subject was right on target in its analysis of the existing record of human rights in the Muslim world, it lacked the necessary grounding in the religious tradition to challenge the traditionalist apologetics and essentialist reading of Islamic heritage frozen in time.

Any student of Muslim theology can attest that historically Muslim theologians were interested in understanding human-divine interaction and its implications for human moral-spiritual development. As a moral agent, endowed with freedom of choice, a human being is endowed with intuitive reasoning—a major source of ethical cognition. There is hardly any discussion of the religious sources for human responsibility in terms of interhuman relationships in this secularist scholarship. Was it not the rational or traditional theory of ethics that made it possible to uphold human freedom of choice or lack of it when it came to human obligations and claims? Was it not a rationalist-objectivist estimation of human action that allowed Muslim jurists to develop a legal methodology to derive fresh rulings by applying ethical norms to relative cultural situations? Many more questions came to my mind, as a student of both Muslim theology and ethics and Islamic jurisprudence, in order to discover the reasons why the traditionalists failed to actively engage the secularists in conversation to develop an inclusive religious-ethical foundation for upholding the inalienable human rights that accrue to humans as humans.

In 2005, the Edward Cadbury Lectures at the University of Birmingham provided me with an opportunity to digress from my major study on Islamic biomedical ethics and concentrate on issues that have been part of my personal struggle as a Muslim and as a human being who believes that no one has a right to deprive any human being of the right to freedom of religion and conscience. More on this will be part of my last chapter. In 2006, I received a Carnegie Foundation Fellowship to complete the research and writing of this book. There are few serious works on Islam and modernity by Muslim scholars in Arabic or Persian. As far as I know, if there is anything worth considering in this area it has been published in Iran by prominent scholars of the tradition. These scholars combine a thorough classical education in the seminary and a brilliant comprehension of modern methodologies that are in place in the academic study of religion in the West. Accordingly, I decided to spend more time in Iran in the spring of 2007 to benefit from personal discussions with at least one of these great minds, namely, Professor Mohsen Kadivar, who teaches at Tarbiat Modares University in Tehran. Kadivar commands respect among the traditional scholars of the seminaries in Qom and Mashhad (not that they all agree with him) as well as modernist intellectuals, mostly apologists for Western culture and human rights traditions in Iranian universities. His analysis of human rights and the fundamental problems the Declaration articles have with Islamic juridical heritage is both authentic and critical. My conversations with him through his writings and personal contact have proven to be a goldmine for my research and writing.

At this juncture it will be useful for me to delineate the direction I am going to follow in this journey, on which I invite you to travel with me with an open mind so that the experience becomes mutually beneficial to all of us. Although I trained under prominent Shīʿite teachers in the traditional seminaries in Iran and Iraq, I am nonsectarian in my approach to Islam. In my scholarly endeavor I retain modern academic methodology, which I learned from my teachers at the University of Toronto. I follow their guidance in my analysis of the classical tradition of Islam. Let me also make it clear where I come from in terms of my personal faith: I am a believer in God, and I worship none other than God; I certainly do not worship Islam. For me Islam is a path among many paths through which God guided humanity to find its perfection and ultimate salvation.

Muslim Scholarship on Human Rights

Since the Universal Declaration of Human Rights, a number of studies on the subject and its compatibility or lack of it with Islam have appeared in Arabic and Persian. There are, generally speaking, two identifiable trends in Muslim scholarship that has investigated the Declaration in terms of its conceptual formulations and effectiveness in Muslim understanding of modern rights language.

The first trend is represented by Muslim scholars speaking for the religious tradition (and not its secular appropriation). This group of scholars, mainly centered in the Muslim seminaries in Cairo or Najaf, did not participate in the human rights formulations when the universal Declaration was being drafted. It is worth keeping in mind that in that formative period the deliberations were not inclusive of all the diverse trends in the traditionalist interpretations of religious notions, including even those of Western Christian theology. The exclusion of Muslim traditionalist representation in the human rights deliberations at this early stage could have been a political decision, since most of the Muslim countries were dominated by Western colonial authorities who had a negative view of Muslim seminarians, whose opposition to colonial political and cultural domination could have simply derailed the secular and antitraditional tone of the human rights deliberations. Traditionalist scholarship, however methodologically problematic and full of self-applauding apologetics, continues to hold sway as the most authentic Islamic scholarship in the Muslim world, which is, by and large, not used to critical scholarship about Islamic juridical and historical studies. More pertinently, traditionalist scholars regard human rights as belonging to the secular sphere of human thought and as an issue independent of the religious sphere. Although they accept the notion of human rights as the struggle to achieve rights and justice to provide protection for the rights of individuals, they regard the struggle for human rights today as the continuation of that essential historical struggle to curb the oppression of tyrannical regimes that culminated in the greatest victory for humanity when nations worldwide endorsed the Universal Declaration of Human Rights in 1948.[15]

The trend of excluding traditionalist interpretations of Islamic foundations of human rights norms persists at the international level today. Not unlike the late 1940s, Islamic interpretations at these international conventions are dominated by secularly educated Muslim intellectuals. This is the second major group, and perhaps the only one known to the Western audience, whose scholarship on human rights remains either oblivious of traditionalist scholarship altogether or simply ignores it as obscurantist. This secularist group can be further divided into two wings: those writing in the Muslim countries in native languages like Arabic, Persian, Indonesian, and so on, in support of the Declaration as it stands; and those writing in the West in European languages, for Western academic audiences and government agencies. Whereas the native interpreters and supporters of the Declaration are fewer in number and have little or no influence in today's climate of political

Islam, the Muslim secular interpretations produced in the West are almost unknown in the Muslim world except among the educated. On a very cursory investigation of the Arabic and Persian translations of these latter studies, I was not surprised to notice that hardly any of these highly acclaimed studies on human rights situations in the Muslim world were translated for the local Muslim readership. While this academic production is highly appreciated in the West for its bold stance against human rights violations in the Muslim world, it barely scratches the surface of the real issues that confront the cultural legitimacy of international human rights.

The secular Muslim advocates of human rights are typically seen as the product of ivory tower elitism, who are recognized and invited by UNESCO or the United Nations Commission on Human Rights, and who represent Muslim interests in these international institutions in the absence of real people on the ground. In the post-9/11 period of Muslim history the situation has deteriorated even further. Hardly any authentic Muslim voice is heard in these international organizations to express the concerns of native Muslim leaders in terms of the protection of their people's basic freedoms in their autocratic and undemocratic political systems. With the almost total absence of intellectual contact between Muslim secularists with a modern education and seminary-trained Muslim traditionalists to steer the critical internal dialogue on the need to support human rights as cataloged in the Declaration in Muslim societies, the future holds very little hope for the improvement of the human rights of all citizens of the Muslim world, regardless of their race, religion, and gender differences.

It is also possible to identify a third trend in Muslim scholarship on human rights that takes foundational sources of Islam seriously and at the same time critically argues for or against liberal interpretations of the second group regarding the compatibility or lack of it by acknowledging substantial differences between some of the fundamental principles set forth in the Declaration and Islamic tradition. Accordingly, this scholarship points out irreconcilable differences between the secular and religious foundations of human rights norms and their origins in secular and Islamic political ideology and theology, respectively.

In the past fifty years, diverse views about human rights have circulated among Muslim scholars that appear to be largely monolithically authoritarian and puritanical to outsiders. This diversity is most vividly illustrated by the divergent attitudes among Muslim thinkers toward the idea of constitutional democracy and its inevitability for the development of a human rights regime in Muslim consciousness. What engages human rights theorists searching for foundational origins of rights language among Muslims is not only the synchronic plurality of attitudes across various groups of traditionally and secularly educated proponents of human rights, living under different political systems, but also the diachronic conglomeration of shifting attitudes, especially in the aftermath of the revival of political theology. Islamic political theology involves metaphysics and carries an underlying assumption that revelation-based certainty guides the move from the ontological-theological level to the ethical-political to create the ideal public order. A number of prominent traditionalist scholars across different Muslim nations with varying seminarian education are now engaged in determining the terms of human rights discourse in Muslim societies. In the last three decades Muḥammad al-Ghazālī, Yūsuf al-Qarāḍāwī, Aytollah Jawādī Āmolī, and 'Allāma Muḥammad Taqī Ja'farī Tabrīzī, among other traditionalist Sunnī and Shī'ite scholars, have enunciated antiauthoritarian and pro-constitutional views that support the spirit of human rights language founded upon human dignity and inviolability as well as the inherence of individual rights. Post-9/11, this trend in support of social and political pluralism and its impact upon the development of the idea of equality of citizenship without insisting upon theological unity has gained momentum. I distinguish the traditional search for Islamic political theology that can support modern concerns for consensual rule and human rights as a critical move from liberal Muslim scholarship in Western academia. The latter scholarship is important in its own ways but has little or no influence in the post-1970 Muslim societies with renewed confidence in Islam's ability to deliver a just social order. Let me reiterate the observation that without the traditional leadership's endorsement of constitutional democracy and a bill of rights in Muslim states, it will be hard to see critically needed changes of attitude regarding the international document to afford it cultural legitimacy in the Muslim world. Traditional Muslim support, in the absence of politically legitimate governance in almost all Muslim countries, is the most important venue left for the human rights discourse to find its proper place in Muslim social and political consciousness.

In connection with the development of human rights discourse, it is possible to identify three major tendencies in contemporary Islamic thought: the tendency to view the discourse in liberal, secular terms; the tendency to compare the UN Declaration with the Cairo Declaration on Human Rights in Islam of 1990 without engaging the philosophical-theological underpinnings of either document; and the tendency, mostly among the traditionalists, to challenge the foundational sources of the Declaration in terms of Western politics against the Islamic world and to present an alternative revelation-based foundation for the inherency of human rights. These tendencies demonstrate the dialectics of the changing attitudes toward the international human rights

Declaration and conventions. My major interest is in the third tendency because it asks the tough questions that Ignatieff, as discussed above, would like us to downplay in the practical interest of protecting individuals' inalienable human rights. Moreover, since the majority of traditional leaders have a problem with the foundational origins of the Declaration, they have worked and reworked metaphysical questions to argue against the authenticity of human rights norms and demonstrate their stark opposition to the secular-political affirmations of the dominant Western culture.

The first academic goal of this project, then, is to identify the overriding ontological issues in the writings of selected representative thinkers of the Sunnī and Shī'ite schools of thought, and explore the way these notions continue to prefigure different ethical-political formulations about the sources of human dignity and human agency. The point to be emphasized and substantiated throughout this study is that the emergence of a new theological-ethical vision of politics among traditionalist interpreters of political theology is basically different from the classically formulated political society in that the new vision of public order is nationalistic as well as self-deterministic. It is no longer confined to the classical division between Muslim and non-Muslim in granting full rights and assessing civic responsibilities. In view of a new political reality founded upon the sovereign state, the new theology endeavors to recognize and affirm the individual's dignity, first as a human person, and then as a member of a civil association founded upon equality of rights and responsibilities within the framework of a modern nation-state. The new political theology is not propounding a return to the classical model of a political system with a charismatic caliph as its head. The despotic rule that sought unquestioning obedience from the ruled in the name of some divinely ordained normative laws, as propounded and supported by traditionalist jurist-theologians, has, more or less, come to an end. In their place, traditional religious leadership is envisioning rulers who are accountable to the public, and is reasserting the traditionally formulated rule of law with an essential difference that this law can no longer discriminate between a believer and nonbeliever, between man and woman. The most critical challenge facing the traditional leadership is to search for an inclusive political theology that no longer discriminates by faith to determine an individual's rights and duties. I contend that in assessing the developing human rights discourse in the Muslim world a major epistemic shift has to occur from a juridical to a theological-ontological status of human personhood. This will in turn contribute to the comparative foundational theory by sharpening the boundaries of secular-cum-religious norms of human rights as well as pointing to different ways that categories of political theology play themselves out in different cultural settings.

Alongside this analytical task, my principal aim is to investigate alternative ways to work out the foundational sources of Islam in order to think through different theological-ontological affirmations concerning universal moral values and the inherent nature of rights that accrue to a human as human—something that will in turn shed light upon different interpretations of values like justice, freedom, and equality, which continue to play a critical role in both secular and Islamic human rights discourse for their universal applicability. This latter aim will involve a critique of the current shape Islamic human rights discourse is taking, especially in regard to the incongruence between its ambition to rework Islamic foundations and its unwillingness to renegotiate the foundations and terms of liberal democratic values that inform the Declaration. I shall argue that, as it stands, the conception of human rights that most Muslim traditionalists speak about remains ethically relativist when compared to a secularist conception of human rights that aspires to be morally universal.

Human Rights Political Theology

The connection between religious universalism and the secular claim to universal morality based on ethical-political dimensions of human rights and their ramifications for the particularistic exclusive claim to scripture-based truth claims has been a theme of reflection among Christian theologians.[16] Can secularly based universal morality transcend cross-cultural disputes about the Declaration's universalistic intent? Can human rights theory on its own, without help from religious inspiration, set the terms of interreligious and cross-cultural dialogue to develop global norms that will foster respect for other humans as equal in creation? A number of Christian theologians have critically evaluated the universalist claims of the Declaration and have concluded with much evidence that without a universalist religious validation, any notion of universal morality is incomplete because secular culture is incapable of generating religion's sense of life's sacredness and human beings' possession of inherent dignity and rights. Religion, with its power of persuasion, not only provides cultural legitimacy to human rights; it can also become its staunchest advocate.

In a number of recent political developments in those regions of the world where human rights violations were rampant, religious leaders have resorted to their religious traditions to inspire resolutions to civil conflicts and foster just human relationships by advocating truth and reconciliation with those who, at one time, had failed to provide basic rights to life and protection from cruelty to their people. In many proven instances the Declaration's inability to appeal to a common moral intuition of human dignity has been compensated by religious morality expressed in what I have termed political theology—a theology that opposes flagrant authoritarianism, whether secular or religious, to seek ways of promoting social justice and democratic governance.

In the Christian context, Max Stackhouse speaks about "public theology" to argue about the importance of theology for public discourse to discern the decisive role intensely personal commitments play in influencing civil society and in the development of democracy and human rights. However, in an Islamic context, I prefer to speak about political rather than public theology because politics determines the action plan for the implementation of religious ideals for a just public order. Moreover, political theology (*al-kalām al-siyāsī*) in Islam correlates reason and revelation in such a way that political jurisprudence (*al-fiqh al-siyāsī*) undertakes to translate personal faith into social action through judicial decisions that envision and endeavor to motivate the faithful to establish just institutions in society so that they objectively reflect God's will for humanity. Islamic political theology based on the central doctrine of a just and merciful God bound by His own moral essence to guide humanity to create a just public order can serve as the major theological-ethical foundation for human rights and its prerequisite, namely, democratic governance in Muslim societies.

Recent trends in Islamic legal-political thought can also be situated within the debates in political theology that regard the challenge posed by modernity as a threat to the traditional and historically enduring synthesis of religion, philosophy, and social wisdom in Islamic civilization. By reassessing this aspect of Islamic thought in a dialogical mode with secular and Christian treatment of human rights concepts and categories, one can begin to render Islamic legal-political thought more comprehensible in the context of epistemological challenges posed by liberal humanism that disregard the ability of religion to transform life for the betterment of all humanity without discrimination at the interpersonal level. Further, dialogical treatment can reveal how those inclusive and pluralist concepts and categories can themselves be creatively renegotiated to respond to the needs of a different time and place.

While the essential comprehension of political association traces social-political allegiances back to their very deepest affirmations, political theology takes the opposite course by raising a fundamental question regarding the ultimate purpose of scriptural allegiance in creating an ideal political society. As a world-embracing tradition, Islamic political theology from its early inception provided religious legitimacy to existing social and political structures by insisting upon certain extraneous characteristics to the public order under divinely ordained legal norms. In other words, it functioned as a rigorous critique of an existing order claiming to be Islamic by evaluating its temporal performance, thereby affording a secular space for assessing a religiously defined public order. The public scrutiny of the political performance of an otherwise spiritually and morally defined polity was the most significant contribution of Islamic political theology that required religious vigilance on the part of the governed to check the excesses of those in power. In this manner, Islamic revealed texts provided the preamble for an ethical political order with important criteria to determine when it was a duty to combat flagrant political authoritarianism that stifled the human ability to respond to the divine moral challenge for establishing justice on earth.[17] Islamic political theology has maintained its vibrancy as a constructive critic without compromising its essential objective of empowering the "downtrodden" to demand the right to be salvaged from the "corruptibility of human order."[18] The impetus for resistance against oppression and the duty to struggle for justice on earth is so deeply ingrained in Islamic political theology that militant Muslims, through their selective retrieval of scriptural sources, have accented the corruption aspect of autocratic political systems in their call to overthrow some Muslim governments in the Middle East, to the detriment of human dignity.[19] Muslim political ethics forewarns against the dangers of endless violent opposition in order to restore violated justice that can, in the long run, undo the actual mandate of Islamic revelation, namely, restoration of balance between justice and compassion in dealing with human institutions that are prone to corruption.

In the present study, I undertake to analyze diverse interpretations of political theology as they impact upon human rights discourse among Sunnī and Shī'ite traditionalist scholars to demonstrate that Islamic revelation has maintained its multifaceted vitality to allow for variant appropriation of relevant texts for radically different political ends. In addition, I endeavor to underscore the relationship between religious and secular universalisms that are conditioned by ethical-political particularities at different times. It is my earnest hope that the reader will begin to appreciate the diverse stances adopted by forms of political theology in the matter of human rights and their validating foundation, which is often treated as monolithic and reactionary.

Can an Islamic Foundation for Human Rights Sit in Dialogue with the Declaration?

In the Western studies of Islamic law (written by Western or secularly educated Muslim intellectuals), and whether or not it is compatible with the human rights values enshrined in the Declaration, one can read severe criticism of the Islamic legal heritage and the human rights record of countries like Saudi

Arabia and Iran where Islamic governments have failed to protect the rights of their respective citizens. While there is much to be admired in these critical studies about irreconcilable conflict between the articles of the Declaration and certain legal rulings in the Islamic juridical tradition that are prejudicial, for instance, to women or religious minorities, what is totally missing in these legal analyses and comparisons is tough foundational questions about the rationale of human rights.[20] In all probability, much of this critical scholarship on Islam's inability to develop an inclusive human rights regime is based on the presumption that just as the philosophy of the Enlightenment in its conflict with Christianity sealed the fate of religion in the public square, modernity has also dealt the same blow to Islamic political theology and its ability to deal with universal morality grounded in the autonomous individual's ability to reason and to negotiate his or her spiritual destiny. To add to this secular antireligious presumption, the religious implications of the Cairo Declaration as it stands, and its lack of any theological-ontological articulation about human personality and its ability to know right from wrong based on Islamic theological doctrines about human nature, dignity, and agency, leaves very little room for any human rights theorist to appreciate the foundational potential in Islam to engage secular claims of universality on their own terms. In other words, according to the Cairo Declaration, the reasons why Muslims ought to implement human rights in their societies is because they happen to be Muslim, and not because they are first and foremost humans. Such a particularistic approach to the bearer of inalienable human rights in the Cairo Declaration as an alternative or as a Muslim response to the universal Declaration actually invalidates its claim to be universal, because it primarily caters for its own members as privileged rights-holders—however large this membership might be—without attending to the foundation that can deliver equally universal rights to all humans qua human. The faith community in this Islamic document does not transcend self-imposed particularity ("Therefore we, as Muslims, who believe . . . in our obligation to establish an Islamic order"), which, in turn, is bound to lead to discrimination against those outside the communal boundaries. My critical assessment of the Cairo Declaration is essentially foundational, because the daunting task of defining an Islamic foundation for human rights can come only from a painstaking analysis of Islamic political theology—a field for the self-critical assessment of the political performance of those in authority—which has remained in abeyance in much of the Muslim world because of undemocratic governance that hampers any criticism of those in power and any attempt to implement basic rights of the governed. It is not surprising that Max Stackhouse, a Christian theologian, who had probably very cursory knowledge of Islamic tradition, regarded Islam as a religious tradition that simply does not maintain the free agency of human beings for freedom of action and association to develop democratic governance in Muslim societies. As a matter of fact, in his study of human rights in three cultures he indicates that Islam, in comparison to Western Christianity, is ill suited to a democratic concept of society.[21] Such a negative evaluation about the foundational inadequacy of Islamic tradition is not limited to Stackhouse. Even Muslim secular intellectuals have not only failed to recognize pluralism in the interpretation of the revealed texts; they have also ignored the anti-authoritarian theological stance adopted by a number of classical jurist-cum-theologians, who vehemently opposed an "official" authoritarian reading of these texts. The absence of a religious institution like a church that represents God's interests on earth allows easy departure and dissension from officially promoted theology among Muslim scholars.

In a well-known Persian women's journal, *Farzāne* (*Intelligent Woman*), when Ayatollah Bojnūrdī was asked about the contradiction between the rulings of Islamic jurisprudence (*fiqh*) and the articles of an international human rights document regarding the human rights of women, he did not hesitate to point out that Islamic jurisprudence is not Islam. Jurisprudence, as Bojnūrdī correctly points out, is the process of extrapolation by a jurist, which is open to change and revision in accord with time and place. The extrapolated rulings are not written in stone; rather, they respond to the changing circumstances in which women find themselves today. Hence, as an example, he brings up the question of whether a woman can inherit her deceased husband's land, which the classical jurists ruled as forbidden. "This is not an absolute opinion of Islam; rather, it is open to change in jurisprudence as dictated by the changed circumstances for a woman today."[22] Another prominent and highly influential traditional scholar, Ayatollah Javādī Āmolī, in his analysis of the moral foundation of the Declaration, makes a revealing observation that clearly presents a different picture of the way traditionalist scholars view human rights issues:

> Some people appear to be saying that they can formulate human rights without any reference to the underlying worldview and the relation between human beings and the world. The advocates of this view formulated the bill of rights, calling it the Universal Declaration of Human Rights. Without consciously or unconsciously desiring it, they neglected to take into account the fact that by merely signing such a Declaration one could not claim that it is beneficial to some or a majority of the peoples of the world. Rights are not a national issue like cultural traditions and customs are, and which might vary from

> culture to culture and people to people. It is worth keeping in mind that the function of a true religion is not to command people what to wear or what to eat, for these things vary in different cultures and places. What a true religion declares includes all the facets of life that apply universally to all human beings without regarding the differences. . . . Human beings cannot acquire a common and universal source for determining human rights without freeing themselves from the shackles of nature.[23]

The above discourse by a leading traditional Muslim authority seems to be conveying that religious discourse in Islam is open to various interpretations. However, at the same time, this discourse is not oblivious to the implications of religious faith that ultimately it is only God who has comprehensive knowledge about all human conditions to exercise self-determination in the area of natural laws that form the divinely ordained source for human rights. Whether one agrees with Javādī Āmolī or not, it is obvious that the issue that confronts the legitimacy of the Declaration among the traditionalists is not reduced to judicial rulings that are conditioned by culture, time, and place. Rather, the issue is fundamentally foundational. Can there be a concept of human dignity based on something inherent in human nature without some sort of existential sacredness connected with the very creation of human beings in God's image? What is the source of human dignity and the worth of human persons that is inviolable? If human rights stem from something deeply ingrained in the human person, is it sufficient to maintain that such rights have their origin in human rationality without any reference to some metaphysical source of those attributes that constitute humanness? It seems that the antireligious and anti-sacred stance of the secularist advocates of the Declaration, however well-intended to steer the document away from epistemological entanglement with theological-ontological comprehension of the status of human beings as part of God's purposeful creation, has actually become a conversation stopper, depriving the international document of its due consideration among serious Muslim, and even Christian, theologians.

I begin with an investigation into the present theory of human rights in order to contrast the claims of universal rights that stem from secular and religious presuppositions of international human rights and Islamic tradition respectively. At the center of the debate is whether human rights ought to remain foundationless, independent of a particular religion that acknowledges a revelatory foundation for such claims. With the rise of religious militancy that has been evinced through extremism and violence, the debate about the theoretical foundation of human rights has assumed some urgency and needs to be resolved without resorting to polemics or apologetics. The two universalisms, one projected by secularism and rationalism and the other by scripturalism and traditionalism, are in competition or even in a state of collision unless a way is found to establish a conversation between the two ideologies. The faith communities cannot afford to ignore the liberal-secular hold over the instruments of the implementation of rights; nor can the secularist advocates of universal human rights afford to isolate and lose support of influential religious leaders to further the protection of the rights of the most vulnerable in society.

The following two chapters discuss the foundational sources of Islamic universalism and whether they can become the source for an inclusive theological and ethical-legal system to change the exclusive juridical tradition that divides humanity into believer and nonbeliever camps to an inclusive system that accepts equality of all citizens as the sole criterion for the holder of rights in the Muslim world. One of the critical questions that needs to be raised in an Islamic context is whether there is any notion of natural rights and natural law in Muslim theology. As discussed earlier in this chapter, Johannes Morsink has demonstrated with much evidence that Enlightenment philosophy provided the drafters with intellectual ingredients to support the inherence of human rights based on the theory of natural rights. If Christianity, with its overbearing emphasis on the Christological Revelation, could derive its theory of natural law through its intellectual assimilation of Hellenism, Islamic theology was even more amenable to the Greek heritage through its systematic absorption of Hellenism in its rationalist and naturalist theology and juridical methodology, to extrapolate universal morality situated in the doctrine of the innate nature (*fiṭra*) of humanity bestowed by God through His act of creation.

Can there be a rationalist-naturalist theology in Islam that can actually support an Islamic theory of natural law and natural rights that can function as the foundation for universal human rights? I raise this question in the context of the prevailing view about Islam among Catholic theologians, symbolized by the papal address in Regensburg, Germany, on September 12, 2006. In his lecture to the academic audience, Pope Benedict XVI attempted to identify the sources of Christian political ethics by underscoring the compatibility of self-communicating reason with mysterious Word in Christianity. This compatibility of Christian revelation with reason is indicated by the reasonableness of the "Christian spirit" and its ability to sit in dialogue with the "Greek spirit" in a context of modernity that has usually denied the rationality of faith in God and its capability to engage secular reason in genuine enlightenment for the sake of seeking to influence civil liberties and peaceful coexistence among nations. Most important, guided by a kind of modern Enlightenment thinking that belittles the role of religion, Hellenistic reason has found revelation-based reason to be nothing more than a faith that affirms God's overpowering will that can be known only through the unquestioning acceptance of and submission to God's commandments, however irrational they might appear. Such a concept of absolute God leads to a kind of impenetrable voluntarism that deprives humanity of its moral agency and freedom to act in accord with its intuitive reason. Further, faith in this absolute, omnipotent God renders the good and the just eternally unattainable to reason without submitting to "capricious" God's transcendence and otherness, which are not bound to any self-evident ethical norms. The Pope then went on to attribute such a concept of a transcendent God to Islam, whose believers, on the basis of comments made by the Byzantine emperor, have resorted to spreading their faith through violence. This violence in the name of God, as the Pope endeavored to argue, is totally against God's nature, as conceived in Christianity. In other words, violence and intolerance among Muslims can be traced back to the very nature of God in Muslim revealed texts, which present the dichotomy between reason, on the one hand, and revelation, on the other. This dichotomy is then related to the concept of holy war—jihad—in the political realm of Islamic civilization, which demonstrates, according to the Pope, the "unreasonableness" of Muslim belief in God's transcendence and omnipotence—the main source for this appalling lack of political ethics in the Muslim world.

The pontiff's negative assessment of Islamic political ethics based on some secondary sources about Muslim political theology authored by fellow Catholics is based on a well-entrenched thesis among Western academicians and policymakers about Islamic tradition's intrinsic relation to violence and its political incompatibility with the context of modern international public order. Further, this thesis was based on the conduct of some Muslim militant groups in both Europe and the Middle East. These militant Muslims' politically unethical behavior perpetrates the notion that without reformation and thorough secularization of Islamic tradition through disestablishment of Islam from the public square, it is impossible to see the development of constitutional democracy based on consensual rule and accountability of public officials, on the one hand, and equality of all citizens, regardless of their religious differences, in Muslim countries, on the other. The most problematic assumption in this thesis is the notion that since in Islam religion and politics are inseparable, the traditional paradigm of Islamic political society based upon a discriminatory principle that divides humanity into believers and nonbelievers is not only incompatible with the modern public order founded upon each person's religious and civil rights guaranteed in a constitutional democracy; it also breeds intolerance and endless violence in the name of revelation-based public order.

In other words, traditionally conceived Islamic political society can never serve as a guarantor of individual liberty and religious pluralism, the two most prominent features of the contractarian theories of public order. Since interaction with others on just terms is conditional on political association based on communal affiliation, Islamic political society is permanently at odds with a contractarian theory of political obligation based on a universal standard of interpersonal justice that was derived from a system of natural law and natural rights of all human beings regardless of their religious affiliation.

To be sure, modern notions of liberty, pluralism, and human rights have their antecedents in the authoritative theological and legal traditions of Islam. Without regarding the human analytical mind as the only arbiter of a just public order, and without denying revelation the power of correlating the human understanding of justice with revelatory guidance in the matter of a just social order, it is plausible to argue that there is consonance between the truths of the revelation and the demands of human intelligence in discovering a standard of just interaction that could be universally recognizable. Historically, Islamic public order accommodated default separate jurisdictions for the religious and the temporal through its notions of human–God and human–human relationships. Consequently, it accommodated the separation of religion from the everyday workings of politics without depriving revelation of its religiously conceived role as the major source for a comprehensive doctrine to guide the moral and spiritual lives of the people living under its public system.[24]

The fourth and fifth chapters expound the problem of inherited tradition and its cultural manifestation by focusing on the human rights of women and minorities, and the need for communitarian ethics to move toward the recognition of individual rights as the starting point of all other collective rights within the Islamic system. The sociopolitical realities that render religion and politics intertwined in Muslim societies have grave consequences for the exercise of basic freedoms. As long as democratic governance remains a remote possibility in Muslim nations, equality of all citizens as rights holders will also remain implausible, unless an indispensable rethinking of Islamic political theology to challenge autocratic rule is revived and made part of democratic politics. However, the liberal democratic precondition that deals with setting aside religious reason based on Islamic comprehensive doctrines about a just political order and promotion of the common good in the context of Muslim communitarian ethics is unnecessary because Islamic theology explicitly correlates religious and secular reason to deduce its political theology. In order to develop a public political discourse that is inclusive of all citizens of a nation-state without any discrimination, Muslim societies need to adopt public reason that guarantees human rights based on secularization of public space through default separation of religious and political in Islamic jurisprudence. The proposition to separate religion and politics in liberal democracy is based on the assumption that by adopting secularism as an organizing principle, Muslim societies could establish a responsible and just government for a citizen body composed of all humankind through public rather than religious reasons, and public rather than religious consensus. Furthermore, such an assumption about democratization through the separation of church and state is based on the Enlightenment philosophy that rules negatively on the role of religion in a modern nation-state. As long as religion determines the nature of justice and the human good, it is impossible for an inclusive secular consensus to emerge as part of the modern political culture. Religion must be privatized and limited to the domain of individual lives and religious institutions.[25]

From its inception, Islam saw itself as deeply involved with the creation of a just public order. Hence, its comprehensive doctrine claims to govern comprehensive human life in all its manifestations in this world and the next. This political phenomenon connected with Islam has been identified by Western social scientists as political Islam (which I have identified as political theology in this chapter). So interpreted, political Islam is an activist ideology seeking to respond to the internal decadence and political corruption in Muslim states. Further, political Islam functions as a militant strategy to press for political and social reforms in order to make them compatible with Islamic teachings about the Muslim public order, which also includes the implementation of the divinely ordained Sharīʿa in it.[26]

In the growing manifestation of extremist militancy in the Muslim world in the post-9/11 period, traditional Muslim leadership has demonstrated little intellectual or political imagination to deal with internal challenge posed by extremist elements and the challenge posed by modern, liberal notions of democratic governance or protection of human rights instruments in Muslim societies. At the global level there is a need for a cautious and yet constructive evaluation of the role a political religion like Islam can play in affirming at least some universal rights that accrue to all humans qua human. It is important to keep in mind that contemporary secular validation of human rights denies religious universalism and when it comes to specifically dealing with fundamental freedoms, it has always maintained incompatibility between relatively conceived religious tradition and the universal, secular notion of inalienable rights and individual freedoms. This secular validation of universal human rights, despite its claims to transcend the exclusionary boundaries of a religiously constructed vision of human communities, is actually based on short-lived and culture-bound norms. In addition, the secularists' criticism of religious universalism based on absolute truth claims and the universality of religiously promoted moral values as major obstacles to world peace and sources for the violations of minority rights in countries where religious tradition dominates public institutions neglects to assess the performance of those countries that are dominated by secular norms and institutions. In general, secular human rights theorists are biased against religion and its capability of defending the moral worth and inalienable rights of the individual, and, therefore, they dismiss the role public theology can play in advancing human rights. In contrast, religious human rights theorists call for an alliance between religious and secular advocates of human rights based on serious metaphysical or epistemic ground so that both Western and non-Western societies can work together to implement the universal intent of the Declaration.

In view of the above claims and counterclaims about universal morality, whether religious or secular, a critical question can be raised here: Is there a neutral way of supporting the priority of human rights without garnering the support of other value systems in domestic societies, including religiously derived values? Here is the source of tension: How can we reconcile universal human rights with the principle of toleration in those societies where human rights violations are endemic?

A number of Muslim governments have tried to cover up abuses using an argument based on their citizens' primary identity as Muslims and providing a list of rights that are guaranteed in Islamic tradition, which, in principle, as they claim, rejects gross abuses of basic human rights. Hence, there is no need for them to adopt universal human rights principles within their cultural boundaries. Moreover, they have resorted to cultural relativism by arguing that since values are relative to circumstances that define culture, Muslims cannot be expected to adopt the rights that Western culture has defined in relation to its own circumstances. This argument also assumes that the principles of toleration will be applied to Muslim societies whose actions cannot be judged by outsiders simply because there is no universal moral standard against which Western countries can judge the Muslim world. Undoubtedly, the argument about cultural relativism is a reaction to the colonial and imperialist past of the Muslim world, which has also treated liberalism with much suspicion. But what leads to further contempt for the Declaration is the epistemological denial that morality or jurisprudence has serious metaphysical or epistemic grounds to serve as a foundation for human rights. If the secular intent of the Declaration is defined by circumstance and history rather than any metaphysical notions such as human nature and the inherence of rights, what is so universal about the Declaration's intellectual and moral appeal that it can reach out to other cultures in a global context today? The need for urgent dialogue between Muslim and non-Muslim nations to discover universal moral concerns and principles cannot be sufficiently emphasized when the entire project of implementation of the international document is dependent upon it.

The goal of the present study is to build upon the classical heritage of Islam to convey the theology, metaphysics, and natural law that facilitate the acknowledgment of universal human rights without neglecting to point out the duties that Islamic legal-ethical sources emphasize in regulating human relationships. Human relationships, outside of natural bonds, are based on contractual agreements that require a logical connection between duties and rights. The inclusion of duties along with rights is the framework of religious life and, therefore, within the framework of the assumption about a just society. Accordingly, a detailed legitimation and rational, legal justification is necessary to encourage Muslim participation in the global implementation of human rights. The burden of this research will be to identify and articulate Islamic foundational sources that could establish a legitimate correspondence with secularly derived human rights. Both advocacy and the regulation of human rights are essentially matters of religion and ethics. It is religion that teaches universally recognized principles of conduct, which have a basis in elementary truths about human beings and the purpose for which they have been created. Religious teachings about humanity endowed with ends anticipates teleological notions of nature that stem from common morality shared by two dichotomous universal claims, one founded upon secularism and the other on scriptural sources. Even the Qur'an insists upon interdependence between claims and duties.

The language of human rights, as pointed out earlier, is modern, in which accruing responsibilities that come with the claims to entitlements are underemphasized. This is the source of tension between universal, secular claims of the Declaration and the religious-cultural specificity that demands a responsive voice in fulfilling duties that are imposed on humanity by the simple fact of being God's creatures. This does not, however, mean that religious language limits itself to the performance of duties to the exclusion of rights. Rather, a religion like Islam is interested in striking a balance between claims and duties to establish a viable ethical order on earth. Diverse world communities are engaged in searching for this balance.

To put forward an adequate paradigm that suits the needs of the faith community without losing sight of its relation to other communities in the international order, it is imperative that Islamic discourse receive an independent, detailed treatment in the context of Western-dominated discourse on human rights. The real issues connected with dichotomous relationships between secular and spiritual, universal and relative aspects of moral norms that seek application in specific cultural contexts with a view to search for an overlapping consensus over values that touch all others outside the specific community should assume a critical spot in this discourse. At the international level, two apparently dichotomous universalisms—secular and religious—are in competition for cultural legitimacy by appealing to two sets of normative sources: reason and revelation. Islam, with its world-embracing ideology and historical standing as a highly successful civilization, more than any other religious tradition, claims to present an alternative universal paradigm of political-religious civilization. As such, we need to engage Islam on its own terms, without imposing categories of discourse on the debate between Islam and human rights externally. To begin with, Muslims need to abandon the between-the-lines reading of the colonial-colonized relationship between the West and the Muslim world that has led to a negative evaluation of the Declaration as a hegemonic ploy to impose Western domination on the rest of the world.

Yet the universal elements of Islamic human rights discourse can hardly benefit from the hermeneutical move to bring the normative tradition in line with some of the rights that are derived by reference to the geopolitical context rather than some abstract notion of justice without a serious assessment of the situation on the ground. The real test for any document of rights remains its practical implementation in the community of nations. Many Muslim countries are ruled by autocratic regimes, mostly supported by Western countries, that have suspended their people's basic rights to freedom of conscience and expression under flimsy excuses of nonapplicability of human rights principles or excuses that democratization will threaten the region's political stability. Ironically, it is this kind of support of these autocratic regimes by some Western powers that has done more harm to the credibility of the Declaration than all the arguments based on the inconsistencies between religiously and secularly derived rights or moral relativism.

The Problem of Foundationless Human Rights in Building a Secular-Religious Alliance

If the goal of the present study is to work toward identifying Islamic sources for building an overlapping consensus that could form the foundation for a critical alliance between the secularist and traditionalist scholars of human rights to further the aims of the Declaration, then it will be important to argue for those foundational notions, whether secularly or religiously derived, that have universal appeal. In deriving universal human rights norms, many human rights theorists have argued for a foundationless model of human rights. The basic assumptions underlying this model are twofold: on the one hand, a foundational model, in particular a religious one, appears to be limited to the faith community application, hardly suitable for generating international consensus on human rights norms across traditions. This assumption is also responsible for the secularization of the international human rights document. On the other hand, since there is a sharp distinction between liberal Western and nonliberal cultures, especially Muslim cultures, the foundationless model will achieve better results by focusing on practical issues that arise when these states do not provide instruments of human rights to defend their citizens' rights. Such practical considerations have also led these secular theorists to avoid focusing on philosophical or religious foundations of human rights principles. The problem that faces Muslim supporters of the Declaration is that without due consideration of religious or philosophical sources, it would be difficult to garner the support of Muslim communities to work toward improving human rights instruments to effect the necessary implementation of the Declaration. Evidently, emphasis on the secular-religious dichotomy will necessarily lead to a foundationless model, which actually stifles critical dialogue between secular and traditionalist theorists. In addition, Western-Islamic polarization in terms of liberal and nonliberal societies is also detrimental to the need for international consensus on protecting a number of basic freedoms, including freedom of conscience and religion. An Islamic model for democratic pluralism, as I have argued, for instance, is not inherently antithetical to a central concept of human dignity and an individual's inalienable right to determine his or her spiritual destiny without interference. I am convinced that in Muslim societies, enforcement of human rights will be taken even more seriously if, using the foundational model, one can derive the inherent worth of the individual and argue for freedom of religion. Human rights is in origin a Western concept that needs to become Islamic in all its ramifications. With this in mind, let me very briefly demonstrate a revelation-based foundation for a foundational model that is not oblivious to the concerns raised by the supporters of foundationless theories, and yet able to derive a comparable, and even equitable, conception of human worth.

In order to liberate human reason to make it the sole criterion for moral cognition, the secular model of human rights had to separate reason from its divine origin. Reason was also severed from its bedrock in natural law, which provided all the necessary guidance to achieve the divinely ordained purposes for human life on earth. Secularization of reason coupled with economic and social development led to depreciation of the role of natural law and its religious and metaphysical foundations. This undermining of the revelation has been gradual and almost concealed until more recently, when questions about a fundamental agreement on values and demands of reason between peoples and across cultures have flared up between Western powers and Muslim nations regarding the enforcement of human rights.

In Islam, human ability to know right from wrong is part of the divine endowment for humanity through the very creation of human nature (*fiṭra*), the receptacle for intuitive reason. Moral cognition, in this notion of creation, is innate to human nature and because of it human beings are capable of discerning moral law. There is no discussion about natural law or natural rights in Muslim theology. But the Qur'anic notion of universal morality with which all human beings are blessed and held accountable to God, regardless of their particular faith commitment or even lack of it, as I will elaborate in chapter 3, makes it legitimate to speak about an Islamic idea of natural law. The moral law, then, is universal and can be discovered by all due to the simple fact of sharing a common humanity through creation. Further, the moral law guides humans in all matters, spiritual and temporal, private and public.

The rationalist-traditionalist divide among Muslim theologians did not lead to a drastic conclusion about God's plan for humanity. According to them, religion established the connection between private and public, individual and society, spiritual and mundane. Human progression was guaranteed if they could manage to balance contradicting demands of various spheres of human existence. Two distinct positions on revelation-based or rationally derived morality did not in any significant way undermine the ability of ordinary people to understand the balance between demands of revelation and reason. Revelation actually depended on reason for its validity; and reason sought to validate its conclusions by showing their correlation to the revelation.

The secular liberal thesis that liberty can survive only outside religion and through secularization of a religious tradition was founded upon historical experience of Christianity and, hence, had little resonance in Islam. The liberal solution was clearly to separate the public and the private in order to guarantee that the public square would remain inclusive and tolerant of differences. The value of freedom had to be raised over and against Christian religious exclusivity. In other words, privatization through secularization of Christianity helped in reducing the hold of religious law and the church over society, thus making pluralism in the public square possible.

That religious experience of those who argue for foundationless theories of human rights is worth keeping in mind, particularly when such a negative evaluation of religion is extended to a different historical experience of Muslim societies. The foundationless theories have one of the most critical concerns to guarantee basic human rights: how to reconcile basic freedoms with the moral worth of all humans as humans. To be sure, in light of the tragic unfolding of human exclusive religiosity and moral absolutism, that concern was and remains real even today.

Was Muslim historical experience any different? Evidently it was, and this is what seems to be the source of an alternative human rights paradigm presented by Muslim apologists. What is missing in this alternative paradigm is the discussion of any foundational capacity in Islamic tradition to sit in dialogue with the secular human rights theorists to make a case for inclusive notions of human entitlements tempered with human responsibilities in maintaining the overall well-being of humanity in all its areas and spheres of existence. I aim to initiate a substantial theoretical discussion of an inclusive foundational conception of human rights that would appeal to suspicious traditional authorities in the Muslim world, apparently threatened by secular ideologies that they believe are determined to destroy the spiritual and moral foundations of a global community to make room for liberal secular ideas of inalienable human rights.

The point of departure for my research is to argue for a foundational theory of human rights based on some of the pluralistic features of Islam and its culture, totally ignored by Muslim traditionalist and fundamentalist discourse. True to its internal juridical plurality, the Islamic tradition was concerned with the preservation of freedom against any kind of legal or political authoritarianism, especially in view of its refusal to afford any human institution such as a church the right to represent the divine interests on earth. Moreover, this default plurality was instrumental in preserving relatively peaceful coexistence among peoples of diverse faiths and cultures under Muslim political domination. Functional recognition of separate jurisdictions for the spiritual and the temporal was also instrumental in affording fundamental agreement on public values and in meeting the demands of multifaith and multicultural societies of the Islamic world to regulate human relationships between peoples of different faiths and culture. Hence, the Western experience of separation of religion and politics by default remained alien to Muslim political experience.

It is this difference in the historical experience of the West and Islam that makes my project a viable proposition in the ongoing debate over whether a foundationless secular model can on its own provide universal standards that can be applied across cultures, or whether it needs to look at the foundational religious model with its own universal claim to offer a more comprehensive understanding of what it means to be a defender of human rights today. Religion cannot and will not confine itself to a private domain where it will eventually lose its influence in nurturing human conscience. It needs a public space in the development of an international sense of a world community with a vision of creating an ideal society that cares and shares.

2

The Nature of Islamic Juridical-Ethical Discourse

In my search for universal dimensions of Islamic tradition that could engage in a meaningful conversation with liberal secularist proponents of foundationless human rights, I begin with a critical assessment of Islamic juridical tradition—a formidable obstacle to a number of articles of great consequence for the protection of individual rights that are enshrined in the Universal Declaration of Human Rights.[1] My aim is to explore the ethical doctrines that undergird the legal tradition in Islam, because, as I argue in this chapter, it is the ethical dimension of Islamic legal methodology that holds the potential for an inclusive universal language that can engage the universal morality of the Declaration. What is critically needed in the Islamic context is to demonstrate to traditionalist scholars that Islamic ethics shares common moral terrain with the Declaration on several levels, and that to disregard the Declaration's foundations as antireligious would be to foreclose any opportunity to dialogue with liberal secularists on the need to protect human dignity and to advance peace with justice in the world.

In general, ethical inquiry connected with moral epistemology or moral ontology is underdeveloped in the Islamic seminarian curriculum, which is in large measure legally oriented. This lack of interest in the theological-ethical underpinnings of juridical methodology is a major drawback of seminary education in the major centers of Islamic learning. A number of Western scholars of Islamic legal tradition, following the antirationalist attitude of mainly

Sunni jurists, have erroneously excluded any organic relationship between theological and legal doctrines in shaping legal methodology and application. In contrast, Shīʿite legal studies have not severed their epistemic correlation with, for instance, the theological question of whether good and evil are objective categories that can be known intuitively by divinely endowed reason to the agent or not. The moral consequences of raising such questions about ethical epistemology are enormous, since they lead to larger issues about human ability to comprehend justice and to assume the moral responsibility to effect changes in social and political realms. Moreover, theological-ethical deliberations have led to the moral categorization of human acts based on rational understanding of one's duties and reciprocal responsibilities. Legal categorization in jurisprudence has simply followed what was intuitively assessed as necessary (*wājib*), recommended (*mandūb*), or forbidden (*ḥarām*).

My other aim in investigating the ethical foundation of Islamic juridical tradition is to emphasize the human dimension of the juridical enterprise in Islam, so that the normative essentialism attached to the interhuman relationships in the juridical corpus of the classical age is understood in its historical, cultural, and social contexts. Having spent more than four decades of my academic life mastering the Islamic legal tradition, I have concluded that the reason legal reforms in the Muslim world during and after the colonial age lacked cultural legitimacy was because reformers ignored the task of rethinking legal methodology to appreciate the universal content of its ethical underpinnings in favor of seeking textual proof for fresh rulings in the area of interhuman relationships. Modernization through Westernization forced Muslim countries to adopt Western civil codes to respond to the changing social and political conditions of modern men and women living as citizens of nation-states rather than as believers in the community. There was no dearth of conceptual resources in theological ethics for deriving universal moral principles to guide the life of a citizen who needed to be treated equally, first as a human being endowed with dignity, and only then differentiated as a member of a specific faith community. But these resources were neglected.

Not surprisingly, the same neglect of Islamic ethical resources occurred in drafting the Cairo Declaration on Human Rights in Islam in August 1990. The superficial citations from the Qur'an and the Tradition merely disguise the lack of interest in the intellectually demanding task of defining moral reasoning in Islam, a task that chronologically precedes and substantially supplements the scriptural sources by correlating the conclusions of two foundational sources—revelation and reason—for the establishment of a just public order on earth. An Islamic human rights document that fails to articulate universal appeal that ought to go beyond the boundaries of the faith community to include all human beings regardless of their race, creed, or color, based on their inherent dignity, could hardly convince the international community of the universal intent of Islamic revelation, much less about the drafters' commitment to protect the human rights of all humans as humans. Not unlike the Cairo Declaration, the history of legal reforms in the Muslim world is replete with examples that needed internal response from Muslim jurists to develop an expansive legal methodology that could extrapolate from classical legal theory to offer solutions within the larger context of the new political reality of modern nation-states. Without arṭiculating and recognizing the moral worth of all humans based on Islamic revelation, it is ludicrous to speak about inherent human dignity and inalienable human rights. The credibility of the Muslim claim to offer an alternative to the UN Declaration depends upon rigorously overcoming the restrictive provisions of the Islamic juridical heritage to derive a new concept of citizenship based on equality of all humans as humans.

So this neglect of the ethical presuppositions of the Islamic juridical tradition has become endemic among Muslim jurists in dealing with the dignity and rights of the religious "other." But an equally problematic situation exists among those academicians dealing with the Islamic tradition who, in principle, reject any suggestion that Islam has intellectual resources to deal with the demands of international secular order. Whether or not constitutional democracy or human rights are compatible with historical Islam, the important thing worth exploring is whether a form of religious reason based on a comprehensive doctrine can effectively demonstrate its capability to engage public reason to build an overlapping consensus in the public domain. Nevertheless, without articulation of the all-pervading and inclusive notion of the moral worth of all humans, authentically derived from Islamic revelation, we cannot speak about an overlapping consensus to defend a political proposal of a universal morality that can recognize all humans as bearers of equal rights.

To clarify where I am coming from on this issue, let me interject here a well-entrenched thesis among many Western academics and policymakers about the Islamic tradition's intrinsic relation to violence and its political incompatibility in the context of modern international public order. This thesis—grounded on the basis of the conduct of some Muslim militant groups who have disregarded a long and well-established Islamic tradition of just public order founded upon principles of coexistence and God-centered pluralism—argues that without the reformation of the juridical tradition and the thorough secularization of public space through the disestablishment of Islam, there will be no development of constitutional democracy based on the equality of all citizens in Muslim countries.

In my view, the most misconstrued assumption in this thesis is the idea that since in Islam religion and politics are inseparable, the traditional paradigm of Islamic political society (based upon a discriminatory principle that divides humanity into believers and nonbelievers) is incompatible with a modern public order founded upon each person's religious and civil rights guaranteed in a constitutional democracy. In other words, traditionally conceived Islamic political society can never serve as a guarantor of individual liberty and religious pluralism, the two most prominent features of the contractarian theories of public order. Moreover, by this interpretation, since just relationships with others are conditional on political associations built on religious commitment and affiliation, any Islamic public order is permanently at odds with contractarian theories of social cooperation based on accounts of justice as fairness. By this account, the principle of justice must be founded upon a standard of just interaction based on a system of natural law and natural rights of all human beings regardless of their religious affiliation.

In the following section, I want to argue that modern notions of liberty, pluralism, and human rights have their antecedents in the authoritative theological and legal traditions of Islam. Without succumbing to the temptation of regarding the human analytical mind as the only arbiter of just public order, and therefore without denying revelation the power of correlating the human understanding of justice with revelatory guidance in the matter of a just social order, it is not far-fetched to argue that there is consonance between the truths of revelation and the discoveries of human intelligence as regards a standard of just interaction that would be reasonably accepted by all in some suitably defined public order. Moreover, although traditionally Islamic public order has accommodated by default separate jurisdictions for religious and temporal spheres through its notions of human—God (*'ibādāt*) and human—human (*mu'āmalāt*) relationships, it has carved out a special role for religious premises with political conclusions as an important source for guiding the moral and spiritual lives of the people living under its public system.[2] It is this legacy of the traditional reconciliation between religious premises and political development that can provide indigenous sources for modern notions of liberty, pluralism, and human rights.

Religious Reason in Muslim Polity

The sociopolitical realities that make the religious and political spheres inseparable in traditional Muslim societies call for serious rethinking regarding the preconditions set by the theorists of liberal democracy for the establishment of democratic governance in the Muslim world. Such theorists demand that those societies set aside religious reason based on Islamic comprehensive doctrines about a just political order and the promotion of the common good in the context of Muslim communitarian ethics. In order to develop a public political discourse that is inclusive of all citizens of a nation-state without any discrimination, such theorists argue, Muslim societies need to adopt public reason that guarantees human rights through the secularization of public space through separation of religious and political spheres. These theorists assume that, by adopting secularism as an organizing principle, Muslim societies could establish a responsible and just government for all citizens through a public rather than a religious rationale, and a public rather than a religious consensus. The operative hypothesis in this secular assumption about democratization through the separation of church and state is that as long as religion determines the nature of the just and the human good, it is impossible for an inclusive secular consensus to emerge as part of Muslim political culture. Religion must be privatized and restricted to the domain of individual lives and religious institutions to allow for an inclusive and equal citizenship built upon the inherent moral standing of persons.[3]

Of all the world religions, Islam, with its comprehensive doctrine about the moral duty to institute good and prevent evil, is most identified with attempts to govern human life in all its manifestations in this world and the next. This ethical-political obligation connected with public order in Islam has been identified by Western social scientists as political Islam. So interpreted, political Islam is an active response seeking to counter internal decadence and political corruption in Muslim states. Further, political Islam is open to manipulation as a militant strategy to press for political and social reforms in order to make them compatible with Islamic teachings about the Muslim public order, which also includes the implementation of the divinely ordained Sharīʿa.[4]

Undeniably, it is necessary that the political agenda of ideological religiosity must question both the authoritative claims and the substantive content of its traditional sources that must now take into account new political realities that demand just solutions to the problem of accommodating modern concepts of democracy and human rights. Today, with the prevalence of autocratic governments in most Muslim countries, democracy cannot simply be taken to mean the ability to vote for or against potential political leaders. Mere electoral selection of state leaders has led to neither consensual rule nor accountability of these elected leaders to the people. In the context of our search for ethical resources of public order in Islam, our working assumption is that a democratic system is one in which the consent of the governed, the rule of the people through their elected representatives, and basic human rights and equality of all citizens within a religion-based ideology are promoted through constitutional guarantees. Inasmuch as political Islam treats the two spheres of religion and politics as integrated, it is not unreasonable to assert that it is least prepared to be democratically inclusive and tolerant of the religious diversity prevalent in most countries in the Muslim world.

Liberal theorists' assumptions about political Islam and its presumed incompatibility with liberal democratic values or secular human rights norms, and such theorists' assumptions about the necessary secularization of religious space in public life, can be challenged. They need to be examined in light of the foundational religious texts of Islam, which, as I contend, reveal a complex and at times contradictory relationship between the religious and the political in Muslim history. Traditional understandings of Islam did not rule out a noninterventionist role for religion in public space; nor did the juridical endorsement of the separation of human—God and human—human relationships overlook the pluralistic approach to religious diversity or intercommunal relations. Islamic civilization, despite its favored treatment of Muslims over non-Muslims, was very much committed to peaceful intercommunal relations. In fact, Islam's ability to live with other faiths and peoples was underscored by its universal narrative of creation of the first man and woman on earth with its ethical implications for interpersonal justice, which deserves to be reexamined, however briefly, for its universal undertones.

Theological-Ethical Implications of the Creation Narrative in the Qur'an

In light of the inevitable linkage between the religious and the political in Islamic thought, and the centrality of theological resources to provide the moral basis of legitimate political authority and individual rights in Muslim culture, it is important to emphasize that it is only through the retrieval, further interpretation, and reappropriation of these religious ideas that the necessary political reform in the Muslim world could take firm roots. Right from its inception as a public religion, the Qur'an underscores the need to develop a universal discourse of moral awareness as its foundation for an inclusive human community, guided by both an ethical necessity grounded in intuitive reason and supernatural revelation brought by God's prophets. The creation narrative in the Qur'an offers few details of how the universe was created—the central piece of the Book of Genesis's creation stories. Quite to the contrary, human creation is the main subject of the Qur'anic genesis story, with total attention to the development of moral sensibilities that speak to a future ethical order for a human body composed of diverse human communities sharing the same parentage. The human being is in constant need of guidance, which comes both in its universal form as innate moral sensibility and in its particularistic form in the revelation that reconfirms and sharpens the general intuition.

The theological-ethical implications of this creation narrative assume great significance as a counterpoint to the secular project of abandoning the particularistic traditional linkage of morality to religion. The secular theory of moral development favors exclusively reason-based morality founded upon human experience in the context of everyday life situations. In contrast, moral development, as it emerges in the Islamic creation narrative, takes revealed guidance as well as naturally endowed intuitive reason as two interrelated sources of moral knowledge that humanity needs in order to avoid moral perdition.

The universal dimensions of the creation narrative in the Qur'an become even more significant when examined in the context of another unique cosmic event, namely, the offering of the Trust (*amāna*). Apparently, the theme covered in this event forms part of the creation story, but it precedes the actual creation of the first human. It deals with the offering of the Trust and its ultimate acceptance by humankind:

> We offered the trust to the heavens and the earth and the mountains, but they refused to carry it and were afraid of it; and human being carried it. Surely he is unjust, ignorant. (Q. 33:73)

Muslim scholars have speculated on two related issues in this passage. First, what exactly was the nature of the Trust that the awesome heavens and the earth and the mountains refused to carry it and were afraid of it? Second, if the human being, who in comparison to the tremendous heavens and the earth is physically so insignificant, demonstrated the courage and daring to accept the Trust, why was he being criticized as being "unjust" and "ignorant"? Did he not instead deserve to be praised for his willingness and daring to take up the challenge?

God's Trust in this passage, as asserted by a number of classical as well as modern exegetes of the Qur'an, symbolizes God's power to rule on earth on God's behalf as God's deputy (*khalīfa*). God's decision to commission humankind to rule on earth is linked to humankind's ability to carry out the two prerequisites of exercising God's authority, namely, justice and knowledge. As God's deputy, the human being is commissioned to assume authority and to exact obedience with justice and knowledge about the consequences of political decisions for the good of all humanity. The relationship of authority with justice and knowledge renders God's deputyship as importantly political: the one who accepts its burden becomes the bearer of the moral vision of the Qur'an about a just polity. In this sense, human involvement in public life is an inevitable projection of a personal faith that demands taking up the moral challenge of creating a divinely ordained public order on earth.

In light of the creation narrative and the appointment of humanity as God's deputy, the Trust belongs to God and must be returned to God. In other words, essentially, power belongs to God; and when human beings exercise it while on earth, they must exercise it with justice. God's criticism leveled at humanity as being "unjust" and "ignorant" has an intrinsic connection with the potential for abuse of the Trust (power), which lands humanity in the court of political ethics for judgment. Since only human beings took up the moral challenge, it is only human beings who are endowed with intuitive reason to judge the rightness or wrongness of their actions and face the consequences of their choice accordingly. It is indeed through the acceptance of this Trust of God's rule on earth that human beings acquire both their distinct moral worth and responsibility for their choices, as well as superiority over all other creatures in the world. God's deputyship both enables and obligates them to order society in accordance with their unique comprehension of the realities and challenges that face humanity in the exercise of limitless power in the name of God.

An element of tension enters the narrative of the deputyship of humanity with the appearance of Satan—the one who has caused humanity to slip. The Qur'an underscores two contradictory characteristics in the human being: on the one hand, the Qur'an demonstrates the human being's cognitive ability and asserts the human's superiority over the angels who proclaim God's praise and sanctity; on the other, it reveals the human's vulnerability to satanic temptation and ensuing misguidance that can hinder the development of an ethical society on earth.

Nevertheless, in these narratives the Qur'an honors the whole of humanity without drawing lines between believers and nonbelievers. The source of human dignity (*karam*) is provided in the creation narrative, where it evidently points to the human ability to know right from wrong. The story relates the effect of tasting the forbidden fruit, which apparently damaged human moral awareness. According to the Qur'an, when "they [both] tasted the tree, their nakedness revealed to them, so they took to stitching upon themselves leaves of the Garden." The couple's innate knowledge and reaction to the nakedness being revealed to them evidently reveals a naturally endowed ability to know right from wrong. However, the couple's reaction to the knowledge of nakedness has a concrete and historical context of the Semitic moral sensibilities connected with rules of decency. This relative cultural dimension of the Qur'anic ethics suggests an important caveat in the search for universal morality. If a paradigm for universal morality is to emerge both as a source of human dignity and as a principle of human interaction in society, it has to acknowledge the communitarian boundaries of its application within different cultural and historical experiences of the communities. In other words, there will always remain a tension between a particular revelation, with its specific appeal to the community of the faithful, and a universal morality that requires the community to relate itself beyond its communal affiliation to the larger world community.

This tension is inevitable, because in Islam the first human is not only God's deputy; he is also God's prophet, sent with specific guidance at a certain point in history. The historical relativity of God's guidance to human beings at a particular time leads to the problem of raising a particularistic moral language in the Qur'an to the level of universal application when it comes to Muslim public order. For the particularistic, and in some religious sense exclusive, language of Islamic revelation came at a certain time in history to guide a specific ethnic group; in order for it to serve as a communitarian as well as inclusive normative source for organizing a just and equitable public order, it needs to include a universal dimension that can be appropriated across human communities as part of their social-political consciousness. Religious reasons based on revelation that seek to influence political conclusions are necessarily ethical norms that derive their inclusive validity by appealing to the followers of various cultural and religious traditions who share, at least minimally, common views of the just and the good. Hence, in advancing human rights discourse among different cultures and traditions, it is imperative to develop an inclusive discourse founded upon universal morality that does not deny religious premises their due position in deriving political conclusions that speak to all humanity. In searching for such premises that can engage public reason on its own turf, one can evoke notions like inherent human dignity, which is deeply rooted in religious reasons and which serves as an important backdrop for approaching the question of the relevance of such norms in the pluralistic setting of the majority of Muslim countries today. No traditionalist Muslim authority can afford to ignore the fundamental connotation of the Qur'anic narrative of creation in the realm of ethical necessity connected with the inherent dignity of all human beings as the Children of Adam.

Human Dignity and Religious Particularity

The Qur'an is concerned about the tension between universal and communitarian ethics and undertakes to address the issue on several occasions. The strategy employed by the Qur'an to connect humanity as a single community, even as it recognizes the plurality of scriptural guidance given through various prophets, is to relate them through an "innate nature" that is capable of recognizing a moral good (*al-khayr, al-ma'rūf*). This innate nature is the source of the very first qualities by virtue of which someone becomes human:

> So set your purpose for religion, a human by nature upright—God's original [nature] upon which He created humankind. There is no altering [the laws of] God's creation. (Q. 30:30)

In addition, God also honors humanity with "noble nature" (*karam*). As part of their noble nature, all humans are endowed with an innate scale with which they can weigh the rightness and wrongness of their conduct. This innate scale is connected with a kind of universal ethical cognition, as stated in another reference to human creation:

> By the soul and that which shaped it and inspired it [with conscience of] what is wrong for it and [what is] right for it. Prosperous is he who purifies it, and failed has he who seduces it. (Q. 91:7–10)

Hence, the "human by nature upright" or as created in "original nature" (*fitrat allāh* = God's nature) is endowed with a morality that cannot be arbitrary. Ethical knowledge that is "inspired by God" does not require any justification independent of the naturally endowed innate measure. The Qur'an guides humankind with its upright nature to achieve a balance between "known" (the convictions determined through the process of reflection) and "unknown" moral judgments by placing the known moral solutions in history and culture at the same time. Consequently, the Qur'an anchors moral norms in the reflective process and invites human beings to deliberate about the consequences of their actions and to learn to avoid any behavior that leads to perilous ends. Moreover, it appeals to the human capacity for learning from past destructiveness in order to avoid it in the future. The assumption in the Qur'an is that there is something concrete about the human condition that cannot be denied by any reasonable person endowed with the "heart to understand," that is, the conscience to judge its consequences (Q. 22:46).

Accordingly, the concept of a known prerevelatory moral language in the Qur'an acknowledges the concrete historical and social conditioning of moral concepts, while still insisting that different cultures must seek to elicit the universal ideal out of the diversity of concrete human conditions. This offers a common foundation upon which to construct an ethical language that can be shared cross-culturally in the project of creating a just society. Both the known and the unknown moral principles in the Qur'an point to concrete ways of life constructed in different cultural idioms, idioms that must be understood in order to discern universals and to apply them in similar contexts. The moral and spiritual awareness that ennobles human existence and leads it to carry out duties to God and other humans functions as a torch of the divinely created innate human nature, enabling it to discover the universals that can build bridges of understanding across cultures.

It is true that Muslim societies are, culturally speaking, religious-minded. This means that a religious worldview comprising Islamic beliefs about the supernatural and everyday religious practices has traditionally shaped social and political attitudes and interpersonal relationships and has provided existential meaning as well as security in the ever-changing relations of modern life.

The other source for the liberal-secular suspicion of a religious worldview in general and Islamic tradition in particular is the historically disruptive character of religion and the endless religiously inspired violence in many parts of the world. In *Political Liberalism* (1993), John Rawls identifies the origins of liberalism in the aftermath of the wars of religion and maintains that one of the significant achievements of liberalism is advancing religious tolerance by privatizing religion and clearing the public domain of religious interference.

While I cannot dispute the secular claim that religion in the public domain has been disruptive, I would argue that modern life has reached a point where existentially it has not been able to provide the necessary resources to motivate humans' active response to the demanding responsibilities of human relationships. At the core of Islam's message is a concern with developing just and fair relationships among peoples. Coexistence and cooperation among human groups with differing beliefs is so central to the advancement of religious faith and its spread among all peoples that the scriptural sources of the major faith traditions all contain rules that govern just and fair dealings among the followers of a particular community and with those outside it. Yet these very sources have been misappropriated to impose discrimination against and unfair treatment of religious and cultural others. The Islamic juridical tradition is just one example of the way that a universal tradition, which can treat all humans as humans, can, for whatever reasons, end up becoming a source of institutional discrimination against some, who are religiously reduced to some sort of second-class citizenship.

Hence, the purpose of this chapter is not so much to challenge the liberal conclusion about the role religion has played thus far as to argue for rethinking the role it is capable of playing in the context of advancing the protection of human rights. In the Islamic context, I want to critically assess the problems before I can advance solutions to the lack of commitment and skepticism that

Muslims in general, and their traditionalist leaders in particular, have shown to the secular international movement. The problem, as a number of non-Muslim and Muslim authors on the subject have pointed out, is with the Islamic juridical corpus, which stands in stark contradiction with the major articles of the UN Declaration when it comes to extending human rights to all, first and foremost, as humans. While it is true that Islamic juridical sources should be meticulously reinvestigated for their discriminatory laws based on religious and gender differences, in my opinion, it is the investigation of the ethical underpinnings of the revealed texts that can usher in the necessary reform of these laws to meet the universal standards recognized in human rights norms.

The major objective of this chapter, then, is to explore the theological ethics that serves as the foundation of Islamic legal thought. Muslim theological ethics, in its deontological-teleological forms, promises to bring to light a universal language of ethical necessity in Islamic revelation—the language that has the potential to become inclusive of all human beings, just because all human beings are endowed with the ability to know right from wrong.

The other related objective of this chapter is to revive the right kind of political theology based on a political-ethical assessment of human institutions to further respect for the humanness of all, regardless of creed, color, or gender differences. My working presumption, in the context of human rights discourse, is to reassert the secularity of the public domain in order to establish the equality of all citizens based on human dignity irrespective of religious confessions. Public space must remain immune from exclusionary and disruptive politics of the religious-minded—the group that seems to be in ascendance in the Muslim world.

Islamic religious thought is based on the human ability to know right from wrong. Through God's special endowment for all of humanity, each and every person on earth is endowed with a nature (*fiṭra*), the receptacle for intuitive reason, that guides humanity to its spiritual and moral well-being. On this notion of divine endowment, moral cognition is innate to human nature and gives human beings the capability to discern moral law. There is no discussion of natural law or natural rights in Muslim theology. But the Qur'anic notion of universal morality with which all human beings are blessed and held accountable to God, regardless of their particular faith commitment or even lack of it, as I will elaborate in chapter 3, makes it legitimate to speak about Islamic idea of natural law. The moral law that is discernible through the naturally endowed minimal knowledge of good and evil, then, is universal and can be discovered by all due to the simple fact of sharing a common humanity through creation. Further, the moral law guides humans in all matters, spiritual and temporal, private and public.

The thesis that is to be propounded in this chapter, that Islamic and secular presuppositions about universal human rights are in agreement about innate human dignity, human moral agency, and the role intuitive reason plays in ethical cognition, received its main thrust from my argument founded upon comprehensive doctrine about God's purposive creation with political implications. In this sense, religious premises in Islam carry political implications. However, there is no standardized Muslim theology representing the "official church" of Islam, because there is no church in Islam to represent God's interests on earth. In fact, God's interests are commensurable with human interests in the Qur'an. Although claims of official creed are not lacking among some Muslim traditionalists, who downplay any plurality of religious thought based on different interpretations of the Islamic revealed texts, it is futile to search for a generic or official Islam that can be regarded as the standard version, applicable to all places and circumstances.

Islamic Governance in Seminarian Culture

In the seminarian culture across the Muslim world, there is a deep-seated suspicion of modernity and its damaging impact on the sacredness of the revealed texts—the very foundation of traditionalist legitimacy. Modernity has imposed secularism on religion to make it compatible with democratic politics. Further, it has legitimized the role of human reason in extracting the relevant meaning of the sacred texts, giving rise to relativity of interpretations by human agents. More important, modernity has promoted the diversity of opinion and tolerance of that diversity through democratic politics. Consequently, both modernity and democracy are construed as major threats to the integrity of the Islamic revelation and the form of government it is to support.

To combat the negative impact of the relativity of religious meaning and the growing dissension because of divisive interpretations, traditionalist Muslim scholars have, on the one hand, asserted the conclusiveness of the traditionalist interpretation as the only valid interpretation of Islamic thought, and on the other, they have regarded democratization as a major source of political and ethical instability in society. This traditionalist strategy has led them to denigrate the role of human reason in deriving an authentic interpretation of authoritative religious texts. Whether in support of the congruency between some common concerns for justice and fairness shared by modernity and Islam, or in support of building a political system based on constitutional democracy in Muslim countries, traditionalist scholars have construed modernist arguments in support of pluralistic interpretations and democratic systems as a threat to the religious integrity of an Islamic public order.

Consequently, when a revelation-based political system like an Islamic government is engaged in assessing the legitimacy of and compliance with the Universal Declaration of Human Rights (which has from its inception avoided entanglement with religion and God's rights over humanity in its drafting) and the secular norms that undergird it, it must determine how the compliance with the secular Declaration will not lead to damaging one's faith in the absoluteness of God's revelation. The common lack of confidence in the secular foundations of the Declaration gives rise to the tension and disagreement between religious wielders of power and advocates of human rights in the Muslim world. Islamic government discerns a hidden threat to its faith-based character if it were to work toward the implementation of human rights by complying with democratic politics. In fact, those who legitimate their political might in religious terms maintain that such a political process will end up denying the religious basis of Islamic governance, which in turn will lead to rejection of a very public role for religion. It is for this reason that they have preferred nondemocratic religious governance, and they have denied the Declaration of any cultural legitimacy among the traditionalists.[5]

It is true that Islamic theology, based on its readings of the revealed texts, allows or denies the concept of an autonomous individual, freely exercising his or her rights and determining the course of his or her life, to evolve. The tension between those who regard human beings as free agents of God, naturally endowed with the capacity to choose and act, and those who deny their autonomy to negotiate a moral course of action except through divine commands, has had a crucial impact upon the formulations that are crucial in understanding the Islamic sources for democratic governance and human rights. A commitment to human rights is necessarily tied to a legitimate political system that recognizes its limits and that empowers its citizens to seek remedies for the violation of their human rights. Consequently, a human rights regime is logically connected with a democratic system of governance that treats its citizens as free and equal rights bearers.

But to derive this latter interpretation from within Islamic normative sources is a challenge for any Muslim thinker, and requires a fresh interpretation of the tradition. It is important to keep in mind that when encountering the Declaration, traditionalist Muslim scholars have raised the following two points.

The first point deals with Article 18 in the Declaration, on freedom of religion, which states: "Everyone has the right to freedom of thought, conscience and religion; this right includes freedom to change his religion or belief, and freedom, either alone or in community with others and in public or private, to manifest his religion or belief in teaching, practice, worship and observance." The right to freedom of religion, according to these scholars, only takes one aspect of human faith into consideration. Although they have no problem with this one aspect covered in Article 18 on the grounds that it is part of an inherent right of all human beings, this right overlooks different aspects of the freedom "to manifest one's religion" in public.[6] The article, for instance, neglects to acknowledge that religious belief is at all times based on conviction, and theoretical conviction constantly generates practical decisiveness in the performance of one's duties, in both public and private. In a specifically Muslim case, sometimes the duties performed in public implementation of the Sharīʿa, and at other times they prompt people to uphold retributive and restorative justice as part of the defensive *jihād* undertaken to restore violated justice. This sense of religious duty might appear to outsiders as exaggerated devotion leading to violence and intolerance.

In addition to Article 18, Article 11 of the Declaration states: "(1) Everyone charged with a penal offence has the right to be presumed innocent until proven guilty according to law in a public trial at which one has had all guarantees necessary for his defense. (2) No one shall be held guilty of any penal offence on account of any act or omission which did not constitute a penal offence, under national or international law, at the time when it was committed." This gives rise to a tension created by the implementation of certain laws in the penal system of the Sharīʿa, which would be construed as a violation of human rights in national or international law. Although one has a right to believe what one wishes regarding the implementation of divine norms, what appears to be a predicament for religious-minded people is that, while the Declaration supports freedom of religion, it does not endorse the freedom of decisiveness to act upon one's convictions.[7] This contradiction in Article 18 that upholds the freedom to believe and to manifest one's belief in practice, as religious-minded people argue, is problematic because it seems to condemn religiously inspired political activity. Moreover, any attempt to rethink religious law in order to bring it in line with the universal norms of human rights articles threatens to invest the authority to adjudicate these issues with the secular international law rather than the divinely ordained Sharīʿa from an Islamic point of view, this constitutes actually acting against one's own faith convictions.

The second point deals with the need to democratize Islamic public order so that all citizens may enjoy the protection of their human rights without any discrimination. The question these scholars raise is whether democratization leads to abandoning one's convictions about the public role of religion. In other words, would establishing a constitutional democracy provoke God's disapproval for having abandoned religious governance for a secular state? It is important to bear in mind that democracy here is understood in its liberal version, which advocates that government do nothing to advance or hinder any religion.[8] This question challenges the democratization project in the Muslim world, because it raises a serious question in the faith community whether it is religiously appropriate to reduce religion to an individual's private domain or to the group's religious institutions. To require government and its agents to treat religion separately from politics so as to promote political neutrality in religious matters is inconceivable in Muslim culture where religion has always figured prominently in public debates and political decisions. It is for this reason that the prospects for convincing people in Muslim societies to endorse neutrality in the matter of the role of Islam in public are slim. The major obstacle in the path of affording cultural legitimacy to the human rights document, according to this thinking, is foundational. It is the realization that the international document is unfair to at least some forms of religious expression that causes traditionalist leaders to question the relevance of the document to their cultural and religious situation.

However, an important aspect of democratization of religious governance has been overlooked in these traditionalist concerns. This aspect deals with the malleability of religious interpretations to render religion relevant to contemporary political-social conditions. Democratic processes allow human reason to arbitrate in religious disputes and provide solutions to the problems that linger in the public space. What traditionalist interpreters of religion tend to forget is that it is not religion per se that arbitrates in the public space; rather, it is one of the interpretations of religion that predominates and prevails as authoritative arbiter of political disputes. Understanding religion is an intellectual process, and it is ultimately reason that sits in judgment of the validity of a particular religious comprehension and compares and corroborates its findings with the help of other areas of human knowledge. Hence, if reason discovers that a certain ordinance in the Sharīʿa leads to the violation of human dignity, then it will without doubt work toward admission of this understanding to question that ordinance and to put into action the new comprehension of the classical juridical ruling, which, admittedly, was deduced by intellectual activity of Muslim jurists. In this sense, taking the example of those ordinances that endorse discriminatory treatment of women, one can observe different Muslim scholars' intellectual engagement with these classical rulings and their hermeneutical endeavors to rid Islam of the accusation that its normative texts support such discrimination. More pertinent to this research, it is worth keeping in mind that the juristic methodological approach to resolve the traditional constraints in connection with a woman's position is a historical one, anchored in ethics, in which one reads arguments about the irrelevance of the tribal context which at one time Islam inherited from the ancient world and which smacks of violation of human dignity and the respect that must be owed to all humans as humans, including women.

The fundamental question that needs to be raised in the context of the public role of Islam today is not very different than the one that has been raised in the context of liberal interpretation of secularization of public space by excluding religious reasons from political debates. However, whether religious convictions should be allowed to engage public reason in a political debate about a certain policy that affects all human beings, regardless of their diverse religious or cultural affiliations, needs to be closely examined so that people with religious convictions do not become estranged through unfair denial of their right to express freely what deeply touches them as members of the human race. In other words, it will be unfair to deny religious convictions a voice in the public domain to determine the course of political decisions that deal with interhuman justice—the sore point in human rights protection today. Nevertheless, a religious conviction that neglects to update its sociological context by engaging in a meaningful interpretation of the religious heritage by going beyond the normative texts might become irrelevant to the emerging consensus about citizenship as the sole criterion for protecting equal rights in a nation-state today. As such, this fresh interpretation is not possible without taking into account all other forms of human knowledge that actually clarify and enhance the understanding of the normative texts and their application in a totally different sociological context. In working out the details of Islamic law, Muslim jurists in their own time and place went beyond the authoritative texts to find solutions to pressing issues in the community as it expanded beyond the Arabian Peninsula. Today, more than ever, Muslims are in search of the correct interpretation of Islamic revelation to make Islamic interhuman ordinances more humane and inclusive in those sections of juridical tradition where there have been problems of discriminatory justifications to make Muslims a privileged class.

My overall objective to uncover the foundational sources for human rights norms in Islam, then, depends upon unfolding the universal content of some key Islamic concepts so that it can stimulate and engage the secular advocates of human rights in a meaningful conversation to appreciate an inherent secularity that exists in the Qur'anic concepts of human dignity and moral worth of all human beings without any extraneous conditions.

Ethical Necessity in the Context of Human Dignity

Let me delineate the outlines of a secular model of human rights so that I can explore whether such universality can be joined with a particularistic religious discourse. According to secularist advocates of human rights, human beings are endowed with reason and possess natural rights, which in the social contract between the individual and political authority is meant to protect. This doctrine also serves as the foundation of secular rationalism, with its emphasis on individual entitlements independent of obligations or socially assigned roles, and unconditioned by status or circumstance.[9] On this view, human reason, liberated from its religious or metaphysical antecedents, is free to negotiate its potential and creativity without any restrictions. The human, with the ability to reason, is the ultimate locus of knowledge, including knowledge about moral truth, which empowers human beings with moral reasoning to determine the parameters of the moral life that incorporates responsibilities along with rights to advance political justice.

In the secular model of human rights, then, in order to derive a universal principle that could serve as the criterion for the equal moral worth of all human beings, human reason was made the sole source for moral deliberation. Furthermore, to avoid any confusion with religious reason, public reason was also severed from its anchor in natural law, which provided all the necessary guidance to achieve the divinely ordained purposes for human life on earth. Secularization of reason, coupled with economic and social development in the context of the modern nation-state, led to the depreciation of the role of natural law and its religious and metaphysical foundations. This undermining of the metaphysical aspects of human rights discourse has been intentional and almost forgotten until recently, when questions about the universal application of human rights and cultural relativity have flared up between Western powers and Muslim nations.

In Islam, reason is the divine endowment of humanity through the very creation of human nature (*fiṭra*), the receptacle for intuitive reason. Moral cognition is innate to this nature, and through it human beings are capable of discerning moral law. This law is universal and can be discovered by all, due to the simple fact that all share a common humanity. However, such an inclusive and universal view about the reality of moral law outside of the revelation has not been endorsed by all Muslim schools of thought, especially when such a view is perceived to separate morality from its religious bedrock and render superfluous religious formulations of a just public order. In general Muslim theologians, even the rationalist-naturalists among them, could not endorse a separation of religion and morality in the public domain when the Prophet's political career had set the precedent for the integration of the religious and the political to establish a just public order. Hence, Muslim theologians, whether proponents or opponents of a substantial role for reason in moral epistemology, were thoroughly grounded in revealed texts that were appropriated through a rational or traditional methodology to support their theses. The core issue that engaged Muslim theologians was God's justice, which means (among other things) God's purposes for humanity in attaining prosperity in this world and the next. If as a human being I ought to espouse a religious life based on scriptural guidance in my personal life as well as in the public domain, how should I act if I had never encountered a revealed religion or an inspired prophet who could guide me? This particular question arose in the pluralistic sociological environment of Islamic civilization where different Abrahamic and non-Abrahamic religious traditions had established their communal presence from an early stage. Surely Islam was not the only religion in Baghdad or Damascus of the eighth and ninth centuries. How was Islam then to maintain relationships with other religions in the public domain?

The dominant view among traditionalist scholars was to make Islam the sole repository of religious truth, and therefore of political guidance to regulate Muslim dominance over non-Muslims in the public domain. On this view, the only way of maintaining good relationships among all races and creeds in the empire was to seek a comprehensive doctrine that could override the particularist bent of the dominant theology to make room for acceptance of other faiths and peoples as equally blessed and in possession of a guidance that did not solely depend upon scriptural sources to derive moral norms. These moral norms guided intercommunal and even intracommunal relations in Muslim societies.

At the risk of oversimplification of the complicated theological debates among different scholars living under different political circumstances, I have identified two major trends among Muslim theologians. The first trend was set by the majority Sunni-Ash'arī thinkers, who denied human reason any ability to understand the rightness or wrongness of an act independent of God's revelation. Consequently, the concept of autonomous individuals, freely exercising their rights and determining the course of their life to evolve, was rejected by these theologians. Human beings were born to obey God, who alone determined what was good or bad for them. In fact, without God's intervention there was no way for a person to know the moral worth of his or her own actions. God's commands and prohibitions establish the good and the evil, respectively. The logical conclusion of such a doctrine about human moral cognition and volition was to legitimate the authoritarian politics of the

Muslim empire and its autocratic dominance over its subject peoples. This traditional, majoritarian Sunni position lacks any inclusive doctrine of human moral worth and denies inherent human dignity outside the faith's communal boundaries. It is not far-fetched to suggest that religious extremism in the Muslim world today can be traced back to this hegemonic theology, which does not hesitate to treat dissenting groups within the larger community (like the Shīʿites, for example) as less than human and, hence, worth killing. Whether in Afghanistan, Pakistan, Saudi Arabia, or Iraq, untold atrocities and violence against minority Muslim groups in the last four decades have gone unnoticed by such human rights organizations as Amnesty International.[10]

The second trend was set by the Sunni-Muʿtazilite and the Shīʿite theologians, who form a minority theology in Islam. These theologians both recognized reason as God's gift to humanity to develop their moral consciousness, and acknowledged human moral agency. The main doctrine propounded by these scholars was about God's justice. God is just, and part of God's justice requires God to guide humanity to attain the goal for which it is created, namely, to establish justice on earth. The theological doctrine of justice is a comprehensive notion that specifies an entire program for the spiritual and moral development of an individual in society that reflects God's will and especially God's purposes for humanity. Accordingly, God's purposes for humanity include providing necessary guidance to all human beings, without exception, to achieve the stated goal of establishing a just society. Humanity's endowment with innate moral cognition and volition to carry out its intimations is part of God's justice, so that no one can escape the responsibility for working toward a just public order, regardless of religious affiliation. This doctrine is foundational for a comprehensive political system based on the equality of all human beings; all are endowed with minimal moral apprehension as part of their nature, that precedes the revelatory guidance that comes through God's envoys, the prophets. Muʿtazilite and Shīʿite natural theology, although attuned to the innate human capacity to know right from wrong, did not develop a theory of natural law as such; but their doctrine of human moral agency explicitly made humans the locus of reason and the moral law by the very act of God's creation. Moreover, human nature was acknowledged as essentially social, requiring the fulfillment of moral duty to institute the good and prevent the evil (*al-'amr bi-l-maʿrūf* and *al-nahy ʿan-l-munkar*) in both personal life and the public domain. In fact, this latter doctrine was one of the major principles of Muʿtazilite-Shīʿite political ethics.

The history of Islamic theology traces the development of these natural-rationalist trends among Muʿtazilites that conferred on human beings the innate ability to know right from wrong and the freedom of will to follow or reject it, and the ultimate defeat of this theology (except for its survival among Shīʿite theologians) by the traditionalist Ashʿarites. The Ashʿarites emphasized God's absolute will and humanity's duty to simply submit and carry out God's commands through revelation or be prepared for eternal damnation. The traditionalist thesis denied moral law an independent existence outside of revelation. Reason was circumscribed by the authority of revelation as the final judge of the moral worth of human action. Although the Muʿtazilite rationalist thesis was defeated by Ashʿarite divine command traditionalism, their attribution of legitimacy to human reason as a critical source of moral epistemology has resurfaced among Sunni Muslim modernists and continues to influence their advocacy of human rights based on inherent human dignity today.[11]

Nonetheless, the two positions, as they stand, are both based on a selective retrieval of Islamic revealed texts, which deprives a modern reader of the ability to gauge an overall worldview of the Qur'an and its impact upon two contradictory interpretations. It is important to point out that even when the Muʿtazilite rationalist-naturalist interpretation of the inclusive moral language of the Qur'an resonates well with the universal morality that undergirds the secular international document, it is on its own insufficient to convince those traditionalist theologians whose divine command ethics is also thoroughly anchored in the revealed texts. What is evident, however, is that without reconciling the two positions on human moral agency to a common denominator needed to garner the support of a significant number of Muslim scholars to accept the human rights norms in the UN Declaration, it would be difficult, if not impossible, to encourage the traditionalists to engage in conversation with the secularists to protect the basic freedoms and moral worth of humans as humans.

Internal theological contradictions regarding the status of reason notwithstanding, it is not possible to dismiss the theological enterprise as insignificant in formulating a foundational theory of human rights in Islam simply because it cannot resolve its internal contradictions. As a matter of fact, both theological positions were compatible with the complex portrait of humanity presented by the Qur'an—in which, on the one hand, God's overpowering will was in control of everything God created; and on the other, human beings, endowed with cognition and volition, interacted with God's will to assert their ability to choose among the possibilities offered by the earthly contingencies. The revealed texts demonstrated the multivalent connotations, open to variant interpretations, as part of the divine purpose in endowing humanity with intuitive reason as a critical instrument for comprehending the purposes of creation. Rational inquiry into the meanings and connotations of Islamic revelation was an individual endeavor and naturally prone to divisive subjective interpretations. Controversies and disputes among various scholars served as a critical intellectual exercise to uncover God's purposes for humanity. Further, these disputes led to the formulation of a theoretical apparatus for extrapolating principles and rules for the derivation of laws that regulated all interhuman relations, both interfaith and intrafaith. Hence, in the context of the specific political climate of Muslim society in which the hold of religious law, the Sharī'a, was necessary to provide order and stability, theological disputes underscored the pluralistic nature of Islamic religious inquiry. In this pluralistic sense, belief in the omnipotent God who required people to obey divine commands could not rule out human moral agency as an integral part of the Qur'anic doctrine about human accountability. If the Qur'an included a doctrine about human belief as governed by divine guidance, it also recognized the human's freedom to negotiate spiritual destiny without any compulsion.

It is important to keep in mind that social-political circumstances alone were insufficient to legitimize tolerance and acceptance of the religious and cultural other without the theological discussion and justification of autonomous human moral agency in the Qur'an. Absolute inclusive values based on an affirmation of inherent human dignity in the Qur'an, in large measure, were responsible for disciplining and regulating the natural tendency to denigrate minorities, not least by providing sanctions for trampling on the rights of others. The notion of the entitlements of any group was founded upon the religiously declared inherent dignity of all Children of Adam equally honored and provided for by God:

> We have endowed the Children of Adam with dignity [*karam*] and carried them on land and sea, and provided them with good things, and preferred them greatly over many of those We created. (Q. 17:70)

The rationalist-traditionalist divide among theologians did not lead to a drastic distortion or conclusion about a divinely ordained plan for humanity. According to them, religion established the connection between private and public; individual and society; spiritual and mundane. Human progress was guaranteed if they managed to balance the contradicting demands of various spheres of human existence. Two positions on the sources of moral knowledge did not in any significant way undermine the ability of ordinary people to understand this balance between demands of reason and revelation. Revelation depended on reason for its validity, and reason sought to validate its conclusions by showing their correlation to the revelation.

The secular liberal thesis, that liberty can survive only outside religion and through the secularization of a religious tradition, was founded upon the historical experience of Christianity. There the solution was clearly to separate the public and the private in order to guarantee that the public domain would remain inclusive and tolerant of differences.[12] Secularization, founded upon the principle of separation of church and state, helped reduce the hold of an exclusive religiosity over society, thus making pluralism in the public domain possible. Evidently, in this context, religion rendered people less tolerant of other faith communities and of other denominations within the Christian faith.

The social-political experience of those who argue for avoiding any discussion about the moral foundations of human rights is worth keeping in mind, particularly when the liberal negative evaluation of religion is extended to a different historical experience of Muslim societies. One of the most critical concerns for human rights drafters in the 1940s was to avoid entanglement with the metaphysical and theological foundations of morality in order to bypass religious controversies among different Christian denominations and world religions over the sources of a universal morality that recognized moral integrity of all human beings across different cultures and religious traditions.

The Muslim experience in building Islamic political structures was different, and this is reflected in the alternative human rights paradigm presented in 1990 by Muslim apologists in the Cairo decalration. What is seriously missing in this alternative paradigm for universal human rights is the mention of the theological-metaphysical sources in the Islamic tradition that can serve as a basis for a theory of an inclusive, universal Declaration for all human beings, regardless of whether they are Muslim or not. The only way to engage secular human rights advocates in a meaningful conversation about Islamic universal discourse is to make a doctrinal case for an inclusive picture of human rights, connected with human responsibilities, in order to maintain the overall well-being of humanity's social and political existence. At the same time, a substantial theoretical discussion of an inclusive foundational conception of human rights would, I believe, convince traditionalist Muslim scholars to make room for the idea of inalienable human rights based on human dignity and moral agency from Islamic theological sources. The point of departure for my research is to argue for a foundational theory of human rights that is based on some of the pluralistic features of Islam and its culture, features that are totally ignored by Muslim traditionalist and fundamentalist discourses. True to its internal plurality, Islam's concern with the preservation of freedom against an authoritative theology, especially in view of its refusal to afford any human institution like the church the right to represent the divine interest on earth, was less of a problem in preserving peaceful coexistence among peoples of diverse faiths and cultures. Functional separation of the spiritual and temporal was institutionalized, in order to guarantee fundamental agreement on public values and meet the demands of multifaith and multicultural societies of the Islamic world. Hence, the Western experience of collective intolerant religion remained alien to Muslim experience.

It is this difference in the historical experience of the West and Islam that makes my project a viable proposition in the ongoing debate about whether the secular model can on its own provide universal standards that can be applied across cultures, or whether it needs to look at foundational religious models with their own universal claim to offer a more comprehensive understanding of what it means to be a defender of human rights today. Religion cannot and will not confine itself to the private domain, where it will eventually lose its influence in nurturing human conscience. It needs a public space in the development of the international sense of a world community with a vision of creating an ideal society that cares and shares.

Theological Underpinnings of Juridical Discourse

In Islamic theology, the contradictory conceptualization of human moral agency and ethical responsibility has paradoxically served as a conversation stimulator among both modernist and traditionalist thinkers.[13] These thinkers have confirmed or resisted Islam's ability to withstand the demand for the reformation of classical juridical formulations about interhuman relationships in order to accommodate constitutional democracy and a doctrine of universal human rights. The ongoing debates among traditionalist and modernist scholars about the relevance of certain discriminatory juridical decisions in the area of intercommunal relations, and their disagreements regarding the extension of the notions of human dignity and the ensuing equality of all humans reveal a complex and contemporary development of Islamic religious thought's historical preoccupation with individual autonomy and human rights.

As Muslims understand it, Islam is a comprehensive system of beliefs and practices that relates private and public, individual and society, spiritual and mundane. The best interests of humanity can be preserved when the two realms of the spiritual and the temporal work together to cultivate the values that regulate human relationships in the public sphere. Human relationships are at the heart of this religiously inspired morality; through it people learn to balance the challenging demands of mutual rights and obligations toward one another. Contradictory theological doctrines about moral epistemology do not undermine the need for fairness and justice in building social and political institutions that sustain that balance.

The groundwork for an inclusive foundational conception of human rights in Islam, then, can begin with a search for pluralistic formulations of the public good in the juridical tradition, and for affirmations of inherent human dignity and moral agency in theological formulations. That there is room for such a foundational source for universal morality and human moral worth grounded in the pluralistic features of Islamic revelation and Muslim culture, relies on the authenticity of my presentation of the aspects of the inherited tradition that have been deemphasized by contemporary traditionalist Muslim scholarship. Such scholarship on Islamic creed and practice is oblivious to the Qur'an's universal, and yet particularist, message for humanity. It has intentionally overlooked or ignored the Qur'anic impulse that inspired the juridical formulations about interpersonal justice in all religiously and morally required conduct. More important, a political theology that was once geared toward internal criticism of Muslim social and political performance, has been turned into a justification of discrimination against perceived enemies of the community.

The political-ethical movement that was spurred by the Qur'an in its early years was founded upon the preservation of the message's phenomenological integrity about the soteriological interdependence of this world and the next. But it also acknowledged a need to provide principles that would regulate fair and just relationships between Muslims and non-Muslims in this life. Since there was no way to impose a uniform spiritual response to God across all individuals, a functional recognition of separate jurisdictions for the religious and the secular law to regulate interhuman relations was the only way to guarantee peaceful coexistence between peoples of various religious traditions. The Qur'anic emphasis that not even the Prophet could compel people in choosing their spiritual destiny was the cornerstone of the Islamic notion of tolerance in the public domain. The Qur'anic declaration: "No compulsion is there in religion" served to found a distinctively Islamic functional secularity. This notion still marks the enormous potential of Islamic political theology to provide a doctrinal validation for the sort of institutionalization of ethical consensus on public values that was and is still required by the demands of the multifaith and multicultural realities of the Muslim world.

World religions have a lot to say about human dignity and inalienable human rights. In the continuing debate over whether the relationship between the idea of human rights and the various and potentially divisive religious perspectives that may offer justifications for such rights, the point that needs to be emphasized is that religions can create and sustain communities with a vision, a sense of unity, and an ability to relate positively to other faith communities. The secularist emphasis on social contract theory as a universal, rational foundation of human rights fails to see that there were already tolerant communities founded by religions before anyone thought of a social contract. Religions brought together the bearers of different cultures to form a universal community, bound together in faith and practice. There was already an "overlapping consensus" in place that regulated relations between different communities believing in different comprehensive doctrines, long before the call to abandon the particularities of these traditions in order to endorse moral universality of human rights was raised in modern times. Prior to doctrines about "the priority of the right to the good," various goods were making room for the right.

The functional secularity instituted within these communities made it possible for them not to press for unanimity in matters of faith beyond one's own community. Instead, human relationships were allowed to determine the degree and quality of cooperation within and between faith communities. This was the practical solution to avoid entanglement with the ontological foundations of one's tradition, which would have made moral cooperation impossible without imposing doctrinal uniformity on others. The secularist approaches to moral universality outside religious doctrines for the protection of human rights needs to sit in dialogue with the religious ideas and comprehension of inherent human dignity as the sole criterion for claims of inalienable entitlements. Islam, with other Abrahamic traditions, has something to say about a just society, good government, and the rule of law. No religion will accept a secular solution if that solution will privatize its voice and eventually cause it to lose its influence in nurturing compassion and forgiveness as keys to sustainable human relations. On the other hand, religion needs to voice its concerns for justice without becoming self-righteous and self-congratulatory for its glory in the divine. The public domain provides an opportunity for religion to become a source of moral guidance that is conducive to just human relationships. Let me now turn to the Islamic juridical-ethical tradition, where I hope to find evidence for my thesis.

There are two general themes to which I want to draw attention. The first is provocative, since it challenges the notion, advocated mainly by the religious establishment in Iran, that the role of Islam is to govern. Clear and unbiased thinking about Islam as a religious tradition will reveal that governance or the form it should take was never the goal of the Qur'an. The Qur'an simply laid down the purpose or the end of governance, namely, to establish justice on earth. The second theme is equally challenging to the traditional sensibilities of the Muslim religious establishment. This is the functional secularity of Islamic tradition, which has significant implications for the development of a pluralistic world order and the universal human rights regime in the context of Muslim cultures. At this time, the establishment rejects both pluralism and human rights as hegemonic tools of dominant powers. I will come back to pluralism as it relates to the freedom of religion and conscience in my last chapter. Here I want to present my central theme, by arguing that the original task of the Qur'an was to guide rather than govern humanity in order to establish justice on earth. I need to disentangle the function of guidance from governance, which became naturally institutionalized in the juridical tradition.

In recent decades, the public role of religion in general and the role of Islam in particular has been revisited by a number of Muslim and non-Muslim scholars. In Afghanistan and Iraq, constitutional debates have yet to tackle the role of religious convictions and values in the development of democratic institutions that would guarantee basic freedoms and human rights. The major problem faced by constitutional lawyers has been to include local jurisdiction for universal human rights statutes founded upon an inclusive sense of citizenship. In both these countries, religious leaders have demanded that the religious law of Islam, the Sharī'a, be the principle source for defining freedoms and rights in the national constitution. While the leaders have acknowledged that in the personal status of a Muslim man and woman the Sharī'a could continue to provide judicial decisions in the area of personal law, a number of reform-minded leaders have raised concerns about the way traditional juridical formulations define a woman's social and political rights.[14] More important, the religiously pluralistic nature of Muslim societies require them to take into consideration not only Sunni—Shī'ite but also interfaith relationships.

The challenge that faces the Muslim community today is to determine whether Islam as a religion came to guide humanity, or to govern it. There is a historically inherited dogma among faithful Muslims that as a comprehensive guide to human life Islam must not only guide but also govern Muslim majority states. Is this plausible in view of the challenges that must be confronted in order to institute democratic politics and implement human rights? Are there, within the historical Islam, paradigm cases that can inspire and inform the creation of a nation-state that is also a member of the international public order and a signatory to the universal human rights conventions? In other words, in the light of the changed circumstances under which modern nation-states conduct their affairs today, is religious governance conceivable? Earlier in this chapter I indicated the seminarians' attitude to democratic politics and to some of the articles in the UN Declaration. My own reflections on the Qur'an and the Tradition, which continue to be held in high esteem by the community, enable me to offer my thesis and explore its ramifications for democratic governance based on some sort of functional secularity (*ṣifa madanīya*) in the Islamic juridical tradition.

Let me make it clear from the outset that, being fully aware of the problems of cross-cultural translation and terminology, I am not imposing a functional secularity on the Islamic tradition; rather, the organically Islamic idea of separate jurisdictions (*niṭāq sulṭa*), and not the separation of church and state, is what is acknowledged in the sacred law of Islam, the Sharīʿa, and it is on this that my proposal is built. As a matter of fact, there was never a church in Islam that represented the divine interests on earth. If there was any power struggle to represent God's interests in the Muslim empire, it was between the rulers and the religious leaders in the seminaries (*madrasa*). As far as the public was concerned, it was the seminary that represented the authentic transmission of the Islamic tradition. The state always suffered from lack of sufficient legitimacy to exercise its will with public consent. Hence, it resorted to political authoritarianism.

The historical development of the Islamic tradition reveals that Islam has motivated a public project founded upon the twin principles of justice and social pluralism, a project that recognized the diversity of self-governing communities, and affirmed their right to run their internal affairs within the various communities under a comprehensive religious and social political system. Of all Abrahamic religions, Islam has been from its inception the most conscious of its earthly agenda. Islam has been a faith in the realm of the public. The Sharīʿa regulates religious practice with a view to maintaining the individual's well-being alongside his or her social well-being. Hence, its comprehensive system deals with the obligations that humans perform as part of their relationship to God and duties they perform as part of their interpersonal relations and responsibilities. Order must be maintained not only in the public domain but also in all other arenas of human interaction, including places of worship. The Sharīʿa provides an ethical standard of conduct and enforces the law by taking into account only what affects just human interaction. Consequently, the administration of public justice does not extend into the private domain, unless some infringement of rights occurs there and is brought to the judiciary's attention.[15]

However, the problem with historical Islam begins as soon as the classical juridical formulations that treat Muslim–non-Muslim relations on the basis of a religious doctrine regarding the superiority of the believers over nonbelievers are examined in the context of modern nation-states. These rulings with negative political implications for full recognition of those outside the faith community run contrary to the emerging global spirit of democratization, a spirit that acknowledges the reality of religious pluralism and the equality of all citizens in a state. At the very core of this emerging democratic pluralism is respect for the human rights of the non-Muslims living in Muslim societies.

Since the beginning of the twentieth century, Muslim religious and social thinkers have wrestled with the question of Islam's capacity to create a political society that would not be based upon the traditional boundaries between believers and nonbelievers and thus allow for human dignity to emerge as the sole criterion for social and political entitlements.[16]

Although I discuss the Islamic notion of natural law in chapter 3, let me briefly underscore the significance of Qur'an's universal command that humanity hearken to its original natural capacity to discern rightness and wrongness. No human endowed with reason can fail to understand this moral language. More important, as a source of unity that transcends religious differences, this language establishes the necessary connection and compatibility between a private and particular spiritual framework, and a public and universal moral guidance. Hence, the Qur'an binds all of humanity to its natural predisposition not only in order to be aware of the meaning of justice, but also to will justice's realization. In this universal idiom, no human being, then, can claim ignorance of the ingrained moral sense of wrong and right; none can escape divine judgment of the failure to uphold justice on earth.

The Qur'an allows nonbelievers to be "other" in the sphere of ethics, where the natural knowledge of good and evil makes injustice in any form inexcusable. No matter how religions might divide people, ethical discourse focuses on human relationships in building an ideal public order. Human relationships at the interpersonal level provide us with a framework for defining the religious or cultural other in terms of "us" and "them." Muslim self-identification as a process of self-understanding becomes accessible to the outsider through his or her conceptual description of and relation to the other.

However, in a multicultural and multifaith society, insistence on uniformity of belief as a precondition for social organization is highly problematic. The solution offered by secular advocates of democratic politics is that effective governance arises not from shared beliefs, but from a system of government incorporating a pluralistic politics. International relations today are conducted without any reference to the substantive beliefs of the member states, because religious premises are considered nonpublic. Whatever their irreconcilable differences in matters of faith, all communities are legally bound to do their part in maintaining peaceful social relations. The resolution of conflicts does not require people to uphold certain religious beliefs, nor does the existence of conflict mean that they do not or cannot share a vision of a future community that is inspired by the belief in transcendence. According to such secular thinkers, religiously grounded moral judgments are inaccessible to people outside the faith community because "some of the crucial premises that underlie such judgments are not the subject of general acceptance or of persuasive demonstration by publicly accessible reasons...."[17] Islamic political theology has much to contribute to our understanding of the prospects for an inclusive universal project, founded upon a spiritual-moral challenge, which will guide human cooperation in establishing a just public order.

Let me reiterate that the purpose of divine revelation is to provide norms and values that will guide humankind toward constructing a viable system of governance. When the Qur'an honors human beings with divine deputyship, it is speaking about the potentialities and challenges that await humanity as it struggles to establish a just order. A political theology that endorses human moral agency that is purposive as well as responsive to duty underscores the fact that it is going to be a struggle rather than a predetermined success. In order to reach its final end, humanity will have to utilize all its divinely-conferred abilities and potentialities to assume the critical responsibility of exercising authority in order to establish a just political order. Religious guidance aims to help moral agents to habituate themselves to a virtuous life. The Qur'an's vision of the moral life requires a continual responsiveness and vigilance to God's guidance in order to fulfill the morally commendable end and to overcome the tendencies that hinder the realization of an ideal society—one in which all people are treated fairly and one that respects and protects the rights of those who stand outside one's kindred and faith community.

Like all other world religions, at one time or other, Islam has succumbed to the political ambitions of Muslim rulers; in doing so, it has sacrificed its core values of interfaith tolerance and coexistence. Such an alliance between an exclusive and hegemonic theology perpetrated by the court theologians and political power has actually led to the denigration of the universal, inclusive ethical foundations of Islamic tradition. Surely, Islam includes among its theological doctrines of divine justice and human moral agency concepts of individual and collective responsibility to further a divinely ordained ethical public order. In Muslim theological ethics, moral agency is both teleological and deontological. In its teleological emphasis, human beings are called to realize their full potential as spiritually moral persons by undertaking acts of worship as part of God's right (*ḥaqq allāh*) on them; in its deontological emphasis humans are called to acts of interpersonal justice as part of the reciprocal rights of human beings (*ḥaqq al-nās*) toward one another.

It is remarkable that the violation of fundamental human rights usually occurs when comprehensive religious-secular power is concentrated in the hands of an exclusivist leadership whose views of autonomous individual morality are divorced from the communalistic vision of society. The mistreatment of those within and outside the community who reject that community's religious exclusivist claims also occurs under such autocratic rulers. Monotheistic communities have from time to time denied their individual members a right to dissent from the communalistic interpretation of their respective traditions because of the fear that such internal dissension (usually labeled apostasy) is potentially fatal to the collective identity of the faith community and its social cohesiveness.

There is a strong desire among Muslims to prevent any form of internal dissension. Conflicting and even incommensurable theological positions, for instance, on freedom of religion or the rights of women, have led to the oppressive use of force to ensure adherence to a single comprehensive religious doctrine supported by a powerful religious authority. The ensuing intolerance has also manifested itself in intrafaith relationships. Whereas Muslims often treat other religious communities with relative tolerance, they often treat their own sects with abominable disregard. Thus under various powerful Sunni Muslim dynasties, the Shīʿite minority suffered more oppression than did Jews or Christians.[18]

The Iraq-Iran war in the 1980s, the Gulf War in 1990–1991, and the American invasions of Afghanistan and Iraq in 2002–2003 brought home a realization that even secular ideologies like nationalism, socialism, and more recently democracy did not advance the cause of pluralistic, tolerant political cultures. Furthermore, the imported ideologies, lacking native cultural legitimacy or institutional infrastructure, were enforced from above without people's participation in political processes in order to generate necessary consensus, which led to even more oppression.

The Qur'an does not teach that humanity has fallen through the commission of original sin. But it constantly warns human beings about the egocentric corruption that can subvert the determination to carry out divine purposes for humankind. Human pride infects and corrupts undertakings in politics, scholarship, and everyday conduct. The last is the most sinful aspect of egocentric corruption because it is done in the name of God.

Besides stressing the noble nature (*fiṭra*) that promotes human sociability and a positive bond between persons based on the common ethical responsibility toward one another, the Qur'an emphasizes mutual expectations and relations fostered by our common descent from a divinely endowed parentage. There is no mention of the creation of human beings in the image of God in the Qur'an, although there are traditions that speak about that.[19] A focal point of Muslim political theology, one that confers an intrinsic and universal value to human beings, is the concept of *karam* (human dignity). Human beings are endowed with distinctive qualities by God through this dignity; it enables them to exercise the capacity to perform obligations as God's creatures and relate to one another as members of the universal human community. In this sense human dignity is inherent in human nature and the object of human existence and purposes. This signification of human dignity has obvious implications for an Islamic justification of human rights. Each individual has value and dignity by nature; and as a member of the larger human community, every person is the bearer of inalienable rights.

The Qur'an gives importance to interpersonal relationships in order to establish an inclusive ethical order, an order that would create the institutions and culture that promote the creation of a spiritual-moral community made up of individuals willing and able to take up the challenge of working for the common good. It is for this reason that the moral performance of an individual in society is to be evaluated not so much by an essential dignity of persons, as by whether their actions advance the establishment of those religious-moral institutions through which history has shaped the community's experience of living together, as well as ethical aspirations and sources.

The question that needs to be raised in the context of secular conception of public domain is this: Can a just public order be realized without considering religious ideas about the highest end of human existence on the earth? Further, can such an ideal be accomplished through communal cooperation for the collective good or widely different and even irreconcilable individual interests? How can a religious community remain neutral and noninterventionist in the public domain on ethical issues that from the individual's point of view might run counter to one's sense of the highest end in life?

The secular prescription of liberal democracies seems to suggest that religious toleration is achieved only when the idea of freedom of religion and conscience is institutionalized in the form of a basic individual right to worship freely, to propagate one's religion, to change one's religion, or even to renounce religion altogether. In other words, the principle of toleration is equated with the idea of religious pluralism and the individual freedom of religion and conscience.[20] Moreover, secularism confines the role of religion to the private domain, which is clearly demarcated from the public one, requiring people in public to appeal to "public reason" when dealing with matters of constitutional essentials and basic justice. This is the separationist position with respect to governmental action. Whereas one has the freedom to choose between competing doctrines and pursue one's belief in private life and religious institutions, in the public domain, where one is linked in common citizenry, one must select fair and equally accessible principles that would support a system of social cooperation. This is the secularist foundation of a public order in which, in pursuit of the public good and matters of justice, the state must avoid all considerations drawn from belief in God or other sacred authorities in the administration of public life.

The Abrahamic traditions are founded upon particular scriptures that locate justice in a particular history through distinct communities. This ideal, of a divinely ordained and just community is the natural outcome of a belief in an ethical God who insists on justice and equality in interpersonal relations as part of the believer's spiritual perfection. The indispensable connection between the religious and ethical dimensions of personal life in these traditions inevitably introduces religious precepts into the public arena. In other words, for these traditions church and state are completely related, requiring the involvement of the religious community in taking responsibility for law and order.

Freedom of conscience and religion has been correctly recognized as the cornerstone of democratic pluralism.[21] A pluralistic social order needs to create principles of coexistence in which freedom of religion must be articulated on the basis of both reason and revelation as part of the divinely granted rights of the individual. The question of individual autonomy and human agency might seem peculiar to the modern vision of a public order in which a group of individuals share core ideas, ideals, and values geared toward maintaining a civil society;[22] yet such a pluralistic order also existed in traditional communities founded on revelation. Human sociality necessarily requires mutuality, not only in matters of commerce and market relations; but also presupposes a shared foundation of binding sentiments that unite autonomous individuals who are able to negotiate their own spiritual space—and these criteria apply to all societies in all eras.

In general, by virtue of the natural human urge to social interaction, diverse groups fall back on their religious teachings to derive and articulate the rules affecting public life. The recognition and implementation of the religious values of sharing and mutuality create a "civil religion" that encourages coexistence with those who, even when they do not share the dominant group's particular vision of salvation, can share in a concern for living in peace with justice. Hence, I shall contend, the concern for human autonomy, especially freedom of worship (or not to worship), is as fundamental to the Qur'anic vision of human religiosity as it is to the moral universality of human rights. The Qur'an requires Muslims to sit in dialogue with their own tradition in order to uncover a just approach to religious diversity and interfaith coexistence. Moreover, a rigorous analysis of the Qur'an will demonstrate that, without recognition of freedom of religion, it is impossible to conceive of religious commitment as a freely negotiated human—divine relationship, of the sort that fosters individual accountability for one's acceptance or rejection of faith in God, or one's commitment to pursue an ethical life, and willingness to be judged accordingly.

Although the Islamic tradition weaves the spiritual and moral together as part of its comprehensive response to the Qur'an's commands, the difference between a moral and religious response to God's guidance is critical here. In relation to the divine purposes for humanity, according to the Qur'an, God provides two forms of guidance: a universal moral guidance that touches all humans qua humans, and a particular scriptural guidance that is given to a specific faith community. On the basis of the universal guidance, it is conceivable to demand uniformity because an objective and universally binding moral standard is assumed to exist that guarantees true human well-being. In enforcing that basic moral standard in the public domain, resort to compulsion through legitimate enforcement is justifiable as long as it does not lead to violent confrontation. However, on the basis of particular religious guidance, it is crucial to allow human beings to exercise their freedom in matters of personal faith, because any attempt to enforce religious conviction would lead to its negation. Moreover, although the comprehensive nature of scriptural guidance provides a detailed description of the ideal for human life on earth that is consonant with the historical and cultural considerations of community life in Islam, the public domain necessitates separation of strictly religious actions performed as part of the God-human relationship from human jurisdiction.[23] So construed, the God-human relationship in the Qur'an is concerned with reminding and warning people to heed the divine call through submission to God's will, whereas interhuman relationships are concerned with regulating those relationships in the public domain through cultural and political institutions. As the head of the community, the Prophet could not use his political power to enforce a God—human relationship that was founded upon individual autonomy and human agency. In fact, the Qur'an repeatedly reminded the Prophet that his duty was simply to deliver the message without taking it upon himself to function as God's religious enforcer (Q. 17:54, 50:45).

Nonetheless, the tension begins to be felt as soon as the Qur'an speaks about the just political order. There are numerous prescriptive propositions that deal with the creation of a just social order. Under certain conditions the Qur'an gives the state, as the representative of society, the power to control "discord on earth," a general state of lawlessness created by taking up arms against the established Islamic order.[24] The eradication of corruption on earth, taken in light of the Qur'anic principle of instituting good and preventing evil, is a basic moral duty to protect the well-being of the community. In the Islamic polity, personal faith is intertwined with social ethical commitment, to leave adherents of competing doctrines free to pursue their beliefs inevitably engenders tensions regarding individual and group rights and obligations, and these tensions must be resolved through state regulation.

Dissent within the Muslim community was treated with a great deal of intolerance and was thoroughly institutionalized in the laws dealing with apostasy and religious rebellion. Juridical studies have amply shown that Muslim jurists did not engage in a conceptual investigation of the ethical-legal presuppositions of certain commandments in the Qur'an. In particular, the absence of a thorough analysis of the Qur'anic ethical-legal categories on the one hand, and its ethical-religious categories on the other, has generated rulings that fail to recognize separate jurisdictions for human—God and interhuman relationships. For instance, the Qur'an assigns Muslim public order the obligation of controlling "discord on earth." This phrase is part of a long verse that prescribes the most severe penalties for rebellion:

> The punishment of those who fight against God and His Messenger, and hasten to do corruption, creating discord on earth: they shall be slaughtered, or crucified, or their hands and feet shall alternately be struck off, or they shall be banished from the land. This is degradation for them in this world; and in the world to come awaits them a mighty chastisement, except for those who repent before you lay your hands on them. (Q. 5:33–34)

That the Qur'an presents comprehensive commandments in which moral, religious, and civil concerns are not always easy to distinguish is demonstrated by the fact that ascribe equal gravity under civil law accorded to moral and religious transgressions.[25] Moreover, Islamic law treats these transgressions as affecting not only humans, but also God. There is a sense in which both humans and God may have claims in the same infringement, even if the event seems to harm only one of them. Although the punishment of crimes against religion are beyond human jurisdiction, the juridical body in Islam is empowered to impose sanctions when it can be demonstrated beyond doubt that the grievous crime involved the infringement of a human right (*ḥaqq ādamī*, or private claim). The supreme duty of the Muslim ruler is to protect the public interest, and to do that the law afforded him an overriding personal discretion in determining how the purposes of God might best be achieved in the community.

It is important to indicate the way the recent development of a democratic constitution in Iraq has addressed the call for integrating the Sharī'a. At different times, religious leaders, mainly Shī'ites but also some Sunnis, like the influential professor of the Sharī'a and the imam of the Friday prayers in Baghdad, Dr. al-Qubaisī, have affirmed the Islamic nature of Iraqi society and the need to make Islamic social and political values part of the overall new political system of Iraq. To assess the seriousness with which integrating such value is made, one should identify the religious-legal authority that calls upon the drafters of the new constitution. It is not far-fetched to assert that the traditional leadership in Najaf is interested in seeing that the Iraqi constitution reflects the majority Shīʿite view, which wishes to fulfill the religious dream of situating the Sharīʿa law at the heart of political governance.

However, such a call needs to take into consideration fundamental problems that arise in the Iraqi situation as a modern nation-state. First is the fact of the considerable ethnic pluralism that exists there, and the challenge that pluralism presents in developing a sense of national identity. This also has implications for the development of a democratic constitution in which the notion of citizenship becomes the principle for power distribution. Second is the fact of sectarian plurality that informs religious identities within the broad national culture. This latter identity has gained a heightened sense in the context of an enforced Baʿthist, secular ideology during the last three decades. In fact, with the favored status of the Sunni community under Saddam Hussein, a sectarian identity assumed the primary identity, and in many instances the Shīʿites were discriminated against on these grounds by the Baʿthist government. Such entrenched sectarian identities might yet derail any progression toward the democratization of political institutions, transcending the ethnic and sectarian divides of Iraq today.

The democratic constitution of Iraq, which still faces problems in addressing the issues of religious minorities and women, cannot be fully implemented without addressing some of the critical matters that were raised above, particularly in reference to the public domain and the role of religious reasons based on religious convictions. During constitutional negotiations, the question of guaranteeing the rights of non-Muslim minorities came up a number of times. While it was important to ensure that the new constitution guarantees the fundamental human rights of all citizens, the major issue that needs nuanced and even immediate attention is the treatment of women as a minority. Cultural obstacles are imposed by the patriarchal traditionalism that prevails in religious centers like Najaf, while the discriminatory evaluation of woman's personal status is enshrined in the inherited juristic law, the Sharīʿa. Both these elements can cause irreparable damage to the status of women in the new Iraq, for they could deny women a clear and legitimate voice, even though they constitute over half of the Iraqi population.

The moderates or reform-minded intellectuals in Iraq, mostly products of secular educations, tend to ignore the popular voices whose loyalty to their religious leaders is unquestioned. To reach this populace today, these intellectuals should provide authentic information on how Islam or Islamic law can and cannot become the source of governance in modern Iraq. To ignore this important ingredient in building support for the political system may actually lead to the rise of militant responses, influenced by some politically opportunist religious leaders, intent to fill the power vacuum.

There is little doubt that a fresh understanding of the Sharī'a in the public arena should develop in order to further pluralistic democracy's gradual acceptance by the people. With its insistence on the separation of church and state (seminary and state in an Iraqi context), secularism is not responsive to those popular voices that demand the explicit presence of religious values at the core of the emerging national culture. At the same time, the main problem that haunts any religious system, including the Sharī'a in a multifaith situation, is its claim to exclusive loyalty. It is worth keeping in mind that, as discussed above, the Sharī'a does not advance a concept of egalitarian citizenship—the core of civil rights and responsibilities in a modern nation-state. It simply divides the populace into Muslim members, with full privileges, and non-Muslim minorities, with protected status under its divinely ordained system. Furthermore, since the Sharī'a ordains laws for both the private and public domains, using explicitly religious premises to regulate social-political aspects of everyday life within the Muslim community and outside it, its simple imposition creates a major conflict with the modern democratic understanding of nationals as equal citizens, with equal rights and obligations. More important, in the area of gender relationships, its ordinances have instituted inequalities between men and women that derail the democratic system built on equal rights of all citizens, regardless of their gender or any other differentiations.

Hence, the Islamic juridical tradition today seems unable to offer realistic solutions to the Iraqi situation, solutions of the sort demanded by its ethnically, culturally, and religiously pluralistic population—unless, as demonstrated above, a fresh reading of this heritage is undertaken. Since the majority of the population is Muslim, one can begin to explore the possibilities of retrieving the core values of the Islamic system to offer this fresh Islamic paradigm. This paradigm is actually derived from the religious law of Islam, the Sharī'a itself. Let us consider this in the context of Iraq's need for a democratic constitution.

To begin with, we need to search for freedom of religion to secure an individual's right to adhere to any or none of the confessional communities, without interference from the state. In other words, the foundation of a democratic Muslim state is that religious freedom is offered to all citizens without any coercion or discrimination. With the well-established secularity in the Shari'a ordinances dealing with the human-God relationship, in which the state must maintain neutrality by refraining from intervening or imposing doctrinal uniformity, it is possible to conceive the paradigm of a civil religion. The principle of secularity (*ṣifa madanīya*) allows religion to manage humanity's relationship with God without interference from any human institutions, including the mosque and the seminary. All the laws that regulate the God—human relationship transcend adjudication by human courts. There are no secular penalties for missing the obligations that one performs as part of his or her relationship to God. Only God can demand an explanation for such a breach between an individual believer and God. This area of the law covers the *'ibādāt*—that is, all those actions that are done clearly with the intention of pleasing God.

However, the inbuilt separation of jurisdictions in the Sharī'a empowers the government to regulate interhuman relations with justice in the public sphere. This is the second major area of the Sharī'a. All laws regulating human relationships are covered under this section. This area of the law must be conducted between individuals and groups, including the state, in keeping with the demands of justice in all areas of human existence and interaction. Here human courts have jurisdiction to enforce their judicial decisions and to demand obedience. More pertinently, it is in this area of the law that reforms affecting social issues have taken place through the reinterpretation of religious sources. Hence, the theoretical immutability of the sacred law does not extend to this area.

This separation of jurisdictions is the closest that Sharī'a comes to the secularism often adopted in the West's received understanding of universal human rights. It allows for a functional secularity that can recognize and cultivate civic equality and mutual responsibilities between humans, while acknowledging the particularity and independence of the religious tradition from state administration. In other words, the separation of jurisdictions in Islamic law can respond to the needs of the modern nation-state, where the state must adopt noninterventionist policies in the matter of the religious convictions of its citizens but guarantee civic equality on the basis of interhuman relationships, as required by the Sharī'a. In the context of constitutional democracy, this aspect of interpersonal relationships could be advanced for the improvement of women's moral and political equality with men, especially when the Sharī'a concedes that women have sufficient capacities to enter contracts as equals. In the classical juridical formulations dealing with relations between sexes, there is insufficient recognition of the equality of men and women that should be corrected.

Concluding Remarks

The foundational question about the character of universal morality in Muslim political theology has provided us with an opportunity to delineate the relative adequacy of teleological and deontological models of human moral agency that undergird the legal tradition in Islam. As I have argued in this chapter, the ethical dimension of the Islamic legal methodology can develop and sustain an inclusive universal language—a language that can engage the secularly derived universal morality of the UN Declaration. Islamic ethics shares common moral terrain with the Declaration on several levels, and to disregard the merit of the Mu'tazilite and Shī'ite deontological-teleological models that shape human action that is responsive to duty or purposive would be to foreclose any opportunity to dialogue with Muslim reformist and traditionalist scholars on the need to protect human dignity and to advance peace with justice in the world.

The Qur'an emphasizes moral activity and creativity in human beings as part of their innate responsiveness to the nature with which they are created. It is this nature that affirms virtue (*al-ma'rūf*) as a "known" orientation in society, and that leads a person to rise above preoccupation with his or her own prosperity to working toward the common good. Religious responsiveness then becomes a major source for political activism in the cause of justice and the common good, and for creating a two-pronged relationship between two senses of devotion—devotion to one's political order and devotion to one's religious tradition. A tension arises when the two sources of Muslim identity, revelation and reason, make incompatible and incommensurable demands upon an individual, demanding that she or he hold exclusive and inclusive membership in the community and modern nation-state, respectively.

The solution is provided in the recognition of a principle that can serve as the foundation for a civil society. The principle is enunciated in one of the administrative documents of classical Islam. The document that comprises the principle recognizes the equality of human beings in creation, regardless of one's membership in a religious community. This administrative document was written by the caliph 'Alī (d. 660) at the time when he appointed his governor for Egypt and its provinces. It is important to bear in mind that Muslim conquerors were a minority in Egypt. Egypt had a large Christian population, to whom a proper status had to be granted for administrative purposes. To reduce the majority to a non-Muslim tolerated people was detrimental to the development of a sense of civic responsibilities to the conquering Muslim army. In this context, the idea of civic equality was introduced in the document written by the caliph himself to underscore the fact that communitarian membership was not incompatible with civic equality based on human dignity. As long as the role of faith was to instill moral and spiritual awareness leading to responsible behavior in society, governance could be founded upon a more universal principle of recognizing other humans as one's equal in creation.[26]

The recognition of non-Muslims as equals in creation is certainly a status that can be accorded to a citizen regardless of his or her religious affiliation. The role of religion, then, is to foster norms, attitudes, and values that can enhance peaceful relations among different ethnic and religious communities. The norms like "your brothers in religion or your equals in creation" can and should serve as the founding principle of governance through the creation of a civil society.

Can conventional nonreligious theories of human rights serve as a self-sufficient canon for the universality of contemporary international human rights without a full assessment of the psychological and religious appeal of the religion-based moral universality of the common humanity of equals in creation? As a matter of fact, 'Alī's concept of equality in creation simply reiterates the Qur'anic foundation of the plurality of religious paths of salvation while endorsing the common moral grounds that could function as the fundamental source of human cooperation:

> For every one of you [Jews, Christians, Muslims], We have appointed a path and a way. If God had willed He would have made you but one community; but that [He has not done in order that] He may try you in what has come to you. *So compete with one another in good works.* (Q. 5:48, emphasis added)

This passage from the Qur'an underscores the divine mystery that allows pluralism in matters of faith and law to exist in human society. What unites peoples of different faiths is the call to make a common moral cause and advance the common good of all. This is the foundation for moral universality of human rights.

3

Natural Law and Knowledge of Ethical Necessity

Islamic political theology, with its goal of establishing a just public order, had laid the doctrinal groundwork for the Muslim community to work toward reaching a consensus about the need for peaceful and just relationships with other faith communities on the basis of a common humanity under divine guidance. For the Qur'an it was a given that different communities and groups ought to come to terms with the fact of cultural and religious diversity and regulate interhuman relationships on a dictum that functioned as a tolerance-generating principle among various claims of exclusionary truth, namely, "To you your religion, and to me my religion" (Q. 109:6). In God's wisdom, humans were to be left alone to exercise their volition in the matter of religion (Q. 2:256). Nonetheless, even though coercion in the matter of one's choice of spiritual path was ruled out, the Qur'an did not overlook the necessity of providing some workable principle to serve as a foundation for interhuman relations. To avoid any dispute about whose religion is superior, the principle aims to bring peoples of diverse religious and cultural backgrounds to respect and treat one another as equals had to be based on some extrarevelatory notion. Providing such an extrarevelatory principle, acceptable to all faith communities and groups, was a challenge for the Qur'an, which included both universal and particular aspects in its message. The manner in which the Qur'an addressed the generality of humanity was clearly identified by the universal address: "O humankind!" When the substance of the message was inclusive of all human beings, then the Qur'an proceeded with its universal evocation, as the following passage explicitly underscores:

> O humankind, We have created you male and female, and appointed you races and tribes, that you may know one another. Surely the noblest among you in the sight of God is the most morally and spiritually [*atqā*] aware of you. God is All-knowing, All-aware. (Q. 49:13)

In contrast, the particularist aspect of the Qur'anic message specifically meant for the Muslim community was addressed, "O believers!" The following passage underscores this particularity:

> O believers, be aware of your spiritual and moral duty and fear God as He should be feared, and see that you do not die save in submission [to God]. (Q. 3:102)

Hence, the Qur'an is engaged in guiding all humanity as well as its particular faith community, making sure that the latter group becomes exemplary by avoiding extremism of all sorts and following the path of moderation to earn the title of a "median community" (*umma wasaṭa*) so that it can serve as God's witness to other people (Q. 2:143).

The two forms of Qur'anic address evidently point to the comprehensive ambition of the Qur'an to serve as the reminder to all human beings, regardless of their color, creed, or race. Although submission to the divine will together could serve as a uniting principle, God's decision was not to coerce people into accepting religion under duress. Consequently, the Qur'an sought to provide a source of guidance which any person with common sense could adopt as a strategy for their own benefit and for the benefit of the larger community. Such a universal dimension of Qur'anic guidance always appears with God's creation of humanity—a humanity endowed with a moral consciousness, a humanity that shares a common parentage to claim equality, a humanity that is endowed with nobility and dignity to undertake God's work on earth. Even more in the tone of universal concern is the moral admonition that calls upon all human beings to work for the common good (*al-khayrāt*) of all beings in the natural world, despite their religious differences (Q. 5:48).

To be sure, Qur'an's universalism is thoroughly spiritual in the sense that it essentially responds to the claim of God as the Creator. But this claim of God requires humanity to respond to its own nature in relation to others in the temporal order in order to actualize God's purposes. The divine purposes in religion are closely linked to the perfection of the temporal order in which human beings, assuming moral agency, strive (the true sense of the term *jihād*) to become fully and authentically human by undertaking the duty to be virtuous:

> God commands you to deliver trusts back to their owners; and when you judge between the people, that you judge with justice. Good is the admonition God gives you; God is All-hearing, All-seeing. (Q. 4:58–9)

The substance of the divine command here reflects social responsibility based on rationally derived sense of duty toward delivering trusts back to their owners, and of justice in dealing with others. At the same time it appeals to the community of the faithful, since it has responded to the call of faith and accepted living under the religious system that also regulates the community's relations with other communities living under its governance. This characteristic of Islamic public order seeks to build a common ground, and is similar to the modern search for an overlapping consensus. This characteristc was underscored by the Muslim theologian al-Ghazālī (d. 1111). Speaking about the absolute necessity of political power to manage human affairs, he writes:

> Exercise of authority (*sulṭān*) is necessary in managing the religious public order (*niẓām al-dīn*); and secular public order (*niẓām al-dunyā*) is necessary in managing the religious public order (*niẓām al-dīn*). . . . Surely, religious public order cannot be achieved without secular public order. Moreover, secular public order cannot be achieved without the imam (leader) who is obeyed (*al-imām al-muṭā'*).[1]

This statement by Ghazālī suggests that while religious faith is essential for managing the success of religious public order structured on the principles of secular order, it will be insufficient to manage an inclusive religious public order, if it attempts to build political consensus on religious premises only; rather, it must look for public reason to legitimate its power structure. Remarkably, the source for public reason in Islamic public order is equally derived from the scripturally prescribed moral duty to exercise authority with justice.

It is important to emphasize that this arguement for an overlapping consensus among traditional communities was derived from the scriptural sources, collectively labeled as divine revelation, which, on the one hand, excluded other communities from its particular brand of salvation, and, on the other, intimated to its own community that they could use the innate sense of human moral worth to forge a practical consensus to treat other faith communities with respect and fairness. I return to this inclusive theology in the last chapter.

In chapter 2, I demonstrated that the purpose of revelation is to provide norms and values that will guide humankind toward constructing a viable system of governance. When the Qur'an invests God's deputyship in human beings, it is speaking about potentialities and challenges that await humanity as it struggles to establish a just order. The function of religious guidance is to provide social and legal enactments in light of its general moral teaching and particularly under the impact of its stated objectives, on the one hand, and against the background of their social milieu, on the other.

But how does universal religious guidance become accessible without appeal to a specific revelation sent through the founder of a religion? This is an epistemological inquiry about the source of human morality in divine revelation. Are human beings inclined to apprehend moral truths or develop moral virtue regardless of the quality of human education or moral sensibilities and the demands of divine revelation? Is natural reason, unaided by revelation a sufficient and adequate guide for the moral life? These questions lead to teleological understanding of nature and form the basis for establishing universal norms that appeal to all peoples across cultures and traditions. Further, this moral universality makes it possible for universal human rights to claim international legitimacy. More pertinently, it is this morality that propounds a kind of natural law suitable for dealing with those with whom a person does not share anything more than his or her humanity.

My thesis thus far has contended that religion and human rights norms are two solvents of human life, two interlocking sources and systems of values that have existed side by side in all human communities, regardless of time, place, and culture. Every religious tradition is endowed with both universal and particular ethical norms that have, on occasions, reinforced or contradicted each other. Throughout their history of interaction with the realities of human existence, religiously inspired rights have caused fresh thinking in the area of application in social and political contexts, requiring the emerging legal tradition to stand in dialectical harmony with religion. Religious tradition, for its part, has strived to come to terms with the legal tradition by striking a balance between the ideal and the real and linking communal beliefs and ideals to the formal legal structures and processes for the implementation of concrete solutions to the problems in human relations.

In Islamic tradition, the Sharī'a developed a refined legal structure that developed the enduring principles of Islamic faith into evolving precepts of human action. It sought to imbue Islamic ethical standards in the form of injunctive propositions to emphasize the logical character of juridical categories for indicating the relevance of certain situations and facts from a given normative angle. However, Islamic jurisprudence has always faced the problem connected with the inherent religious nature of its system, and its relevance in changing social-political conditions. In the modern period when

Islam had to deal with a restatement of the inherited tradition that strikes a balance between religious authenticity and the forces of social evolution, Muslim jurisprudence was faced with the challenge of redefining the relationship between the normative standards ("oughts") required by the revealed texts and the mundane forces ("actual realities") that shape society. How was it to avoid the secularization of the religious system through the inevitable adoption of Western legal rules and principles, which were alien to the comprehensive spirit of Islamic legal thought?

The majority of modernizing, secular Muslim jurists proceeded without understanding a theoretical discussion on the juridical methodology that was in place among the traditionalists.[2] Perhaps bypassing serious theoretical discussions was the only way to avoid conflict with the religious leaders, the ulema, who could easily derail the entire reformation based on an innovative method to revise the juridical tradition by individual judgment and by outwardly maintaining some sort of historical continuity with the terminology that was familiar to the ulema. But by avoiding to undertake critical discussion of the highly technical principles in Islamic legal theory, modernizing Muslim jurists failed to garner the support of the traditionalist jurists whose knowledge of the Islamic juridical sciences was not only impeccable, but also an important source for the legitimacy of the modernists' project of legal revolution in the Muslim world. Historically, the early Muslim community was committed to a revelation-based legal system by working toward a theory that would, at least, make it possible to make predictable judicial decisions in all areas of interpersonal relations. But any time, the inherited juridical tradition ceased to be the primary source of precedents that were based on moral-legal analysis, and, insofar as its rules survived in modern codes, they ceased to be legitimately founded upon paradigmatic cases or deduced with some sense of conclusiveness.

Apart from this theoretical weakness regarding the modernization of the Muslim legal heritage, the persistent problem among the traditionalists has been the avoidance of discussion of philosophical issues related to religious thought in terms of prevailing modern philosophical and historical ideas. At the foundational level, it is fair to say that there is no unequivocal language of human rights per se in Islamic sources. As typically understood, "human rights" envision equal citizens endowed with inalienable rights that entitle them to equal concern and respect from the state. But the modern concept of citizenship is conspicuously absent in the traditional sources of Islam. In addition to this conceptual insufficiency, at the political level the human rights record of contemporary Muslim governments has not been exemplary.

To be sure, the language of Islamic juridical tradition is primarily the language of responsibilities and obligations rather than rights or liberties.

A human being is not the ultimate referent of moral agency. It is God who is the end of the moral life. The majority of the Sunni ulema, in line with the Ash'arite theological voluntarism that vindicated the primacy of God's will over the intellect (which led to identifying morality with divine positive law and denying that ethical values can have any other foundation but the will of God), resisted the rationalist impulse of the Qur'an that enabled the Mu'tazilite and Shī'ite theologians to speak about the innate moral worth of humanity and autonomous agency. For the Sunni ulema, nature and reason were insufficient for ethics. An action is not good because it is construed so by the essential nature of a human being, but because God so wills. Consequently, a natural system of ethics was construed by Sunni scholars as alien and was rejected as un-Islamic, which ironically denied that Islam could offer the measure of human beings' dignity and capacity to participate in that moral order. There was no standard of good and evil, however minimal, available to all rational creatures. The notion of God as an unlimited and arbitrary power implied reduction of all moral laws to inscrutable manifestations of divine omnipotence.

The Mu'tazilite and Shī'ite theology, with its emphasis on a substantial role for human reason to discern moral truth, and with its potential to expound a thesis about the teleological understanding of nature within the parameters of revelation, was abandoned in favor of a divine command ethics. In this way the majoritarian political theology denied the human ability to recognize the true values in life by unaided reason and any inclination to pursue these as part of the human capacity to be primarily responsible and responsive to God's commands and God's purposes. As a consequence, it also refused to recognize moral agents willing to fulfill their duty to the welfare of their community as a whole, as well as to its individual members. Recognition of human dignity as sufficient grounds for its inviolability, regardless of differences in creed, color, or sex, had to await a modernizing human rights discourse.

Modern Muslim Human Rights Discourse

Muslim engagement with modernity has been sluggish, to put it mildly. A systematic working out of Islamic religious thought taking into consideration the inherited duality between the religiously eternal and the secularly changeable, has progressed slowly, if at all. A more systematic interpretation is imperative in order to derive an Islamic worldview that is consonant with new intellectual synthesis between a relatively static traditionalist, historical Islam and the constantly changing situation of the modern world. For Muslim scholars, entry into modern human rights discourse depends upon clearly restoring the Qur'an and the Prophetic teachings so that the conformities and deformities of historical Islam may be distinctly judged by the original intent of the Islamic revelation. For instance, some recognition of the epistemic function of human conscience in moral valuation, and the universal dimension of common human nature in deriving legal-ethical decisions would have provided Muslim jurists with a teleological justification for some positive legislation required to improve upon classical solutions to interhuman and international relations. More important, understanding the fundamental equality of all human beings based on their intuitive capacity for moral discernment would have served as an important source for those judicial decisions that require the faith community to work for the common good of all human beings. A rationally apprehended just social order, however abstract and inconsonant with human nature seeking to assume responsibility for creating an ethical political order, would have prepared Muslims to enhance the Qur'anic demand for justice as an overall minimal structure that is required for healthy interhuman relationships built on the equality of all human persons regardless of their creed or race.

In this sense, Muslim thinkers working on human rights must engage Islamic theology rather than Islamic law to challenge the secular advocates of human rights to take minimalist Islamic universalism seriously. Islamic theology in general, and theological ethics in particular, can potentially develop the thesis about natural law in Islam and its connection with the natural, inalienable rights of human beings based on human equality. After all, the idea of natural law as an indication of what is intrinsically good or intrinsically bad is the cornerstone of Islamic theological ethics. Moreover, the locus of concern, in much of the natural law theory, with the question of the common good (*al-ma'rūf*), toward which humanity is invited to act in building intercommunal relations beyond those which the Sharī'a norms project for the Muslim community, is a logical starting point in searching for human rights foundations in Islam.

The articulation of humankind as a universal community (*umma wāḥida*), the central doctrine of the Qur'an (Q. 2:213, 5:48, 10:19) based upon the common, immutable, and eternal nature of human beings, is correlated to the reformulation of the Islamic theory of natural law, which has the potential for universal application of values connected with relationships between God, society, and individual. Reformulating the sources of human equality in Islam means finding ways of effecting change in contemporary Muslim thinking about the emerging patterns of relationship by integrating the inherited patterns into new social and political relationships in the context of human rights discourse. As such, Islamic natural law theory can inescapably touch not only the human's relation to God, but also the human's relation to truth, government, family, and neighbor. It can effect both private and public domains of human existence. It is for this reason that in developing and founding universal human rights norms in Islam, Muslim thinkers not only must contend with the historical juridical system that was fixed and frozen in time; they must also revisit the theological-ethical basis of juridical sciences, firmly extrapolated from the moral world of the Qur'an. This moral world was unusually supple and adaptable in providing fair rulings requiring equal treatment of all humans as the direct consequence of their being born with universal nature.

As expected, the intellectual challenge of modernization, affecting the reformulation of the past heritage, to derive the universal potential of theological ethics in Muslim societies, has involved a selective retrieval of the traditional past and articulation of the insistent new in relation to the overall purposes of Islamic revelation. While the fresh retrieval of the revealed text and its interpretation to confront the challenges of the new era has been feared as a threat to an existing pattern of values and meanings, it has sometimes been hailed as a challenge to create new values and meanings, especially in the context of democratic governance and protection of human rights. In order to restore confidence in the substantive role of reasoning in discerning moral values and its impact upon a rational basis for equality of all humankind sharing moral worth, Muslims cannot afford to ignore the correlation between theological ethics and modern secular values that demand recognition for separate jurisdictions in dealing with religious and mundane, private and public. Understanding and communicating about the crisis of modernization for Islamic religious thought, and the role a religion like Islam can play in negotiating its ethical public order, is extremely crucial to an inner Islamic reformulation based on the core doctrines in the social and political settings of a modern nation-state. Consequently, intellectual cooperation between modernizing and traditional elites in the Islamic world is critical to neutralize any negative effects of traditional religious and cultural values that hamper the emergence of a necessary consensus in resolving the crisis of modernization and the emergence of a political environment conducive to the securing of human rights.[3]

My argument, to be presented with much technical and nuanced discussion of juridical tradition, is built upon a very straightforward thesis: there is a crisis of epistemology in Islamic religious sciences. This crisis is the result of a self-cultivated dislocation between theology, ethics, and law in Islamic tradition. Unless the doctrinal and ethical presuppositions of the early juridical tradition are investigated and expounded afresh, the crisis will continue to produce apologetic, intellectually impoverished, and, most important, ethically counterproductive Islamic scholarship. Moral sensibilities and demands of Islam's revealed texts can work together to resolve the epistemological crisis. Lack of historicism in analyzing the primary materials with sharp ethical tools has led to the devaluation of human life, caught in the crossfire of political conflicts. When a tradition that once taught respect for even the dignity of an animal becomes the source of legal opinions that justify the suicide bombing of innocent bystanders, then it is time to reexamine the moral directives of the Qur'an and the teachings of the Prophet, who is reported to have said: "I was commissioned to complete the noble virtues [in humanity]."

One of the fundamental noble virtues that the Prophet came to teach was the dignity of human persons as human. According to the most revered compilation of Sunni traditions, the *Ṣaḥīḥ* of Imam al-Bukhārī, one day the Prophet was sitting in the company of his close associates when a bier carrying a Jew passed. It was his custom to stand up when a bier passed. So he stood up. His companions pointed out that the dead person was a Jew. To this he retorted: "Is he not a human being?" Traditions like this reveal the conceivability of the human rights regime in the Islamic tradition since they convey the sufficiency of human dignity, regardless of creed, for respect.

Ethical Necessity in Islamic Theory of Natural Law

Ethical necessity is an action that is rationally required (*wujūb 'aqlī*) because it is based on moral norms that follow from human nature—the underpinnings of natural law. Rational duty entails an objective moral order grounded in divine will and justice, whose valuation is discernible to human reason. In comparison to a rationally inferred obligation, the doctrine that God's will is the ultimate source of morality conceives of revelation-based obligatory action (*wujūb shar'ī*) as an expression of God's absolute will. According to the Mu'tazilites and the Shī'ites, the rational and free intellect (*al-'aql*) provides the justification to conceive habitually performed duties as part of the fulfillment of God's will, namely, the revelation-based necessity (*wujūb shar'ī*) in order for persons to attain prosperity (*falāḥīya*) in this life and the next. The difference between reason and revelation-based duty is that an action based on a moral sense of duty, according to the Qur'an, is part of the divinely ordained eternal tradition (*sunnat allāh*), which is the law of nature, and which is a permanent object of human reflection (Q. 33:62, 48:23, 17:77); whereas a revelation-based duty is taught by the prophets to their followers in fulfillment of God's will for human prosperity. In the former sense, moral action is based on ethical and social norms that are universal and applicable to all humans as human. Moreover, in terms of its goal to further just interhuman relationships, ethical obligation is derived on the basis of moral norms that follow from essential human nature. Revelation-based action leads to the discovery of religiously required duties that are by necessity both exclusive, in that they are applicable only to the membership within the faith community, and inclusive, in that they have common concerns in furthering the community's relations with other communities.

This rather oversimplified description of these two types of necessary action might lead the reader to regard revelation-based moral obligation in Islam to be as comprehensive and with great capacity to be inclusive in the public domain. As a matter of fact, the Cairo Declaration on Human Rights in Islam is based on such an assumption that, as a comprehensive system, historical Islam is capable of becoming a source of universal human rights. The critical issue that has been intentionally sidestepped by the Cairo Declaration, however, is the political dimension of theological evaluation regarding human nature and the just public order in the historical Islamic tradition. The majority of traditionalist Muslim leaders not only refuse to regard human beings as rational beings, capable of guiding themselves and deriving from their reason a standard to judge their environment; they also deny that there is anything intrinsically good or intrinsically bad that can be apprehended by human reason and, as such, does not depend on the will of God. Further, and perhaps negating the document's claim to be universal is the denial of a doctrinal basis for the notion that a human is born free and is equal to all other humans in creation.

Whether Muslim theological ethics can serve as the foundation for human rights discourse in Islam or not, the crux of the problem in speaking about the relationship between Islam and human rights reverts to historical apathy among Sunni jurists toward rational theology and its organic relation to ethics in Muslim religious discourse. The Ash'arite doctrine that the will of God is the ultimate source of morality and that law is an expression of the absolute sovereignty of God paradoxically provides justification for the absolute sovereignty of Muslim rulers as the manifestation of God's absolute power. The Mu'tazilite doctrine of human free will and moral agency, on the other hand, vindicates the real task of ethics and ethical necessity, namely, to understand and assert moral life as a manifestation of the rational will conferred on humanity as part of God's purposive creation. In this sense, law and ethical necessity are linked to morality, which is the source of values discernible to human reason. This law is characterized as natural law, whose essential tenet is the equality of all human beings as recipients of a divinely-endowed nature.

Humankind is one community (*umma wāḥida*) based upon this understanding of the common nature of humans and their rational ability to be moral. Accordingly, the essence of humanity cannot be at variance with this common nature, which is also the source of social common good and the human responsibility to God for upholding it. It is this moral structure of human society in terms of the common good in the Mu'tazilite doctrine of justice that needs to be emphasized in Islamic human rights discourse. To be sure, the Mu'tazilite doctrine of justice does not prescribe the manner of achieving a just society; it simply underscores the human capacity and responsibility to establish a just public order where respect of individuals is ensured on the rational basis of ethical necessity, which rules out discriminatory and unfair treatment of a religious or cultural other.

It is not hard to see why Muslim traditionalists have not treated Islamic theological ethics as an independent discipline, distinct from juridical studies that deal with God's commands and prohibitions, and why Muslim scholars never developed a systematic theory of natural law with its outstanding features expressing rationalism based on incontrovertible principles, individualism based on the natural and inalienable rights of human beings, and offering a program of social reform calling for an end of all political institutions that perpetrate injustice in the public sphere. In contrast, Muslim rationalists, both Sunni Mu'tazilite and Shī'ite theologians propounded the rudiments of just such an Islamic theory of natural law when they expounded their moral epistemology in which they contended that ethical knowledge is objective and rationally acquired by unaided reason. This latter doctrine was the basis for human moral worth as well as moral agency—the two prerequisites for a claim of universal human rights.

The modern language of human rights presupposes a person's moral capacities in exercising his or her rights. Consequently, a potential for moral agency is a prerequisite to exercise one's rights. Without the free exercise of will, a possessor of rights cannot be expected to make a moral decision and accept responsibility for his or her actions. A moral right presumes a capacity of acting in conformity with natural law. To possess a right is to have a faculty of acting rightfully in some manner; to act in this way is to exercise this right. As an owner of a house, I have the ability to rent out part of it whenever I wish; if anyone lacking this ownership rents out the place, his act violates the moral law. But how do I make that other person responsible to recognize my right without any power of causing him to act in that way? It is here that social norms become an important source of conformity to the moral code within the limits of natural law. The informal force of society provides the necessary pressures of morality. Society as a whole functions as the protector of rights by regulating the rules of law or morality so that no act of injustice occurs without censure.

Muslim communities around the world need to become collectively and actively engaged in enhancing the human ability to act in conformity to the requirements of what is morally right by challenging the lack of such moral sensibilities among the members of the religious and political establishment in the Muslim world. I regard this as the challenge of human rights to Muslim jurists, who seem to have adopted a passive attitude toward the frequent violations of human rights of non-Muslim minorities or dissenters in the Muslim community within the boundaries of modern Muslim nation-states. This passive attitude, in my opinion, is the result of the uncritical acceptance of the inherited Ash'arite position regarding human nature and the endorsement of the thesis that there is no concept of natural law or any idea of autonomous moral agency in Islam.

Natural Law as a Human Rights Foundation in Islam

The search for a human rights foundation must begin without presenting the historical Islamic juridical heritage as a comprehensive system that is to be maximally applied in the promulgation of universal morality derived from Islamic revelation. It is relevant to point out that even the secular international human rights document does not claim a commitment to more than a noncomprehensive, minimalist foundation. The Declaration, to be sure, is based on a cross-cultural moral agreement about human rights, and, accordingly, it is a warrant for holding people everywhere accountable, regardless of their religious affiliations and disagreements, to the absolute validity of certain moral claims that protect and promote the basic freedoms and welfare of all humans as humans. But, moral standards are derived from distinctive moral experiences that stress the distinctive historicity of every person, and every moral claim becomes intelligible within the cultural traditions that articulate them. The notion of a common morality known to all human beings is, in the context of human rights language, necessarily noncomprehensive, because although the concept of natural rights or duties based on universal reason in Western thought has served as a rationale for a secular universal morality in the Declaration, their cross-cultural application in the context of different religious traditions is seriously contestable.[4] At the same time, there is no need for the Declaration or any such document whose content and justification protect basic human rights to be based on comprehensive doctrines, because what is important is that moral beliefs derived from religious or nonreligious sources should generate a general commitment to the protection of human dignity, not a total morality.

Muslim communities can appropriate this noncomprehensive understanding of morality, accessible to all humans as humans, in terms of the Qur'an's larger conception of human nature and the purpose of creation. In other words, the Qur'anic notions of humanity as one community under God, the equality of all human beings through God's endowment of a constitutional nature capable of intuitively discerning the moral worth of an action correlative with revelation can serve as a minimalist foundation for human rights in Islam. This foundation can then bridge, rather than bypass, the intellectual and moral gap between the secular and religious noncomprehensive universal morality in order to make a common cause for moral education and training about inherent human dignity and moral worth of each person as such.

In my search to discover a foundation for those human rights that accrue to a person simply because of his or her humanity, whether or not he or she accepts Islam as his or her religion, I have identified the concept of human nature (*fiṭra*) as the most logical point of entry in human rights language for Muslims. The notion of a natural or innate constitution of the human being is the core doctrine of the Qur'an that underscores the Qur'an's insistence on God's purposive creation of humanity.

The Concept of *Fiṭra* and Related Notions of Natural Constitution

Sayyid Quṭb (d. 1966), is a major figure in the Sunni reform movement in the twentieth century. In his commentary on the Qur'an, he presents human nature (*fiṭra*) as the locus of the divine guidance of humanity toward the law of order that regulates human action as well as the movement of the entire natural order, orienting the creation toward the Creator.[5] The purpose of creating human beings, accordingly, is to develop their *fiṭra* in such a way that they attain moral and spiritual perfection through the guidance that God bestows in two forms: first in the form of practical intelligence (*al-ʿaql al-ʿamalī*) in order to fortify the soul to fathom the purpose of its creation, the second, in the form of the right path for the individual in order to achieve salvation in the hereafter.[6]

The Qur'an's concept of *fiṭra* in the sense of "creation" is organically connected with the notion of "by nature upright (*ḥanīf*) through creation (*faṭara*)" (Q. 30:30). The act of creation is to cause a thing to come into existence; it also signifies the natural or original constitution with which a child is created in his mother's womb. In this sense, *faṭara* is *khilqa*, that is, "originating a thing" as the Qur'an says when it speaks about "originating creation" (Q. 30:27). A similar meaning of "natural or original constitution" is evident in the Prophet's tradition that states: 'Every infant is born in a state of conformity to the natural constitution (*fiṭra*) with which he is created in his mother's womb, either prosperous or unprosperous [in relation to the soul].' Evidently, there is agreement among classical Arabic lexicographers that the essential meaning of the word *fiṭra* signifies something natural, native, innate, original, or another quality or property with which humans are created by God.[7] As a connotative signification of the word, some lexicographers take the word to mean the "faculty of knowing God," with which God has created human beings. In other words, *fiṭra* is the source of natural religion. God's guidance in the matter of natural religion can be sought in two ways: first by seeking knowledge (*ma'rifa*) through reasoning and evidence; and second by inner purification and ascetic practices (*riyāḍa*).[8]

The first form of guidance bears all the characteristics of something universal, related to human nature before it submits to any formal religion. The evidence comes from those passages of the Qur'an that speak about two forms of "straying away" (*ḍalāl*) from truth or the right path. The first form of straying away causes the *fiṭra* to become corrupted and lose its natural ability to know the right from the wrong, by letting disbelief (*kufr*) and hypocrisy (*nifāq*) find their way into human action. In contrast the second form of straying away reinforces disbelief and hypocrisy in human personality. This is alluded to in the verse that reads: "In their heart is a disease and God increases their disease. A painful doom is theirs because they lie" (Q. 2:10). The first disease is imputed to human beings, and the second to God. "So when they went astray God sent their hearts astray. And God does not guide the evil-doers" (Q. 61:5).

The second form of guidance, on the other hand, is related to the particular revelation that is given to the prophets, the bearers of the divinely inspired message. The guidance through revealed scriptures follows the guidance that is already imprinted upon unimpaired state of *fiṭra* (natural disposition or constitution). The unencumbered natural disposition perceives the need for further guidance that can be attained outside itself and, hence, it prepares the person to accept the existence of the one hidden from sensory perception, who is the originator of everything, in whom everything shall terminate and to whom everyone shall return (Q. 2:156). Just as God does not neglect even the most minute detail that is needed in the creation, so does God not neglect the guidance of humankind in what would save them from destruction of their deeds and morals. This is what is known as conceding voluntarily (*iḍ'ān*) to belief in the oneness of God, the need for prophets, and the Day of Reckoning, beliefs that form part of the fundamentals of religion (*uṣūl al-dīn*). Evidently, by conceding voluntarily to God's guidance through God's prophets, human beings can maintain their nature in an unimpaired state. Moral action performed by human beings is due to the human's station between the two forms of God's guidance: the prior (*sābiqa*) and the subsequent (*lāḥiqa*) guidance—the prior being related to human nature and the subsequent to the revelation. Moreover, faith in religion and commitment to moral action are located between divinely conferred natural constitution and the revelation—the two forms of guidance that are correlated to bring about human prosperity in this world and the next. What proves that the subsequent religious guidance is derived from the prior natural constitution is the verse that speaks about God's providence: "God confirms those who believe with the firm judgment, in the present life and in the world to come, and God leads wrongdoers astray. And God does what He wills" (Q. 14:27). In other words, all guidance is from God, and it cannot be attributed to anyone else except figuratively, as the Qur'an declares: 'And whomsoever it is God's will to guide, He expands his bosom unto submission (*islām*)' (Q. 6:125).[9] Even more poignant is a reminder to the Prophet that 'You will not be able to guide whom you like. Indeed it is God who guides whom God wills. And God is aware of those who are guided' (Q. 28:56).

Hence, God's guidance is well established in both its forms, in the sense of showing the path; and when the Qur'an speaks about God denying guidance to those who do not believe, this denial applies to the purpose of guidance, not to the actual guidance, which is not denied to anyone. In other words, God's denial of guidance pertains to the attainment of perfection through that subsequent guidance, and not to the bestowal of original guidance itself. The law of nature causes a person to pursue and discover the desired goal for which he or she is created. This is God's unchanging law, which is underscored in the above-cited verse Q. 6:125, which also warns those who reject the "original" guidance connected with their natural constitution, which is innately bestowed through creation:

> And whoever it is God's will to guide, He expands his bosom unto submission (*al-islām*),[10] and whomsoever it is His will to send astray, He makes his bosom close and narrow as if he is engaged in sheer ascent. Thus God lays ignominy upon those who do not believe.
> (Q. 6:125)

Human Moral Agency

How does the human being submit or surrender to God, and yet maintain autonomous moral agency? *Islām* (submission) of a person in relation to God indicates the person's acceptance and compliance with God's authority in all those matters that go to form the order of creation (*ḥukm takwīnī*), which includes all the matters that are decreed by God; and the matters that go to form the order of divinely revealed law (*ḥukm tashrī'ī*), which includes the commands and prohibitions that are part of the revelation. Accordingly, submission to God is graded in accord with what is attainable by means of it. Thus, for instance, the first level of submission is the acceptance of the commands and prohibitions of God's revelation by reciting the formula of faith verbally, regardless of whether the mind agrees with it or not (Q. 49:14). From this sense of *islām* follows the first level of faith, which is the voluntary conceding (*al-iḍ'ān al-qalbī*) to the necessity of putting into action most of the religiously required practices. The second level of submission is conscientious compliance which enables the person to advance in true belief, and by performing the good deeds that follow from those beliefs, although it is possible to fall short in some instances. "[These are the ones] who believed Our signs (revelations) and were self-surrendered [*muslimīn*]" (Q. 43:69).

Thus the distinction between two forms of submission is a qualitative one in the sense that the second form of *islām* ensues from the detailed comprehension of faith in religious truth (Q. 49:15, 61:10–11) and compliance with the requirements of it; whereas the first level of submission is simply being guided to discover the latter. This qualitative submission leads to the third level when the soul becomes fortified with virtues and gains mastery over the beastly appetites. It is also at this level that people begin to worship God as if they see God, and if they do not see God, then God certainly sees them. Nothing in the human character at this third level is found to be wanting in terms of compliance with God's commands and prohibitions. It is a state of total submission to God's decree and God's order of creation (Q. 4:65). The corresponding level of faith prepares the believer for the world to come. All acts of personal piety are part of this level of faith (Q. 23:1–5). The person who has undergone transformation in the previous levels of submission has gained the inner strength necessary for this third level, by remaining steadfast in the fulfillment of his or her duties no matter how difficult they were. At this station of absolute submission, divine providence enwraps him or her with God's bounties, which God dispenses universally and perpetually, without restriction and disinterestedly (Q. 2:127–128).

This is captured in God's command to Abraham: "Surrender!" He (Abraham) said: "I have surrendered to the Lord of the Beings" (Q. 2:131). The apparent sense of the command is based on *lex gratiae* and not *lex naturae*, for Abraham had surrendered to God voluntarily, responding to his Lord's call and fulfilling God's command. Accordingly, these commands are directed toward him in the beginning of his spiritual and moral journey. At the end of his life, Abraham's prayer with his son Ishmael to make them surrender (*muslim*) to God and show them the ways of worship (Q. 2:127–128) is a prayer for something beyond his will. Thus, the *islām* requested in this prayer is the meaning of faith at the highest level, that is, at the level when one wants to hold to this state of "active surrender" under all circumstances (Q. 10:62–63).[11]

Our main purpose in bringing the Qur'an's view on submission to God's will into this discussion is to underscore the fact that even when the Qur'an speaks about the entire nature having submitted to God's will, when it comes to humankind the revelation advances the freedom of human choice, for God permits the human to accept or reject the act of submission that God demands. This leaves human beings free to negotiate their religious affiliation in any given faith community, or none at all. But it does not permit them to deny the existence of the moral sensibilities necessary for them to undertake to perform their moral duties in relation to other human beings. Such a denial is construed by the Qur'an as the denial of the order of nature (*ḥukm takwīnī*).

The Qur'an speaks about divine inspiration (*ilhām*) (Q. 91:8) as the epistemic tool for practical reason to get to that which is desirable and which enables the nature to become receptive to moral cognition and volition.[12] In this sense, the human's natural constitution is equipped, through divine inspiration, with the moral sensibilities necessary to discern good and evil, and is enabled to exercise personal choice to follow or reject innate moral guidance and face the consequences accordingly. The human being is, then, a free moral agent endowed with value and dignity intrinsically by nature. Further, according to the verse in Q. 91:8, because of humanity's intuitive reason, human beings possess natural dignity based on the self-evident universality of the moral worth of each person.

Judicious investigation of the Qur'an demonstrates that based on inherent human dignity it is not difficult to establish human moral agency and equality. Besides *fiṭra*, there is another fundamental Qur'anic concept that helps to establishing the notion that God's natural guidance is available to all human beings equally. Such guidance springs from God's special endowment of the *qalb salīm*, a phrase signifying "sound mind, moral disposition, the recesses of the mind [*dākhil al-khāṭir*], the seat of consciousness, thoughts, volitions and feelings, the reason" conferred upon humanity.[13] It is a faculty by means of which a human being distinguishes truth from falsehood, good from evil, beneficial from harmful. It confers on humanity an existential meaning for their life, without which life becomes just physical presence.[14] Accordingly, to deduce a moral foundation for human rights based on religious premises,

Muslim advocates of human rights need to reexamine Qur'anic doctrines that speak about human conscience and its freedom from any coercion.

The basic impulse of the Qur'an is dynamic and action-oriented, and seeks to create a perfect society on earth without turning moral inspiration into institutional power. Coercion is contradictory to the moral quality of action because it destroys a spirit of tolerance within certain agreed-upon limits. Human action needs to be gauged in the contexts that define a person's relation to others, because it is in these contexts (political, familial, and personal) that he or she accepts (or rejects) values and authority, and determines what kind of limits make life with others possible. Action that is informed by one's religious commitment and that carries with it the reality of personal choice must be weighed in the moral scale so that that action's consequences for the development of human conscience become clear to the moral agent. Since the moral agent is endowed with conscience, he or she has a duty to follow unfailingly the judgment of conscience in human action. At the same time, he or she also has a duty to conform to the commonly accepted standards of conscientiousness in arriving at the judgment without compulsion. Freedom of conscience is guaranteed when the agent is not forced to act against his or her conscientious judgment. Each person in conflict situations regarding the dictates of conscience must determine his or her "sphere of duty" without any external pressure.[15]

The Qur'an also introduces a new metaphor of *nafs* ("soul") to supplement the function of the heart as the seat of human consciousness in order to underscore an inner ability in human beings by which they distinguish between what is blameworthy and praiseworthy in their own actions.[16] The morally fortified reason, according to the Qur'an, seeks to direct human life on earth in a spiritual and moral pattern, which it locates in the soul—the realm of human personhood. Human beings need to develop a morally sensitive conscience and unambiguous intuitive reason by continually working on overcoming the weaknesses of their personhood so that reverential fear of God (*taqwā*) leads them to pursue righteous conduct based on justice and honesty. The Qur'an speaks about the source of human responsibility—the element of personal choice, which is never wholly absent but is a variable that determines human action (or inaction). However, it is the sensitive conscience and divinely conferred moral intuition that guard individuals from deciding to commit acts of disobedience by explaining or even suggesting to them what they should fear or from what they should preserve themselves. This is the Qur'anic notion of conscientious action based on reverential fear of God (*taqwā*) (Q. 97:19).

God's primary guidance, as noted above, is universal and given to all human beings in the form of spiritual and moral consciousness. This form of guidance is located in the inherent capacity of the human being to discover the unchanging laws of nature. Spiritual and moral awareness leads to righteous conduct, which actually precedes the subsequent guidance that comes through one's acceptance of a particular faith. Before calling humanity to faith, God confers on it an innate attribute that covers all the levels of potential response to the calling of faith. The highest level of human responsiveness to faith in God is reached when that faith turns into continual moral life. The subsequent guidance that God confers comes after a person has attained moral and spiritual awareness through the naturally endowed attribute of seeking to understand the moral reasoning behind a certain action. This guidance prepares a person to respond to the faculty of knowing God, that is, the *fiṭra*, by declaring faith and by providing him or her with the ability to gain confidence and a sense of inner security (*īmān*) and to remain unshakeable when encountering unbelievers or hypocrites. In this way, the primary guidance takes place in the state of the natural constitution (*fiṭra*), whereas the subsequent form of guidance occurs when the natural disposition becomes fortified with developed moral agent's moral sensibilities and righteous conduct.

The Law of Nature or *Fiṭrat Allāh*

The prophetic statement, that every child is created in a state of conformity to the natural constitution before he or she adopts a religion through parental guidance, must be understood in the context of natural and scriptural guidance connected with creation. The primary form of guidance is found in the law of nature, which is immutable and eternal in the sense in which the Qur'an speaks about God's blessing for people: "God does not change what [God has created as a blessing] in a people, until they change [it by neglecting] what is in themselves" (Q. 13:11). God's purposive blessing in the form of guidance through creation does not change its course in guiding the people who might choose to corrupt the state of nature in which God creates them and accordingly face the consequences of depriving themselves of God's universal moral guidance available to unaided reason. What is critical for the Qur'anic notion of ethical necessity based on the human's natural constitution is that although human beings are free to negotiate their spiritual destiny by accepting or rejecting submission to God's will revealed through a specific scripture, they can neither deny the reality of their inherent capacity to discover moral law nor escape the moral consequences of their actions in all spheres of human interaction. By leaving people free to respond to the second form of guidance based on revelation, the Qur'an is confident that universal morality does not depend on revelation, even when there is a correlation between reason and revelation, and when revelation does not contradict the law of nature. In fact, the Qur'anic metaphor *fiṭrat allāh*, meaning God's nature, through which God has created the universe, implies that the natural world is entirely divine, and reason and faith are not only not incompatible, they are also correlative and partners in guiding human life to a meaningful existence.

Maḥmūd b. 'Umar al-Zamakhsharī (d. 1143), the Mu'tazilite commentator on the Qur'anic notion of universal guidance (*al-hudā*), provides a synopsis of the thesis that the Qur'an describes itself as "the guidance," a means to the desired goal. This is so despite the fact that the Qur'an consists of both clear and ambiguous verses. The latter verses cannot be sorted out without the assistance of reason. Thus it is clear that the desired goal of guidance in the Qur'an does not necessarily mean "to be rightly guided [on the scriptural path]," as some scholars have contended, since guidance to the understanding of the meaning of revelation is possible without "being rightly guided." Without the guidance provided by human reason (*al-'aql*), it would have been impossible to distinguish between the clear and obscure verses of the revelation. Hence, the guidance that the Qur'an speaks about is in actuality the human's universal rational guidance (*al-dalālāt al-'aqlīya*) and not the scripture, which is open to all kinds of interpretations by interested parties. On the other hand, the Ash'arite commentator, Fakhr al-Dīn al-Rāzī (d. 1209), who rejects this Mu'tazilite emphasis on the role of reason in guidance, has argued that the Qur'anic guidance means to be "rightly guided to Islam" and it is essentially revelation that is the main source of that guidance, although reason has a subsidiary role in discovering the intent of the revelation for the desired goal of "submission to God's will" (*al-islām*).[17]

Since the Qur'an makes reason a separate source of moral guidance, not to contradict but rather to complement the revelation, it is possible to speak about a universal morality based on religious premises. Here, religious premises provide the foundation for an ideal public order that acknowledges human moral agency as well as the human's inherent dignity as part of God's natural endowment through equal creation of all humans as human. Such a concept of morality is akin to the secular view of universal morality that undergirds the Universal Declaration of Human Rights. It is in this sense that I speak of "two universalisms" that share a common understanding of what it means to be an autonomous moral agent endowed with inherent dignity, able to claim a set of inalienable human rights simply as humans: a universalism based on a comprehensive moral outlook derived from public reason with its roots in a social contract, and a universalism founded upon comprehensive religious doctrine that calls upon humanity to build a just public order founded upon equality of all humans as humans. The challenge of secularly proclaimed human rights norms to religious communities cannot be ignored anymore; on the other hand, ultimately it is these communities' faith in revelation that must be appealed to in order to demonstrate the compatibility between the two self-proclaimed universal systems of moral values. In this setting, the challenge to Islamic theology is to sharpen its self-understanding in order to contribute constructively to the protection of the norms that are imprinted on the clean slate of human nature (*fiṭrat salīma*).

The time has come to engage the Islamic tradition in order to respond convincingly to the violations of human rights that plague contemporary Muslim societies in three important areas: (1) intolerance and even institutionalized violence against different sects and religious minorities; (2) rampant disregard for the rights of women; and (3) lack of any democratic constitutional and conceptual development of the notion of citizenship. By simply declaring the superiority of human rights guaranteed in the Islamic tradition without accounting for their exclusiveness in the Sharī'a over the current legal protections offered by an inclusive human rights regime, Muslim religious scholars are failing to challenge autocratic regimes in the Muslim world to accept their moral and religious responsibility in protecting the human rights of the people they rule. International human rights guarantee the liberty of religion and conscience and freedom of religious exercise to religious groups, in ways that the inherited juridical corpus denies to anyone outside the community. Not to confront such blatant religious discrimination, in my opinion, does a disservice to the Islamic revelation, which requires its adherents to work for and establish a genuinely inclusive justice on earth. The Qur'an recognizes justice, order, forgiveness, restitution, responsibility, obligation, and other legal ideas based on its understanding of human moral agency as endowed with an innate nature that enjoys moral cognition and volition to further divine plan for humanity. This is the core of the Islamic theory of natural law, in which morals are primarily located in the innate nature of humankind, which is capable of recognizing the true values in life, endowed with the inclination to pursue them, in acknowledgment of attendant sanctions from divine authority that influences humanity to carry out the dictates of the natural obligation to pursue such goods.

It is my contention that without first fully articulating natural law in Islam, Muslim advocates of human rights cannot overcome the religious obstacles, laid down by traditionalist Muslim scholars, to the full participation by Muslims to uphold the Universal Declaration of Human Rights. The natural law idea, if proven as intrinsic to Islam as it is, for instance, to Catholicism, will determine the course of action to revisit and revise the traditional disqualifications for inclusive membership of all human beings on the basis of divinely endowed human dignity. Without recognizing the sufficiency of the principle of human dignity for the rights holder, there cannot be a religiously inclusive human rights regime in the Muslim world. The exclusive ethical underpinnings of the Sharīʿa need to become inclusive before it can bear out the true potential of Islamic tradition to a universally inclusive morality founded upon the sheer humanness of humanity rather than a particular religious identity. It is conceptually inconceivable to speak of an Islamic regime of human rights without first determining the natural endowments of the human person, including universal guidance in the form of moral cognition, independent of the particular guidance in the revelation.

Human beings have always endeavored to regulate relationships on certain norms or prescriptions derived from some sort of obligating authority external to the agent. Appeals to human nature as a source external to the agent that provided conventional mores in a society, have a rich history in world civilizations. If there are laws that regulate natural order to preserve its integrity, then there must be laws that direct human natural functions toward a prosperous life. However, in order to grasp these laws implanted in human nature, human beings need an experience of living that develops their practical reason. But human reason on its own cannot grasp the intricacies of moral law; it needs divine commandments to know the details of moral situations. But are the moral laws to be understood as coming entirely from the revelation that details the commands and prohibitions of God?

Scriptural Ethics

There is a recurring command in the Qur'an to "enjoin the good and forbid the evil" (*al-'amr bi-l-ma'rūf* and *nahy 'ani-l-munkar*). This command to enjoin what is right and forbid what is wrong is a prescriptive guidance to uphold moral values in society and to create institutions that promote these values. These moral values, however, are not presented as arbitrary, but as part of a commonly recognizable moral good (*al-khayr, al-ma'rūf*). They are revealed in the Qur'an against the background of the tribal society of Arabia, and as such the moral exhortations to "establish justice" (Q. 4:135) or to "judge with justice" (Q. 4:58) become comprehensible within the context provided by the common pre-Islamic usage. The Qur'an introduces the prescription to establish justice as an objective moral value, on the basis of which one can affirm it to be a universal and natural mode of guidance to which humankind in general can be called upon to respond. Moreover, justice follows from the precepts of natural law, which are disclosed to a common human nature and are regarded as independent of particular religious beliefs. This observation regarding the objective nature of justice is important to bear in mind, because the Qur'anic notion is built upon a universal standard that is intelligible through some reference to an objective state of affairs.

Elsewhere, the Qur'an recognizes the universality and objective nature of moral virtue, for example, goodness, which transcends different religions and religious communities, and it admonishes human beings "to be forward in good work [*khayrāt*]," and holds them accountable for their deeds regardless of their religious differences (Q. 5:48). This passage provides a clear assumption that certain basic moral requirements, like "being just" or being "forward in good work," self-evidently apply to all human beings, regardless of differences in religious beliefs. Therefore, while ideal human being combines moral virtue with complete religious submission (Q. 2:12), it seems that there is a basis for distinction between the religious and the moral in the Qur'an, where moral virtues are further strengthened by the religious act of submission to sacred authority.

It is in the realm of the cognition of universal moral truth that human beings are treated equally and held equally responsible for responding to the ethical duty of being "forward in good work." Furthermore, it is this fundamental equality of all humanity at the level of moral responsibility that directs humankind to create an ethical order on earth and makes it plausible that the Qur'an manifests some kind of natural law accessible to all irrespective of a particular revelation. The concepts of divine command, wisdom, and guidance all point in the direction of a scripture-based ethics. God endows human beings with the necessary cognition and volition to further their comprehension of the purpose for which they are created, and their achievement of it. However, the Qur'an also speaks about basic human weaknesses: "Surely human being was created fretful, when evil visits him, impatient, when good visits him, grudging" (Q. 70:19–20). Recognition of these weaknesses reveals a basic tension in the scripture-based ethics that must be resolved by further acts of guidance by God. The prophets and scriptures show human beings how to change their character, and to conform to the divine plan for human conduct. The prophets, in their mission, become the source of authoritative paradigms for the perfection of human societies. Their moral conduct becomes a source of emulation for their followers. In this way the scripture and the prophet complement each other in cultivating respect for religious guidance.

Predeterminist Political Theology

So far what I have discussed on the basis of the Qur'anic view of human moral agency and natural law is only a partial assessment of the universal potential of

Islamic revelation. The Sunni Mu'tazilite and Shī'ite rationalist-naturalist theological doctrines were authoritatively extracted from the scriptural sources—both the Qur'an and the Tradition. Yet the majority of the Sunni Ash'arite theologians, who were instrumental in legitimizing the authoritative politics of their rulers and who supported state-sponsored discrimination against non-Muslims, suspected the rational underpinnings of human moral agency. To be sure, human moral worth was constructed over inherent human dignity as well as the human ability to discern right from wrong. Such egalitarian notions were a threat to the special status that was crafted for the believers over nonbelievers in the public domain. How were the unbelievers living under the Muslim political order to be treated? Did they not share the same degree of dignity and moral worth as Muslims? The universal implications of Mu'tazilite theology were obvious to the traditionalist theologians. At the same time, the problem of disbelief and the ability of the Meccan unbelievers to inflict harm upon Islamic public order in the early history of the community could not be ignored. However, the critical question was whether it was justifiable to extend the Qur'anic designation of "unbelievers" and their prescribed treatment to all unbelievers throughout human history. What about their natural constitution (*fiṭra*) through creation and their potential for being guided by God as outlined by the Qur'an in its endeavors to guide all humanity?

The traditionalist theological debates on the status of unbelievers were shaped by God's foreordainment of human destiny and whether human beings possessed free will to negotiate this destiny at all. There was no ambiguity in the Qur'an that human beings exercise freedom to negotiate their spiritual destiny. The entire thesis about human responsibility in this and other human acts and the final day of reckoning was built upon the moral worth of human persons endowed with cognition and volition. As long as that aspect of Islamic morality was overlooked, there was little chance for universal morality to emerge as part of the Qur'an's emphasis on indiscriminate dignity for all Children of Adam. Indeed, the Ash'arite denial of human moral agency meant a radical change in the approach to morality as it applied to humans as human. The vindication of the absolute divine will over the intellect capable of cognizing good and evil led to the denial that ethical values could be discerned by unaided reason. The notion of God as an unlimited and arbitrary power implied the reduction of all moral laws to inscrutable manifestations of God's omnipotence. Such a doctrine meant a serious setback for self-subsistent morality as part of the natural human constitution. According to the Ash'arite theologians, there was neither a natural constitution endowed with moral cognition nor natural law to function as the basis of ethics that directed human purposive existence. Contrary to the Qur'an, which emphasized God's unchanging order of nature, the traditionalist position affords no indication of the existence of an eternal and immutable order. It no longer constitutes a measure of human dignity and of their capacity to participate in that order, nor does it establish a standard of good and evil available to all rational creatures. An action is not good because of its suitability to the innate nature with which God created humanity; rather, it is so because God so wills. God's will could also have willed and decreed the precise opposite, which would then possess the same binding force as that which has validity as long as God's absolute will so determines.[18]

Contrary to this rejection of the Qur'an's notion of moral law as an expression of God's will and the essential recognition of humanity endowed with the same level of ethical cognition and volition to fulfill accruing responsibility for one's actions there were other Muslim theologians who disagreed with this absolutist political theology. For these thinkers the matter of disbelief was relative, since the Qur'an approached the matter of guidance in religion without coercion, leaving it to human self-understanding to respond to the calling. The incongruity of generalizing the word *kuffār* (plural of *kāfir*, meaning unbeliever) as it appears in the Qur'an was obvious, because if the verse that reads, "As for the unbelievers, alike it is whether you have warned them or not, they will not believe" (Q. 2:6), were to be taken as God's foreordaining about the unchangeable status of unbelievers, generalized and applied to all unbelievers at all times, it would lead to the closing of the gates of guidance to them forever. Such an interpretation was against the spirit of the Qur'an, which had come to guide humanity regardless of their acceptance or rejection of that divine guidance.[19]

It is significant to note that the Qur'an uses "disbelief" (*kufr*) in at least three senses: (1) in the meaning of "denial," which signifies rejecting what God had commanded to be performed; (2) in the meaning of denial of God's Lordship, which signifies disavowal of God's authority and rejection of God's blessing in such utterances as, "There is no Lord, no Paradise, no Hell!"; and (3) in the form of rejection of truth, when knowing the truth as self-evident, a person chooses to reject it. In none of these usages does the Qur'an indicate that such a denial was foreordained or that the person committing such an act was not responsible for the choice and was immune from facing the consequences of his or her willful act. In other words, there is nothing in the Qur'an to suggest that unbelievers suffer from lack of ethical knowledge or moral worth.

The political context of these early debates also involved the determination of responsibility for the sinful behavior of those who were in power. After all, people suffered at the hands of these rulers, and religious leaders were keen to hold them responsible for their bad behavior and to require them to compensate the victims. The fundamental question that was raised by the theologians was: Did they act as God's free agents or were their acts predetermined by God's overpowering will? The Qur'an proffered a complex view of God's will as it interacted with human acts. There are verses that speak about God "sealing their hearts" or "When they swerved, God caused their hearts to swerve; and God guides never the people of ungodly" (Q. 61:5). These were taken to imply that God foreordains everything for good or bad. Other verses imputed the responsibility for being misguided to the people, thereby making it possible to speak about human free will. Thus, the Qur'an presented a multifaceted correlation between divine predetermination and human responsibility.

Mu'tazilite theologians, who were also dubbed the people of justice (*'adlīya*), demonstrated with much textual evidence their rational conclusion that God's judgment of human action was inconceivable without the human ability to act freely, that is, without the capacity to will and execute an act. They insisted that in human affairs obedience to rulers is conditional because there is no obligation to obey them if they command things that are unjust. In other words, human responsibility was commensurate with freedom to exercise choice of action.

Inasmuch as human beings are free agents, they can reject God's guidance, although because of their innate disposition (*fiṭra*) prompting or even urging them subtly to believe in God, they cannot find any valid excuse for this rejection. Even then, their rejection pertains to the subsequent guidance for procuring of what is desirable, and not to the original guidance that enabled them to apprehend what is desirable in the first place. Furthermore, when human beings choose to reject this guidance, God denies further guidance to them: "Those that believe not in the signs of God, God will not guide them" (Q. 16:104). This denial of guidance clearly pertains to the guidance that would lead the rejectors to reach their desired end, not to the initial moral guidance that is engraved in the hearts of all human beings, in the form of an innate disposition, to guide them toward the good end.

The question of guidance is related to the source of the knowledge of ethical values, such as justice, in classical as well as modern works on Qur'anic exegesis. Significantly, it is at this point that theological differences among Muslim scholars become striking. These differences are rooted in two conflicting conceptions of human responsibility in the procurement of divine justice: the two major schools of Sunni Muslim theology: the Mu'tazilite and the Ash'arite. (The Shī'ite Muslim theology shared its ethical epistemology with the Mu'tazilites.)

The basic Mu'tazilite doctrine is that human beings, having been endowed with an innate capacity to know right and wrong, and having been endowed with free will, are responsible for their actions. Furthermore, as per their moral epistemology, good and evil are rational categories that can be known by intuitive reason, independent of revelation. God created the human intellect in such a way that, if unhindered by social traditions and conventions, it is capable of perceiving good and evil objectively. In this sense, the moral law is the expression of God's will in creation. Moral epistemology is in reality a corollary of the fundamental Mu'tazilite doctrine, that God's justice cannot be fulfilled without providing access to objective knowledge of good and eviln regardless whether the revelation decrees it so or not.Without such objective ethical knowledge, and with the possibility of lack of any contact with a prophet or sacred scriptures, no human being can be held accountable for his or her deeds.[20] In this way, the Mu'tazilites emphasized complete human responsibility in responding to the call of universal moral guidance through natural reason, which was further elaborated by guidance through revelation.

The Ash'arites rejected both the idea of natural reason as an autonomous source of religious-moral guidance as well as the idea of moral law as the expression of the divine will. They maintained that an action is good not because human intuitive reason says so, but because God so wills. Good and evil are as God commanded them in the scripture, and it is presumptuous to judge God's action restricted by God's justice, on the basis of categories that God has actually provided in scripture for directing human life. There is no way, within the bounds of human logic, to explain the relationship of God's power to human actions. God's absolute will give meaning and moral determination to human action, regardless of whether human reason judges it as good or otherwise. Human action is the result of God's pure will, without any foundation in the essential nature of things.

Both these theological standpoints were based on the interpretation of Qur'anic passages, which is undoubtedly complex as we saw above. On the one hand, the Qur'an contains passages that would support the Mu'tazilite position, which emphasized humanity's complete responsibility in responding to the call of both natural guidance and guidance through revelation. On the other hand, it has passages that support the Ash'arite viewpoint, which upholds the omnipotence of God and hence denies humans any role in responding to divine guidance. Nevertheless, it allows for both human volition and divine will in the matter of accepting or rejecting faith that entailed the responsibility for procuring justice on earth.[21]

Islamic Law: The Expression of Divine Will

The responsibility of procuring justice puts an enormous burden on the traditionalist theology, because its rejection of the natural endowment of innate moral capacity in humanity has led to a detrimental neglect of the ethical presuppositions of the normative juridical tradition. For such theology, an action is not good because it correlates with the essential nature of human beings. It is so because God so wills. What if God wills and decrees the precise opposite of that good? Does it still have the same binding force as that which is now valid because God's absolute will so determines? Muslim traditionalist theologians were inclined to afford validity only to those acts that had the sanction of the divine will in the form of revelation. They ruled out any moral restriction—in fact any restriction at all—on God's sovereignty and absolute discretionary authority to manage human affairs. As a consequence, both the universal moral significance of Qur'anic idiom and its implications for the development of Islamic natural law theory were discarded.

The primacy of the will over the intellect led to the denial that good and evil can have any other foundation but the will of God, which expressed itself in providing the blueprint for human activity in the Sharī'a. The scales of justice that were to be implemented in Islamic public order were not available to human reason, except through the mediation of supernatural revelation. In other words, the Sharī'a is the embodiment of God's will for humanity without any foundation in created reality, without foundation in the essential nature of things—eternal and hence immutable. God's pure will was the pivot of Sunni theology and ethics in a way that decisively impacted the development of the normative juridical tradition.

The normative juridical tradition seeks to address, accommodate, and reconcile the demands of justice and the public good. In dealing with immediate questions about the rights of minorities and religious communities living in the Muslim world, Muslim jurists draw on legal doctrines and rules in addition to analogical reasoning based on paradigm cases in the classical tradition. Their practical judgments reflect the insights of jurists who can connect the contemporary situation to an appropriate set of linguistic and rational principles, principles that can provide a basis for a valid conclusion in a given case. A cursory treatment of the substance covered in these practical decisions shows that they deal with an elaborate system of duties. The conceptions of justice or public good in these practical judgments, even when they appear to have universal application, created institutions and practices that establish duties, not rights. The Qur'anic notion of human dignity (*karāmat al-insān*) was evoked quite often without any emphasis on equal and inalienable rights held by all human beings because of the way God had honored all of humanity. The tradition limited full legal rights only to free adult Muslims. It failed to develop the idea of the moral worth of all human beings through divinely conferred intuitive reason and dignity—notions that would have led it to an affirmation of the equality of human beings as human. Consequently, universal morality founded upon the essential nature of human beings and their human moral worth remained unexplored among jurists until recently. As noted in the beginning of this chapter, the challenge to rethink Muslim theological ethics to elaborate legal principles in light of new concepts like equal citizenship and democratic governance remains unanswered until today.

The epistemic problem that confronts Muslim jurists now is the reestablishment of the historically severed connection between theological ethics based on the moral worth of each human person and prevalent Islamic jurisprudence. How can a juridical ruling permit a Muslim man to divorce his lifelong wife because she happens to be old, without considering the morality of such a legally legitimate decision? Even if the ruling is legally correct, how can it be morally justified? Islamic jurisprudence (*fiqh*) has yet to reassert the notion of the essentially moral nature of human beings and confirm that moral law as the expression of the divine will. Unless the doctrinal and ethical presuppositions of the early juridical tradition are investigated and expounded afresh, this problem will continue to produce intellectually impoverished and ethically insensitive Islamic scholarship.

The enunciation of underlying ethical principles and rules to govern practical ethical decisions is crucial for making any religious perspective intellectually respectable in the contemporary debate about a morally defensible cross-cultural account of human rights. All communities share certain moral principles (compassion, honesty, justice, and so on); all require rules like fairness and just restitution as essential elements for regulating responsible interpersonal relations; yet major global controversies persist on issues such as cultural relativism that hampers the implementation of universal human rights cross-culturally. What kind of ethical resources do different traditions possess that might lead to a common ethical discourse about, and perhaps even a resolution of, global controversies regarding the implementation of the international human rights regime?[22]

Traditional Muslim scholarship often avoids critical assessment of the normative resources that might actually contribute to a resolution of contemporary ethical-legal issues. The treatment of apostates is exemplary here. One of the most controversial articles of the UN declaration that confronts Sharīʿa scholars is the punishment of an apostate. The Qur'an deals not only with individual religious freedom but also with the creation of a just social order. Under certain conditions, the Qur'an gives the state, as the representative of society, the power to control "discord on earth," a general state of lawlessness created by taking up arms against the established Islamic order.[23] The eradication of corruption on earth, taken in light of the Qur'anic principle of instituting good and preventing evil, is a basic moral duty of the state toward the community. In the Islamic polity, where religion is not divorced from the public agenda, to permit adherents of competing doctrines free to pursue their beliefs engenders an inherent tension between religious communities that has to be resolved through state regulation.

The "millet system" in the Muslim world provided the premodern paradigm of a religiously pluralistic society by granting each religious community an official status and a substantial measure of self-government. The system based on the millet, which means a "religiously defined people,"[24] was a "group rights model"[25] that was defined in terms of a communitarian identity and hence did not recognize any principle of individual autonomy in matters of religion. And this communitarian identity was not restricted to identifying non-Muslim *dhimmis*;[26] the millet's self-governing status allowed it to base its sovereignty on the orthodox creed officially instituted by the millet leadership. Under the Ottoman administration this group status entailed some degree of state control over religious identification, overseen by the administrative officer responsible to the state for the religious community. In addition, the system permitted the enforcement of religious orthodoxy under state patronage, leaving no scope for individual dissent, political or religious. Every episode of the individual exercise of freedom of conscience was seen as a deviation from the accepted orthodoxy maintained and enforced by the socioreligious order.

The uncritical approach to the normative sources has deep roots in the theology of revelation in Islam. There are two major trends concerning the meaning and relevance of revelation for Muslims. According to one, the Islamic revelation in its present form was "created" in time and space and, as such, reflects historical circumstances of that original divine command. According to the other, the revelation was "uncreated" and hence its current form is not conditioned by place and time. Most traditionalist scholars reject any hints that the revelation's interpretation is a cultural or historical variable. Quantitative and qualitative changes in the modern Muslim world have raised questions about the relevance of traditional readings of the revelation to contemporary ethical and social exigencies.

Besides the problem with the conservative spirit that dominated the stultifying approach to the normative sources, the scriptural sources themselves could not easily cover every situation that might arise, especially when Muslim political rule extended beyond the Arabian Peninsula and was obliged to grapple with the governance of urban life, commerce, and government in advanced countries. But how exactly was the rational endeavor to be directed to discover the philosophy and purpose behind certain paradigm rulings provided in the religious sources, in order to utilize them to formulate fresh responses to the ever-expanding political horizons and changing national and international relations of the global Muslim community?

There was a fear of admitting reason as a substantive and even independent source for deriving the details of ethical-juridical decisions. This fear was based on the presumption that if independent human reason could judge what is right and wrong, it could render God's revelation merely supplementary for moral cognition. However, it was acknowledged that although reason can aid revelation in cultivating the moral life, it is not adequate for discovering the justification and meaning of the commandments. In fact, as these theologian-jurists asserted, the divine commandments to which one must adhere are not objectively accessible to human beings through reason.

Concluding Remarks about Human Dignity and Justice

The title of this chapter indicates conceptual and historical problems because discussions about natural law, inherent human dignity, or human moral agency are part of modern political and human rights discourse. This discourse has deep secular roots that can be traced back to Enlightenment ways of thinking about universal morality; in contrast, Islamic discourse expresses religious commitments based on revelation-based reasons that are particularistic and therefore incongruent with the universal purport of the concepts under consideration.[27] Since secular public reason denies the effectiveness of arguments based on religious reason in matters with political implications (lest it destabilize public order through its intolerant exclusivist doctrines), the task of this chapter was to provide Islamic perspectives that could speak in a universal idiom to all human beings. This process had to unavoidably rely on two hermeneutical moves applied to normative Islamic sources like the Qur'an and the Tradition to bring the relevant materials in line with modern human rights discourse, which claims to provide a language of universal morality that appeals to all communities across state boundaries. Hence, Islamic discourse on human dignity and related concepts had to at least be inclusive enough to give voice to peoples across religious and cultural boundaries. The first hermeneutical move of necessity involved deconstructing the contextual aspects of the classical juridical heritage of Muslims, by looking at the way religion and politics in Islam interacted to distort the original universal intent of the relevant texts for exclusivist political reasons. The second move involved providing a fresh interpretation that is consonant with the inclusive intent of the religious discourse and relevant to modern discourse on human dignity and justice. However, both these epistemic moves can be criticized for lack of indisputable historical information in determining when such hermeneutical distortions in the original texts were introduced. Moreover, it is not epistemically feasible to claim with certainty that fresh interpretations of classical usage, made to resonate with the universal purport of modern human rights language, now bears the approval of the original denotation of Islamic revelation. Here Islamic discourse is in serious competition for legitimacy with secular liberal political discourse when public reason free from religious premises has convincingly argued for dignity, fair treatment, and justice for all humans as humans.

To be sure, the search for Islamic perspectives on human dignity and justice faces both conceptual and historical challenges. One conceptual challenge, connected with human dignity, arises with the claims by liberal secularists that it was not until secular public reason began to look at individual rights within the context of modern religiously and politically pluralistic societies that a universal source of human rights was identified in inherent attributes based on a belief in the innate dignity of human persons. Similar conceptual reservations are noticeable in the ways in which modern liberal political thinkers have used the term *justice* to argue for a "free-standing political conception" that can hopefully generate the necessary overlapping consensus among reasonable persons in a pluralistic world for social cooperation. Historical problems in dealing with the contextual aspects of Islamic normative texts go beyond the usual historical inquiry that seeks to determine the origins of these concepts—whether they go back to classical sources, which include religious reasons, or whether they simply go back to the European domination of Muslim peoples when Enlightenment thought, with its distinctive claim for locating universal morality outside religion, was in vogue. The idea of human rights as something universal is a distinctive creation of Western culture, which emerged at a specific, identifiable moment in European history. The inherence view of humanity was its most convincing tool to argue that the idea was common to all societies. Whatever the account of the origin and early development of the idea among Muslims, my objective in this chapter was to underscore the difficulty of reading modern discourse into the classical sources, especially when this modern discourse dismisses religious reasoning as unreasonable or irrational.

The first article of the Universal Declaration of Human Rights, for example, reads: "All human beings are born free and equal in dignity and rights. They are endowed with reason and conscience and should act towards one another in a spirit of brotherhood." The article speaks about human being born free with dignity and possessing equal rights that an individual enjoys based on the inherent attributes of his or her person. The inherence view of human rights holds that human rights inhere in people as such, not because of any external causes. The Vienna Declaration and Programme of Action, adopted by consensus of 172 states on June 25, 1993, at the UN-sponsored World Conference on Human Rights, reaffirms the inherence view in insisting that "all human rights derive from the dignity and worth inherent in the human person." But what is the source of such a view? Is it human reason? Then why did it take so long for rationalist nations to do away with racial discrimination? Why does the colonial period appear to be one of the most degrading periods for colonized peoples? The question of these blatant violations of human dignity and equality of all human beings required me to look into a more convincing foundation for human rights than simply the reasonableness of rationally derived notions of human dignity and moral agency. Although fully aware that a number of prominent secularists like Richard Rorty, Michael Ignatieff, and others have for good reasons dismissed any metaphysical reference to a natural constitution of humanity or an inherent capacity of human beings to discover principles of law as a major source for a universal appeal to human rights norms, the only intellectually honest route left for me whereby I might convince traditionalist Muslim opponents of modern human rights discourse was to delve into the depths of classical Islamic heritage to relate Islamic revelation and its political theology to natural law. Are human beings rational beings, capable of guiding themselves and of deriving from their reason a standard to judge their environment? Are the testimony of reason and of revelation correlative? Are faith and reason incompatible? Is a human being free and equal to all other humans?

The Ash'arite theological doctrine that the will of God is the ultimate source of morality played a prominent role in defining human worth in the juridical tradition—the tradition that is under severe criticism for perpetuating discriminatory attitudes toward women and non-Muslim minorities. But there was also the Mu'tazilite doctrine that rejected the extreme Ash'arite view of the absolute sovereignty of God and furthered the human responsibility to meet the dangerous challenge of the absolutist rule of the caliphs and the sultans. Although they did not speak about natural law, their theology was devised to challenge the view that the Islamic Sharī'a was not merely an expression of the divine will. It was also an expression of the divine morality that was conferred on humanity through the very creation of human nature (*fiṭra*). This Mu'tazilite doctrine is truly universal, and, being firmly rooted in the Qur'an itself, it is eternal and immutable. If traditionalist Muslim scholars can be convinced of the authenticity of natural law in Islamic theological ethics, then human rights discourse in the Muslim world can be based on this foundational doctrine, which treats human equality as its first and essential tenet. More important, if it can be shown that the Qur'an neither contradicts the law of nature nor rejects the evidence of reason as unreliable and hence incompatible with the goals of revelation, then one can admit a thesis that the law of nature is embodied in the Qur'an. Natural law goes back to God in the sense that its precepts derive their authority from the fact that they are confirmed and implemented by the revelation as the "eternal, immutable tradition of God [*sunnat allāh*]." Unlike other laws that respond to the human contingencies that change over time, natural law, with its connection to inherent human capacity, has an inbuilt permanence, which renders it absolutely binding and which overrules all other laws.

I believe that I have demonstrated with much evidence that in Muslim theology, especially the theology that was concerned with showing that God's justice was far more central to the moral world of the Qur'an than God's absolute will, to speak about natural law as the source for human rights norms is not only compatible with the overall religious outlook of the revelation, it is the key to exerting new pressure on Muslim jurists to rethink some juridical decisions, both in historical Islam and in contemporary rulings, on the basis of ethical sensibilities that undergird juridical methodology in Islamic jurisprudence. Islamic ethics rather than Islamic jurisprudence must assume a central role in defining human rights that accrue to all humans as human. It is only then that Muslim thinkers can begin to conceptualize a modern citizenship and the equality of all humans in a nation-state today. Such a universal conceptualization is inconceivable without adopting the ethical epistemology embedded in the Qur'an, namely, that what is intrinsically good or intrinsically bad does not depend upon the revealed will of God; it derives from the justice of God, who never abandoned humanity without providing basic moral awareness. It is the acknowledgment of minimal moral knowledge that lays the groundwork for the next chapter on women's human rights, which must consider the extent of the naturally endowed human capacity given to all human beings—both male and female—in assuming responsibility for one's action toward others as equals in creation.

4

The Dignity and Capacities of Women as Equal Bearers of Human Rights

My search for an Islamic theory of natural law in the previous chapter had two objectives. My first, and primary, objective was to demonstrate that there were doctrinal resources within the inherited Islamic tradition that could naturally lend the necessary cultural legitimacy to the UN Declaration by supporting universal morality based on the principle of inherency and the moral agency of all human beings. My major concern here was to search for resources that overcame the relativity of historical Islam and its application in the context of the nation-state today. My second objective was to engage Muslim scholars to acknowledge the larger human community as the bearer of equal rights through God's special endowment for all human beings without any distinction. The Qur'anic idea that all human beings are unconditionally equal in dignity through God's act of creation, in my opinion, is sufficient to convince any Muslim that all human beings, regardless of their race, sex, and creed, are entitled to certain rights as part of their inviolable personhood. This self-evident conclusion of my second objective would have served as an important moral principle to respond to the relativist challenge to the idea of universal human rights when it came to the human rights of women and minorities. But, as I shall discuss in this chapter, even the most persuasive arguments against the moral relativism that afflicts human rights discourse at the international level, especially in the Muslim world, have failed to convince the traditionalist Muslim leadership to acknowledge the full citizenship of a woman as a bearer of rights equal to those of a man.

In general, one of the major challenges facing those who are concerned with human rights in today's world is articulating a position that is commensurate with the Universal Declaration of Human Rights—a position of universal and absolute human rights and, at the same time, of respect and positive valuation of local cultural traditions and religious sensitivities. A number of human rights scholars with religious sympathies have argued with much evidence that the universal and absolute nature of human rights is an almost religious idea.[1] The idea that fundamental human rights stem from "the inherent dignity of all members of the human family" is, at least for the scholars of Abrahamic traditions, based on the religious conviction that every human being as God's creature is inviolable (*dhī ḥurma*). Leading Christian scholars have underscored the religious basis or foundation of human rights and have demonstrated that what renders human rights inviolable and sacrosanct, is their religious origin, and removes them from the contingencies of political calculation and decisions based on expediency or conflicts between pluralism about the human good.[2] According to these theologians, what is absolutely universal must be incontrovertibly linked to the One whose existence does not depend on the play of forces, passions, or calculation that is peculiar to the human sphere of action in this world.

However, making absolute and universal religious claims often involves intolerance toward those others who are not willing to recognize that tradition's religiously premised absolute claims. Such a stance of intolerance is unacceptable in today's culturally and religiously pluralistic world. The universal applicability of human rights has to go beyond ethnic, national, and cultural boundaries and preferences, and their inalienability has to be independent of any contextual factors or other contingencies. The problems arising from the differing definitions of what is congenial to the flourishing of every human being across different cultures and religious traditions seriously affects women's rights in the context of marriage, divorce, education, and legal status. A purported standard of universal human rights and the very diversity of human communities make it much more difficult to ascertain the validity of contradictory injunctions that affect women's rights across different cultures.

This is a contradiction that confronts women's human rights advocates. With the spread of globalization and the increasing interconnectedness among different peoples of the world, issues connected with the human rights of more than half of the world's population—women—grows from day to day. It is no longer a problem encountered only by Muslim women. Global communication and commerce implicate a majority of nation-states in protecting the basic rights of their women citizens. Whereas respect and positive valuation of diverse religious identities, commitments, and desiderata are important issues of women's human rights, all too often Western ideas of gender equality and the universality of human rights of individuals have run aground on the particularity of local customs and prohibitions. Certain practices that appear to many Westerners as discriminatory and oppressive are viewed in a very different light by their practitioners, male and female alike. Thus, for instance, the case of modest Islamic dress, which in many Muslim countries is sometimes willingly embraced by women as a protest against the homogenization of culture through global consumerism and the lifestyle represented by Western ideas and social norms, is mostly viewed negatively by Western commentators on Muslim attitudes toward women. Issues revolving around the status of women are, however, only the most visible of an array of problems connected with the universal application of human rights.

Women and "Islamic Authenticity"

Although historically the language of Islamic revelation, as demonstrated in the previous chapter, has substantively supported the universality of human existence, affording it a meaningful way of relating peoples of different religions and cultures in a single human community, paradoxically, today it is the traditional Muslim appropriation of Islam that is used to disseminate contemporary claims for a more relativistic and culturally sensitive approach to the human rights of women and minorities. It is not an exaggeration to say that it is the particularity of a specific Islamic language, culture, and moral discourse connected with women's position in Muslim societies that has deprived the UN Declaration of cultural legitimacy in the Muslim world. Women's human rights can be identified as the main area of contention between the Muslim world and the West, and one major source of criticism of the Declaration as Eurocentric or culturally imperialistic and, hence, relativistic. Of all the issues connected with different international documents—the Universal Declaration of Human Rights (1948), the International Covenant on Civil and Political Rights (1976), and the International Covenant on Economic, Social and Cultural Rights (1976)—it is issues connected with women's human rights in all social and political arenas that are faced with the cultural and moral relativist challenge.[3]

The implications of the paradox between universal morality and absoluteness of human rights and the implementation of such rights in the context of the particular Muslim culture are for the most part evident in the evaluation of woman's humanity. In fact, one of the major impediments to the universal recognition of a woman as a human person similar to a man in the Muslim world has been the politics of Islamic "authenticity" in the postcolonial age. The failure of imported modern ideologies to implement political and social justice in Muslim societies across the Muslim world has led to zealous support for militant Islamic theology that forcefully prescribes a "return to the Qur'an and Sunna" as a form of rejection of cultural imperialism imposed by the West. Assertions of cultural authenticity and integrity in the face of Western domination and modernization have challenged the universal applicability of Western definitions of rights. Moreover, these assertions, as discussed by Deniz Kandiyoti, have ended up repressing women's rights in the name of Islamic forms of regulation that impose further restrictions on women's legitimate rights as individual citizens.[4] Martha Nussbaum has painstakingly detailed the role local traditions and religious interpretations advanced by male representatives have played in stifling the human rights of women in different cultural contexts with differing definitions of the core coordinates of social life determined by religious beliefs. Authenticity assertions, instead of searching for authentic and authoritative primary materials to advance woman's full dignity and personhood, have ironically led to further discriminations and denial of women's equal rights.[5] The problem of violations of women's dignity and personhood is compounded when such gender discrimination becomes theologically justified. The religiously justificatory language, using threats of divine wrath and punishment, that is employed by religious representatives to coerce women has led to the silencing of women's legitimate complaints against violations of their personal integrity.

The purpose of this chapter is not to marshal all the evidence others have ably produced to make the point that women's human rights in the Muslim world are still being suppressed under claims of cultural distinctiveness and Muslim identity. Since the first United Nations conference on women in Mexico City in 1975, there has been a plethora of scholarship documenting gender gaps in all fields of human interaction, including, most importantly, in education, financial independence, public participation, and women's overall social standing.[6] These studies have been authored by non-Muslim as well as Muslim scholars, men and women, alerting the international community about the situation with women's rights across Muslim societies. In fact, a number of pioneer studies have been undertaken by Muslim women scholars, analyzing the critical situation under which women in general, and Muslim women in particular, continue to suffer discrimination under the influence of major world religions that deny the equal rights of persons and justify violations of women's dignity and their person.[7] These studies on the dismal record of human rights of women have prompted several conscientious Muslim leaders to critically evaluate the juridical tradition for perpetrating prejudicial attitudes against women.[8] It is not an exaggeration to observe that a prejudicial attitude against women has been institutionalized in the patriarchal culture, which shows little respect for women as human persons.

However, Muslim scholarship on this critical chapter in modern endeavors to protect the human dignity of a woman and her inalienable rights has focused exclusively on problematic areas in Islamic juridical tradition, the Sharīʻa, which determines the validity of civil rights guaranteed in the national constitutions of the nations in question and which nullifies these countries' commitment to the UN Declaration. The dominant religious discourse, as demonstrated by this scholarship, is opposed to the liberal language of the Declaration with its emphasis on the equal worth of all individuals who therefore enjoy basic liberties guaranteed in another international document, namely, the Convention on the Elimination of All Forms of Discrimination against Women—a multilateral treaty ratified by majority of the countries.[9]

However, the critical area of Islamic heritage that holds essential keys to reassert the absolute human rights of women based on their inherent dignity and moral worth similar to men is located in the ethical-theological doctrines. Islamic juridical rulings reflect the pragmatism of Islamic political discourse, in which ethical claims that are universal in nature are downplayed in favor of all forms of male dominance in the patriarchal-tribal culture. It is for this reason that thus far there has been little progress in challenging the dominant religious discourse based on these rulings in which women and minorities suffered legal disabilities as "incompetent minors" who always needed to be represented by male near kin. The guardianship (*wilāya*) of the minor in religious law included women, however mature and competent they might be. Most Muslim and non-Muslim scholarship has concentrated on such rulings to speak about the incompatibility between the UN Declaration and the Sharīʻa, without probing into the theological-ethical and philosophical underpinnings of Islamic juridical discourse.

The major analytical tool that can actually lead to the recognition of universal morality from scriptural resources in Islam and its commanding influence over the deconstructing of discriminatory religious discourse is embedded in the Qur'anic doctrine of God's justice and the human capacity to advance in perfecting the living environment with justice and equity. In my opinion, Islamic public theology offers the key doctrinal resources to challenge the traditionalist Muslim leadership that has arrogated to itself some kind of divine authority to enact barriers to the full recognition of a woman's personhood and her fundamental human rights in Muslim societies. In light of this literature, it is not surprising to find the younger generation of Muslim seminarians questioning the absolute validity of the classical formulations about women's personhood and dignity in Islamic tradition.[10]

Women's Rights in Revealed Texts

In some of the recent articles and books authored by traditional Muslim scholars, there has been much debate about whether the paradigmatic status afforded to classical juridical formulations concerning gender differences and the lower status of women in these religiously informed legal enactments can be hermeneutically maneuvered to conform with international conventions on the equality of rights of all citizens as guaranteed in the national constitutions of the modern states. Whereas some scholars have ruled out such a hermeneutical move in the revealed texts for fear of being labeled heretics and condemned to all sorts of social and political disabilities, others have courageously pointed out that not only are the classical formulations discriminatory against women and in need of reform, there are epistemological obstructions in these formulations to bringing woman's status as a full person into accord with the articles of various international conventions.

Muslim traditionalist scholarship tends to treat any academic endeavor that questions its appropriation and interpretation of the revealed texts, whether from the Qur'an or the Tradition, in their historical contexts as an affront to the sanctity and absolute nature of Islamic revelation. The prevalent theological doctrine in this scholarship is that since revelation is from God, it is both immutable and perfect in its specific rulings even when the social-political context of its revelation is culturally specific. This doctrine is the main reason why women's human rights have continued to suffer despite the fact that in the last century Muslim reformers in different religious institutions of Islamic higher learning endeavored to argue for corrective measures to improve upon the classical rulings. In other words, the veracity and absoluteness of the past rulings have been regarded as independent of any context and material condition for their universal applicability in the faith community. Such claims about universal and absolute religious truth often involve intolerance of those others not willing to recognize universal truth claims—a stance that is unacceptable with today's growing awareness about women's human rights and the way the inherited tradition has continued to stifle fundamental reform in this regard.

Like other religious traditions, Islamic tradition emphasizes gender differences as the major source for enacting different laws affecting men and women. In the context of human rights discourse, such a view of gender differences is regarded as the major source of violations of women's human rights, because the laws give preferential treatment to men, taking biological differences as essentially favoring men over women. If racial identity cannot become a source of discrimination, on what basis can gender differences become an essential source of distinction and discrimination against women? The problem reverts to the theology of revealed texts that provide religious premises for discriminatory treatment of Muslim women. Muslim jurists are fond of referring to these texts as "absolutely binding" injunctions (*musallamāt dīnīya*) that cannot be questioned by any believer. If that is the case, then one can, without any hesitation, conclude that there can be no compatibility between the articles of the UN Declaration and other international documents that speak to the inalienable rights of women and traditional Islamic teachings that insist on gender distinctions and use them to discriminate against women. This is what I have identified as "the crisis of epistemology" in Islamic tradition, which, as I argue in chapter 2, cannot be resolved by simply reforming the classical juridical rulings and bringing them in line with the international human rights conventions on the civil rights of all citizens of a nation-state, and not simply its male members. Is the case, then, foreclosed before one can renegotiate the rightful place of women in the religious scheme of individuality and identity?

Women's human rights must be examined in the light of problems arising from the differing definitions of core coordinates of social life and the ways that one can mediate between the rights of individuals and the rights of groups. What are the rights and obligations of the family in relation to the individual, and of the individual to the family? Indeed, women's human rights in the context of the family are contested and differentially defined across Muslim societies. Taking the example of "honor killings" in some parts of the Muslim world, while it is not difficult to condemn the act as a violation of fundamental human rights, issues of divorce, education, and the legal status of the extended family are much more complex when scrutinized in light of international human rights norms. Similarly, the wearing of the head covering, which is seen in the West as discriminatory and oppressive, is sometimes willingly done by Muslim women and is interpreted very differently by them.[11] From a human rights perspective, the wearing of the head covering can be seen as part of an individual's expression of cultural and religious identity, which is actually protected by a number of articles that speak about freedom of religion and expression. A large number of Muslim women regard the act of covering their head as part of their individual and group identity.[12] Hence, I raise the question of women's human rights not as an endeavor to endorse the homogenization of culture and worldview represented by Western ideas and norms. The diversity of human communities cannot be ignored. At the same time, irreconcilable contradictions and tensions in a purported standard of universal human rights and local traditions and cultures cannot be used against upholding women's civil rights or their human personhood.

Islamic discourse is uniquely positioned to critique some of the denigrating tendencies in Western discourse about religion in general and Islam in particular. After all, historically, at least in the Arab context, it was the Qur'an that introduced the language of universality connected with human creation and it was the revelation that for the first time articulated arguments in support of human dignity and moral worth when the tribal culture of Arabia could not fathom core coordinates of social life beyond kinship and tribal genealogy. It is, therefore, contrary to the universal spirit of Islamic revelation when in the context of women's human rights some traditionalist Muslim scholars marshal arguments against the universality of human rights norms and demand a more relativistic and locally sensitive approach to some key articles of the UN Declaration. Nonetheless, the particularity of a specific language, culture, and moral idiom connected with the idea of rights is well established even among those traditionalists who speak about universal religious idiom and who endeavor to reconcile contradictory injunctions to universal and particular application. Accordingly, while there is recognition of moral absoluteness at one level of the application of religious norms, there is also an acknowledgment of relativity at another level that must take particular circumstances into consideration when dealing with relational aspects of religious practice. Women's situation in the core coordinates of social life gives rise to that kind of consideration in Islamic religious thought.

Rereading the Universal Applicability of Women's Rights

The major objective of this chapter is to make possible a different reading of women's rights in Muslim religious sources. As I have stated earlier in this book, the rights-based discourse is modern, and although the moral language of rights shares something in common with the Qur'anic notion of equality in creation, the modern secular and democratic notions of rights is not always compatible with the Islamic religious heritage. I hasten to add here that while the endowment of a natural constitution is deeply rooted in modern natural law tradition, Islamic political theology had worked out its own solutions as regards the overcoming of religious identities and commitments by insisting upon the equality of creation of all human beings by the One God, the Sustainer of the Universe.

In my search for an Islamic theory of natural law in Muslim political theology, I spoke about the crisis of epistemology in the juridical sciences, which need to shake off outdated views about human beings in general, and about nonbelievers and women in particular. There is no other area in interhuman relationships than the treatment of women that presents Muslim jurists with the challenge of rethinking past rulings in the Sharī'a. Whether it is in the area of personal status or laws of inheritance, issues related to women's human rights demand not simply revision but also abandonment of some past juridical decisions. The crisis of epistemology has shaken the confidence of male-dominated Muslim seminaries in which judgments regarding women's concerns and legitimate claims were formulated without a single female legal scholar participating in deliberations that affected women's position in the private and public sectors. Women activists in the Islamic world have correctly pointed out that without women's participation in the constitutional debates, for instance, in Iraq and Afghanistan in recent years, it is impossible to see how certain universal norms of human rights based on recognizing the human dignity and capabilities of women can be implemented without constitutional guarantees promoting a healthy quality of life for women in all Muslim states.

While intelligible reenactment of the subjective experience of woman as the social and religious other through the formation of figuratively represented relations in legal deliberations is not entirely impossible, its cognitive content is not free of suspicion. For instance, in the context of a legal ruling pertaining to a woman's situation in a society, the traditional juridical language constitutes the meaning of utterances about the female other mediated through male representations of interpersonal relations in Islamic jurisprudence. The specific juridical statement in such circumstances is promulgated and interpreted by a male jurist to apply to all women in a society without taking full account of the concerns and conditions peculiar to female life in various familial and social situations. Hence, what we have in the juridical declaration is a partial figurative impression rather than the actual representation of women's situational and objective condition.

To overcome this cognitive impediment, one needs to undertake an analysis of the symbolic network of Islamic juridical discourse. In other words, contextualization of rulings about sexual segregation, for instance, that still stand sanctioned among religious-minded Muslims today cannot be endowed with validity by merely referring to the textual and cultural validation of the practice in Muslim societies. One needs to explore and estimate the intertextual network of symbols expressed by means of the narratives developed through interlocutory devices in which women are represented as actors, as questioners, even occasionally as disputants. To be sure, these narratives extend beyond judicial decisions about male-female segregation. They in fact contribute to the formation of a symbolic configuration of Islamic cultural values as a whole.

Further elaboration on this particular issue of segregation is appropriate. In general, rulings about female segregation are based on the concept of *'awra*, meaning "indecent to expose."[13] On the basis of this concept, jurists regard a woman's body, including her face, as *'awra*. However, there are controversial texts ascribed to the Prophet and some of his companions that regard even her voice as *'awra* and hence, "proper for veiling or covering" at all times.[14] Through such an extension of the *'awra* to include the voice, Islamic law seems to advocate a position in which a woman is legally silenced, morally separated, and religiously veiled.

Clearly, such a reading of the term *'awra* does violent injustice to some of the most fundamental articles of the UN Declaration that guarantee women's human rights. Given that this concept still forms the basis of a number of judicial decisions that restrict a Muslim woman's access to normal channels of communication to voice her concerns, whether in spousal or other familial-social relations, it is necessary to go beyond the text and the context of these rulings to fathom the level of prejudice against women that forms an entire genre in Islamic juridical texts. Such contextual analysis of linguistic as well as cultural usages could direct us to pose a fundamental question to Muslim juridical studies: Can the male-dominated juridical epistemology provide a fair assessment of women's social and familial situation simply by means of the interpretive process connected with the female other? How can male jurists undertake to map the subjective experience of the silent other of a Muslim society without fully accounting for the personhood of a woman?

I am not convinced that the solution to this epistemological crisis lies simply in making sure that women become full participants in the juridical deliberations that affect their rights, if those deliberative processes remain unreformed. The establishment of Muslim women's seminaries in Iran, whose curriculum in Islamic juridical studies is still controlled by male jurists, has achieved negligible progress in making women's representation in matters affecting their rights fair and effective. Until now, institutional development that can include women's voices in juridical and ethical deliberations has been, at most, formal without any substantive result in protecting women from abuse. Thus, advocating some form of feminist jurisprudence to protect Muslim women's human rights, in my opinion, is insufficient. Without a thorough overhaul of the traditional seminary culture, which is dominated by the patriarchal and even Arab tribal values that are part of the religious textual heritage of Muslims, it is impossible to create the necessary awareness among the majority of Muslim women about their basic dignity as human persons. As long as the male-dominated seminary curriculum ignores the sociological and psychological evaluation of a woman's personhood in the context of a family or society, the violation of women's human rights in Muslim societies will continue unabated.

However, it is important to state that a number of religious leaders have endeavored to transmit female existence and experience, however imperfect, by bringing forth that segment of their ideological utterances that consider both genders to be part of humanity. Without such an acknowledgment of the essential humanity of both men and women, it would have been impossible for them to transmit those values in the culture that saw woman and man in relational terms as parents, sister and brother, daughter and father, mother and son, and husband and wife. Islamic legal discourse has not always conceived of male–female relations in terms of a gender power struggle, even when it has engaged in formulating a hierarchical system with man as the head of the household and with the ultimate responsibility of providing for everyone in the family.

There are a number of apologetic studies written by Muslim jurists about how Islam changed the pre-Islamic Arabian attitudes toward women and granted them both personal dignity and equal legal status in a culture that treated its women as tribal property. The Qur'an bears testimony to the horrendous immoral act of infanticide that a baby girl suffered upon birth. Furthermore, it sketches the overall negative attitude that patriarchal tribal culture of seventh-century Arabia exhibited in dealing with its women. Women suffered and continue to suffer under a system that claims normative authenticity in matters of inheritance or rights within a marriage. Any cursory acquaintance with pre-Islamic Arab culture would support the claim that relatively speaking, Islam ushered in a period of great strides in protecting women from abuse by the system that denied them their human dignity. As a matter of fact, the Qur'an provided for the first time a balance between a woman's rights and her duty in the familial context, by explicitly declaring "their claims commensurate with their obligations [as determined] by [universally accepted] goodness (*al-ma'rūf*)" (Q. 2:228). *Al-ma'rūf*, meaning "the known," which I have rendered as "universally accepted goodness" underscores a moral prescription that no human being with sound reason can fail to recognize. "Goodness" is understood as the Arabs understood it conventionally, before the Qur'an was revealed to supplement the common ethical sense of *al-ma'rūf*. In keeping with Arabic idiomatic usage, I have translated the preposition *la*, meaning "for," as claims, and the preposition *'alā*, meaning "upon," as duties. In Arabic usage, the placement of the two prepositions *la* and *'alā* in a single declarative statement indicates the correlation between entitlement and obligation. Since just interhuman relations were at the heart of Qur'anic social ethics, it is inconceivable that the underlining mutuality that regulated interpersonal justice could be proposed without a logical correlation between entitlement and reciprocal obligation. And yet, the Qur'an spoke about these claims in relational situations where social and familial roles were traditionally defined to create a healthy society. The Qur'an did not mark a total departure from tribal culture, whose extremely chauvinistic moral code was at the center of male-dominated tribal dealings. Clearly the Prophet wanted to tone down the pre-Islamic fanaticism, aptly branded as *ḥamiyat al-jāhilīya* (viciousness of paganism, Q. 48:26) by the Qur'an, without totally denying its core moral appeal. He achieved that by appropriating the familiar concept of *al-ma'rūf*, which conveyed a continuity of the well-known standards of civility anchored in the objective state of moral guidance in the matter of what constituted goodness and fairness in interhuman relations.

When introducing reforms in Arabian society, the Prophet was aware of the general tribal trends that determined the practical approach to the power structures prevalent in tribal culture. The pre-Islamic code, known to the social historians of Islam as *murū'a*, meaning "manliness" (a term derived from *mar'*, i.e., man), regulated intertribal relations based on the prowess of male members of the tribe. In the twenty-three years of his mission, as per the Qur'an, the Prophet created a momentum for an Islamic polity founded upon the moral mandate of "instituting the good and preventing the evil," but he could not completely supplant the pre-Islamic tribal system with a new Islamic order. In spite of the Prophet's emphasis on justice and egalitarianism, social distinctions and other forms of discrimination practiced in Arabia continued to influence human relations.

Nonetheless, as the important contemporary source for the study of social reform in seventh-century Arabia, the Qur'an reveals some sort of gradual introduction of reform policy in which divinely inspired social norms functioned as templates for future development of the ideal polity. The prescriptions that regulated male-female relations within a family and all other ensuing interhuman relations that grew out of that fundamental building block of the new social and political order were in some sense time-bound, since they responded to the specific tribal culture in that period. Their culture-specific resolution, for example, to the problem of a wife's demand for more rights in the context of her empowered social status through Islam, and the husband's demand for obedience as a sole provider and head of the household, as the Qur'an shows, were open to further reflection and interpretation to extrapolate relevant directives for a different place and time. I will come back to the subject of women's domestic and social empowerment later on.

Normative Immutability of the Qur'an and Women's Rights

There is no doubt that behind the immediate Qur'anic resolutions were universal moral concerns like fair treatment and justice in spousal dealings that needed to be extracted and utilized as guiding templates for resolving other similar problems. Since these resolutions were part of the divine revelation, the later juridical tradition regarded them as immutable, requiring a wife's absolute obedience to her husband, even if she managed to become a breadwinner for the family. As pointed out earlier, the jurists took biological variations in men and women as indicators of social and functional inequality. Thus when the Qur'an spoke about functional differences leading to different social responsibilities between man and woman, the jurists generalized the specific conditions prevalent in seventh-century Arab tribal culture to argue for the essential superiority of man over woman, as the verse, "Men are managers of the affairs of women for that God has preferred in bounty one of them over another, and for that they [men] have expended of their property" (Q. 4:34) had indicated. The apparent sense of the verse does not even remotely deal with the superiority of one gender over the other.

Now if verses that are culture specific to the tribal norms prevalent in Arabia become the source of laws that are raised to the status of immutable and universally applicable laws at all times and under all circumstances, then it is impossible to see how universal norms in the UN Declaration can find relevance in Muslim societies today. The Qur'an restricted normative immutability exclusively to the order of nature, calling it God's tradition (*sunnat allāh*) that does not change. It never extended that immutability to social laws, which were governed by human conditions. Islamic legal theory developed a justificatory system for religious-moral action that consisted of a dialectical relationship between judicial rulings in specific cases and the generalizations derived from effective causes in new cases in the light of which generalizations themselves are modified. Hence, to derive a specific judicial decision—for example, that treating women with fairness in the distribution of inheritance is obligatory—is to confirm that it satisfies a certain description of religious-ethical notions of justice according to one's commitment to social responsibility. Social responsibility as part of a generalizable command to be just in one's treatment of women could then be applied to other acts.

The convergence between the immutable divine command that human beings must treat each other justly, and the rational cognition that justice is good, underscores the importance of identifying culture-specific rulings first and then deriving the universal principles behind them to apply to new cases. As discussed above, the Qur'an uses the word *al-ma'rūf* (the known paradigms) for these generalized principles,[15] which must be inferred from the concrete ethical practice of everyday life. There is a correlation between known moral convictions related to the manner in which the Arabs treated their womenfolk and God's immutable purpose for improving that situation as mentioned in the revealed Islamic texts. General moral beliefs that are guided by the revelation seek application in specific situations, thereby furthering the authenticity as well as the relevance of religiously based practice.

In this sense, culture-specific rulings are never elevated to immutable moral paradigms that can be grasped intuitively through a reflective process that involves pondering the consequences of human action and their generalizability for the ethics of human relations. Islamic revelation regards human society and interhuman relations in it as in constant flux, with its laws malleable to meet each new day's requirements. While acknowledging the capacity of a human mind to understand the consequences of engaging in unjust acts, the Qur'an appeals to the human capacity for learning from history in order to avoid immoral behavior in the future (Q. 22:45–46). There is something concrete about human conditions that cannot be denied in the name of universal morality. Muslim theologians were divided on the issue of the availability of universal morality, clashing on whether it is totally conditioned by the social and cultural conventions or derived from a universal standard of rationality grounded in human nature. As discussed in chapter 3, Islamic revelation provides a complex moral language that speaks about human beings, who, on the one hand, share some universal values and interests as equals in dignity and conscience, but who, on the other hand, are bound in particular brotherhood as members of distinct communities and nations.

The concept of universal morality in Islam did not fail to acknowledge the concrete historical and social conditioning of moral norms that affected women's human rights across cultures. But it insists that different cultures must seek to obtain the universal moral principle of justice—a common foundation upon which to construct a universal morality that can be shared cross-culturally in the project of protecting the rights of all humans. In this sense, social principles like justice and mutuality enjoyed normative status because of their derivation from natural law that regulated interhuman relationships, even when social ethical prescriptions were relative in application because of the diverse nature of human society. The divinely ordained just social order had to await its realization as the community gradually developed personal and social ethics by growing in faith and in conduct as prescribed by the revelation.

This debate about the mutability or immutability of the Qur'anic prescriptions is at the heart of the crisis of irrelevance of the inherited tradition and the way it negatively impacts efforts to defend the rights of women. The debate can be traced back to a fundamental thesis about the immutability of the Qur'an in Islamic theology. Muslims regard the Qur'an as God's Speech (*kalām allāh*). God speaks to humanity through His prophets, providing them with universal as well as particular guidance to direct human life in order to achieve the divine goal on earth. Whereas the universal guidance in the form of intuitive reason aims to provide directives that can touch all humans qua human, the particular guidance is in the form of scriptures and provides prescriptive directions to organize the spiritual as well as temporal affairs of that specific community under the leadership of the prophet.

In this sense, Muslims have always approached the Qur'an as a living source of prescriptive guidance for the community's well-being. Accordingly, Muslim scholars sought solutions to concrete problems under given circumstances by applying the rules derived from Qur'anic precedents. The Qur'anic cosmos was thoroughly human, profoundly anchored in human experience as humanity tried to make sense of the divine challenge imparted in the revelation to create an ethical order on earth. As long as the belief about establishing the ideal order on earth remained the major component of the living community's faith and active response to the divine challenge, there remained the need to clarify the Qur'anic impetus in order to promulgate it at each stage of the community's drive toward its ultimate destiny.

Hence, the history of the Muslim community provides a creative and fertile ground for an ongoing interpretation of the divine purposes indicated in the Qur'an. However, due to innumerable factors impacting upon a commentator, the representation of the Qur'anic goals for humanity has not received adequate treatment faithful to the text of the scripture. Undeniably, scholarly pretext plays a significant role in the explication of a particular circumstance of the text and its denotation.[16] It is within this interpretive realm that an insightful investigator can discern the authorial pretext of the earlier commentators that led to the distortion of the otherwise objectifiable context of Muslim existence. In addition, it is through the investigation of such distorted explications of the context of the Muslim community that a Muslim exegete today is able to recontextualize the Qur'an and afford a fresh understanding of the divinely ordained Muslim community.

However, the theological doctrine regarding the miraculous nature of the Qur'an as a miraculous word of God gives rise to the problematic issue of historicizing the revealed text in its cultural context. According to this doctrine, it is inconceivable that the timeless prescriptive directives of the Qur'an should be open to an investigation of their cultural variability. The Qur'anic prescriptions, in such a conceptualization, cannot be regarded as relative and as specifically applicable to that century or cultural context only. They are in this sense immutable and universal in their application, even when the relative context of some of them is explicitly enunciated with phrases like, "And when they ask you about such and such tell them . . ." that clearly suggest their particular historical context. As a corollary to this doctrine, all the specific rulings in the Sharīʿa are considered immutable even when the terms of these rulings and their final judgments were deduced by highly sophisticated human intellectual endeavors within their scholarly as well as cultural setting in Medina, Baghdad, or Cairo.

Undeniably, the most challenging aspect of the Qur'an is its invitation to humankind to reflect on the meanings of God's essentially universal message given to different prophets at various times in history. The purpose of this divine message, according to the Qur'an, is none other than to complement the innate reason in human beings, in order to seek right guidance for establishing an ideal society on earth that would reflect God's will for humanity. The divine message, in this sense, seeks appropriation and implementation by human beings through a divinely bestowed gift of reason—the "light" by means of which human ignorance can be turned into redemptive knowledge.[17] The key to human flourishing is the interaction between God's revelation in scriptural mode and the processes of human reasoning that endeavor to unlock the divine mysteries in nature and revelation. In this sense, there has been an ongoing relationship between reason seeking to uncover universal guidance related to the innate nature—the *fiṭra*—created by God in humankind, and the particularity of the revelation given to a specific community to correlate the common goals of reason and revelation in Islam.

As a rule, and as part of their creedal statement, Muslims today do not regard the Sharī'a laws as having been promulgated by the early community and their expert interpreters of the Qur'an and the Tradition by correlating the common goals of reason and revelation. In fact, in the faculties of the Sharī'a in the Muslim world there are no courses on the history of Islamic law, since such an inquiry is superfluous when the system is regarded as totally divinely ordained and, hence, perfect. Such an uncritical approach to the juridical decisions made by learned scholars in the past leaves too many problems in the area of social ethics and interhuman relations unresolved. In other words, by extending the immutability of the Qur'an to the rulings given by Muslim jurists in the area of interhuman relations, including the treatment of women, the community seems to be saying that it has inherited a perfect system that does not need any revision in the decisions that were made by the founding jurists. The point that needs to be reiterated in the context of this chapter is that the inherited juridical rulings in the books composed by Muslim scholars in the classical age were the culmination of Muslim intellectual endeavors in the appropriation of the divine revelation. Both the Qur'an and the Tradition were regarded as foundational and divinely ordained. The goal was to provide a sort of ideal blueprint for the administration of justice in the Muslim empire. The transition from Muslim empire to modern Muslim nation-states is certainly a new political reality that demands a thorough analysis of interhuman relations under these new national and international contingencies. The limited scope of this inquiry requires me to attend to the specific laws affecting women's rights that were extracted from the scriptural sources and raised to the status of divinely ordained injunctions requiring the absolute obedience of the faithful. The court rulings formulated by Muslim jurists into paradigmatic positive laws of the Sharī'a in the eighth and ninth centuries in the Muslim empire need to be sociologically and anthropologically analyzed to provide their cultural and social context. Traditional jurisprudence treated the specific cases dealing with women's issues in the Qur'an as general directives to argue for more restrictive rulings that led to abuse of women's rights even in domestic life.

Advancing Women's Rights in Muslim Nations

Closely related to the epistemological crisis is the predicament of locating the right religious authority in the Muslim community that can speak to the pressing needs of modern Muslim men and women as they try to make sense of modernity and its challenges to their social values. The two power centers in Muslim society, the state and the seminary, have grown to love power and use it as a control mechanism to remain in power. Autocratic governments and authoritarian religious leaders have, at times, joined hands in suffocating any viable alternatives to providing practical guidance in matters of religion and ethics in the community. Ironically, both centers of power, in most cases, lack legitimacy in the eyes of the majority of Muslims, especially the younger, educated and disenfranchised class, who have sought alternative sources to seek answers to the problem of irrelevance of much of what the government-controlled religious establishment teaches about Islam. Unfortunately, this crisis of religious leadership is the major cause for the political rise of extremist, militant elements in the community, who control the pulpits to preach their brand of intolerant and subverted Islam that is totally against women's empowerment through education and economic advancement, as was the case in Afghanistan under the Taliban.

Today Muslim women have every right to question the authoritarian claims made by male Muslim jurists regarding their interpretations of the scriptural sources and their extrapolations dealing with women's rights. The claim of immutability attached to the rulings that were actually deduced by these jurists creates a problem about the authoritativeness of the legal decisions that affect women's rights. This flawed claim, about the absolute applicability of the legal prescriptions that were given at one time in response to the situation in Arabia, can no longer serve any useful purpose for advancing women's human rights today. Thus far, Muslim jurists have concentrated on the Qur'anic prescriptions without adequately contextualizing them to estimate their sociological and anthropological dimensions. The epistemological shift that needs to occur is related to understanding the connotation and denotation of the scriptural sources within their social and political contexts so that fresh rulings can be formulated to modify or correct the rulings that have been treated as immutably inferred from God's revelation.

A thorough investigation of the scriptural sources, especially the Qur'anic commentaries, reveals with much clarity and certainty that the Qur'an treats man and woman as fundamentally equal, with no modifying adverbs such as "spiritually" equal but "socially" unequal, which are commonly found in modern apologetic sources, especially those produced by militant Muslim leaders. This gender equality can be asserted as a decisive feature of the Qur'anic proclamation that cannot be overturned by any hermeneutic move, however intellectually compelling, against its explicit text to that effect. One just needs to read the creation narrative to appreciate the unassailable position on gender equality. The Qur'anic account of the creation of the first human couple, Adam and Eve, reveals in no uncertain terms that as far God is concerned man and woman share equal moral responsibilities for the future of humankind.

According to chapter 4 of the Qur'an, "The Women," Adam and Eve are created from the same being (*nafs wāḥida*). Eve is not created from the rib of Adam and does not suffer eternal inferiority because of that. More pertinently, while in the Garden, both share the divine reproach and both are held equally responsible for having fallen prey to Satan's temptations. Hence, from the very beginning the human couple shared everything as equal, whether it was the divinely taught ability to restore oneself with God through repentance after having fallen short in one's religious performance, or whether it was in the performance of ethical duties as free agents of God with equal endowment of moral cognition and capability to execute a decision, right or wrong, and face the consequences accordingly. However, in the exegetical literature one reads about the permanent inferiority that woman suffers because of her biological creation. Since the purpose of the Qur'an is not to indulge in details of the Genesis (the ground covered in much detail in the Hebrew Bible) but simply to hold both the first man and first woman on earth equally responsible for what happens to humanity in the future, it moves on to draw large conclusions about the reasons why human beings fail to obey God's commandment and suffer as a result. In Muslim sources, in order to lower the status of Eve in comparison to Adam and prove the infallibility of Adam and impute the entire blame for the fall to her, Muslim exegetes had to rely on what has been termed as *isrā'īl īyāt*, that is, biblical narratives and their commentaries among the Jews and Christians. Had this prejudicial evaluation of the first woman on earth stopped at the level of embellishment of narratives for entertainment among the eager listeners in religious gatherings of men, women's legal and social status would not have suffered terribly in male-dominated juridical deliberations.

Let us remind ourselves that the juridical deliberations in the exclusively male-oriented traditional centers of Islamic learning, the *madrasa* and *ḥawza*, have disregarded female voices in the emerging discourse connected with women's issues and human rights. The redefinition of the status of a Muslim woman in modern society is one of the major issues that confront Muslim jurists' claims to be an authority on legal-ethical sources of Islam. But such a redefinition, as I argue, is dependent upon Muslim women's participation in the legal-ethical deliberations concerning matters whose situational aspects can be determined only by women themselves. Without their participation in legal-ethical deliberations, women's rights will always depend on a representational discourse conducted by male jurists who, in spite of their good intentions, treat the subject as absent and hence, lacking the necessary qualification to determine her rights in a patriarchal society.

Let us take the example of the way laws about a woman's testimony were promulgated from the apparent signification of a specific verse of the Qur'an. The estimation of a woman's position in jurisprudence is contextualized in the following pertinent reference, where the Qur'an speaks about a contract for a debt:

> O believers, when you contract a debt one upon another for a stated term, write it down, and let a scribe write it down between you justly, and let not any scribe refuse to write it down, as God has taught him; so let him write, and let the debtor dictate, and let him fear God his Lord and not diminish anything of it. . . . *And call in to witness two witnesses, men; or if the two be not men, then one man and two women, such witnesses as you approve of, that if one of the two errs the other will remind her;* and let the witnesses not refuse, whenever they are summoned. . . . And fear God; God teaches you, and God has knowledge of everything. (emphasis added) (Q. 2:282)[18]

The passage has been used as documentation to extrapolate rulings in an important chapter in Islamic jurisprudence that deals with administration of justice. One of the major issues in the administration of justice is the testimony that proves or disproves the claim of wrongdoing. Although verse Q. 2:282 deals with the writing of a contract and the need to certify the authenticity of the terms of such a document, it has served as the main textual proof for the derivation of the detailed laws of evidence (*shahādāt*) as they pertain to male and female witnesses. In addition, it has been evoked to communicate the inferiority of a woman's evidence as compared to a man's. Exegetical literature discusses variations in the reading of the phrase "if one of the two [female witnesses] errs [*'an taḍilla iḥdahumā*]" and questions whether the subordinate clause is conditional and whether it conveys the superiority of male memory power.[19] In fact, the Shī'ite commentator Ṭabarsī cites a rare opinion, which he rejects, that maintained that the Qur'an made this provision of "reminding" in women's evidence because "forgetfulness overcomes women [inherently] more than it does men."[20]

It is remarkable that major commentaries in the classical age do not go beyond lexical and grammatical exposition of the subordinate clause to establish that women are in need of being reminded in order to render their evidence equal to that of a man, who enjoys impeccable memory power. To be sure, the Sunnī commentator, Bayḍāwī, maintains that the Shāfi'ite jurists implemented the terms of this verse only in the case of business and financial transactions (*amwāl*), whereas the Ḥanafites extended the requirement to criminology and the law of retribution.[21] Yet the syntactical conclusion that the Qur'anic statement "if one of the two errs" is a conditional clause had enormous implications in explicating the nature of divine commandment in jurisprudence. This grammatical specification had been acknowledged despite the fact that only one transmitter among the early transmitters of the Qur'anic text had insisted on reading the clause as conditional. For the jurists looking at the denotation of the statement, the question is: Is the conditional commandment given for the specific situation in Medina society that can be extrapolated as a generalizable, unconditional commandment, evincing the probable conclusion that regardless of whether a woman errs or not, her evidence is to be reduced to half of a man's evidence?

In fact, some later exegetes maintained that the statement is unconditional because woman is inherently weaker in her rational judgment than man, who is intellectually stronger, and forgetfulness is far from his nature.[22] Furthermore, according to Sufyān b. 'Uyayna (d. 198/813), the verse's requirement for two women brings together the evidence of two women and raises it to be equivalent to that of one man.[23] However, both the explicit denotation and the implied context of the verse in the exegetical literature allow for only a conditional commandment to be surmised. It denies the unconditional purport with its damaging implications for the inherent inferiority of a woman that was asserted in legal decisions, including those maintained by the Shāfi'ites in the limited area of financial transactions. As pointed out earlier, the verse simply speaks to the functional aspects of a contract dealing with financial matters and recommends that it be written and properly witnessed by two morally sound male witnesses, or if they are unavailable, then one male and two female witnesses. It does not engage in providing the rationale for such a recommendation, whether biological or functional, except that no injustice should occur in the matter of lending or borrowing money. At that point in the social history of the Arabs, the major concern of the Qur'an appears to be lack of proper documentation for any claim that involves financial exchange. There is nothing in the passage to suggest otherwise. As a matter of fact, one can assert with much confidence that it does not deal with anything remotely connected with gender relations. And yet, Muslim jurists extrapolated discriminatory rulings against women using the passage as an indicator of natural deficiencies in female members of the community in dealing with public life. Such an essentialist reading of the Qur'an is the main cause for the lack of progress in women's rights in Muslim societies.

Today Muslim jurists continue to assess the position of women in public life in the light of past juridical decisions that reflect a totally different social and cultural context. In order to extrapolate fresh rulings about the legal validity of a woman's testimony, jurists need to inform themselves about the sociological and political facets of financial dealings specific to pre-Islamic Arabian culture. More important, those verses of the Qur'an that appear to speak critically about the female gender need to be contextualized and assessed for juridical purposes merely within the Qur'anic polemics against the Meccan negative attitudes toward female children and women in general. Those pre-Islamic attitudes must definitely be rejected if any advancement in women's dignity within Qur'anic teachings is to be achieved. Lack of such an interdisciplinary investigation has led to erroneous opinions about woman's social-biological capabilities, which have adversely affected her performance in the political arena. Determining the equal dignity and human agency of a woman is one of the areas in jurisprudence where certain norms of human capability should be decisive for political purposes in thinking about political principles that can provide the underpinnings for some constitutional guarantees for women's participation in political processes.

Muslim Political Theology on Woman's Capacity

In speaking about human capabilities that function decisively in asserting social and political rights, Muslim political theology provides an untapped conceptual resource to address Muslim women's human rights in the Muslim social and political context. In Muslim theology, the faculty or aptitude to undertake performance of action is known as *istiṭā'a*, meaning capacity to act. It is a technical term that is defined as "the accident created by God in animate beings who, thanks to it, perform acts of free choice."[24] There are variants in the definition of the term that would emphasize that the notion of capacity as a technical term varies with the different schools of Muslim thought, and sometimes with the writers, and that it is always closely dependent upon theses founded on the intrinsic reality or nonreality of human freedom of choice.

The Qur'an speaks about the capacity that is needed to perform certain obligations, but it never uses the term in its technical significance to introduce the concept of capability. Although the Arabic term suggests "faculty" in the sense of potentiality and power, the essential meaning is capacity. In this last sense, power and capacity are identical. The capacity of a human in regard to his or her acts depends above all upon his or her physical aptitude to accomplish them. The Mu'tazilites, for instance, have identified a number of elements that constitute capacity and that must come together to produce the desired act.[25] Some of these elements include health and physical integrity, favorable circumstances, the desired time, instruments, and motivation. The act is produced when all these elements are present. Capacity, however, is created by God for the act and at the instant of the act whose accomplishment it governs.

In contrast, according to the Ash'arites, the capacity is created directly by God "with the act and for the act." It does not preexist, a point of difference from the Mu'tazilite thesis. A man who does not have the requisite physical integrity is stricken with powerlessness; he would certainly be incapable of performing the act, but that is not the true conception of capacity. If, on the contrary, the power to act fails a person (whatever his physical integrity may be), it is because God has not created in him the corresponding capacity. For the Ash'arites, like every accident, capacity is directly created by God and, like every accident, it does not last. Therefore, it does not precede the act, as the Mu'tazilites would have it, but is concomitant with it.[26]

This insightful theological discussion about human capacity (*istiṭā'a*) occupies a serious consideration in assessing the moral worth of human action. Without recognizing capabilities, how can one speak about free will and the ultimate moral responsibility of human agency? Obviously those who rejected human moral agency, like the Ash'arites, spoke about God's limitless capacity to do what God willed. There was little room to speak about human capacity in a theology that was guided by the dictum "Might makes right." But for the Mu'tazilites, the question of basic human capacity in the sense of physical integrity that renders an act possible was critical to their thesis about God's justice. If God is just, then God has to create equal capability in all humans to carry out the requirements of innate moral guidance. Human moral agency gives humans a natural claim to demand capacity to carry out a moral imperative. How can a just God ask a human being to climb to the roof without first providing the ladder and the necessary potency to climb it? With ethical cognition humans are provided with volition; and with volition there is the capacity to realize an act.

The divine endowment of the human's capacity to act provides me an opportunity to assert that at the level of capacity, all humans are treated equally by giving them minimal conditions to enable them to pursue their own respective vision of what it is that makes life worth living. Since the capabilities were given individually to each person, each person had to find that life individually in some sort of private space. The public space, created through collective agreement, had to allow every person and every group to pursue their own vision of that final good without interference and without imposing their vision on others. Claims or entitlements are the criteria by which public space is to be maintained by respecting the private space of every person and group. This is the foundation of a pluralistic society that can emerge from the theology of human capacity to pursue the intimation of intuitive moral cognition to work for both private and public space consonant with peaceful coexistence. In such a society, tolerance is extended to anyone who is respectful of the basic capabilities afforded to all humankind and the minimal law promulgated to allow these capabilities to flourish under universal moral guidance.

What I want to suggest at this point in my inquiry, is that we need to find an inclusive theological doctrine that will be responsive to the need for a clear statement about women's human rights in Islam. Here theoretical unanimity on the first principles derived from the Islamic theory of natural law, as discussed in chapter 3, is a significant source for creating the necessary consensus on male–female interaction within the system of values that is conducive to fair treatment without resorting to flimsy notions about a woman's dependent role or incapacity to manage her own affairs. The Qur'an supports the unconditional equality of the capacity that God has created in all human beings, regardless of their sex, race, or creed. In order to make a strong case for women's human rights today, Muslims need to focus on capacity language, which cannot be easily dismissed by the traditionalist jurists entrenched in their ideological and male-dominated juridical tradition in the Muslim community. Such a focus on human capabilities, to which man and woman can claim equal access as per God's endowment in the natural constitution (*fiṭra*), will allow for minimalist as well as pluralist teleology anchored in the basic commonalities between man and woman through their equal creation to determine universally accepted equal rights.

Here my efforts to search for a pluralist teleology are not diverted by the need to develop a case for women's human rights that is compatible with the Muslim cultural legacy. I recognize the plurality of capabilities in human persons, who develop these variable ends, not necessarily congruent with the religious or secular ends of humankind. Quite to the contrary, there is a natural tendency in human groups and individuals to autonomously negotiate their ends within the available social, political, and cultural institutions to foster the proper functioning of men and women in different familial, social, and political settings. The minimalist search for commonalities between competing groups and individuals provides the culture with a common goal and its unique characteristics. I do acknowledge that cultures are complex and cannot be pigeonholed in a single typology because they are fluid complexes of intersubjective meanings and practices. At the same time, I do not wish to confuse the diversity of human cultures with cultural relativism, an argument that one reads against the moral universality of human rights put forward by a number of Muslim autocratic states.

Nonetheless, I do submit that in comparative studies that are used to assess the performance of different societies in promoting the quality of women's life, it may be problematic to use concepts that originate in one culture to describe and assess the realities in another, especially in the present climate of suspicion about the political aims of economic globalization. As shown by a number of studies dealing with the anthropology of human rights in the context of ceremonies involving genital alterations in a number of African countries, for example, one can notice insufficient ethical attunement to cultural variety and particularity in these comparisons that use either absolutist moral language to condemn the practice or revert to moral relativism to justify tolerance of traditional practices that are, in some cases, inhuman in their treatment of female members of the society.[27] Whether it is a culturally sanctioned practice of female circumcision, or, as labeled by its opponents, "female genital mutilation," the practice needs to be assessed for its harm to a woman's dignity and identity. Calling for cultural eradication of the practice without fully understanding what the practice does to enhance gender identity in some cultures, where the ceremonies involving genital alterations are embraced by some women, could lead to violation of other people's valued way of life. However, any campaign for tolerance versus eradication of morally abominable practices like honor killing of women in some Muslim cultures could lead unwittingly to moral relativism and total disregard for a woman's life and personhood.

Islamic culture contains authoritative norms of female modesty, deference, obedience, and self-sacrifice that have defined women's lives in Muslim cultures for centuries. To dismiss these norms as traditional and incapable of providing a good life to women in modern times would be to miss an opportunity to sit in dialogue with women who have chosen a traditional lifestyle, to understand their capabilities and expectations in life. There is no doubt that one cannot take these choices at face value, without fully assessing the opportunities and obstacles that are in place for women to achieve their ends in those societies.[28]

Let me clarify my stance on cultural relativism and the way that argument impedes the advancement of women's human rights. The major problem that I have with the argument about cultural or even moral relativism is the phenomenological integrity it lacks in assessing the variables of human behavior. More pertinently, and rather unfortunately, it supports tolerance of a morally unacceptable position, whose immorality is obvious to any person of sound mind. In the global context today we are often told that relativism with tolerance of diversity is imperative on the grounds that we should show respect for the ways of others. What if the ways of others are humanly unacceptable? Should we not search for a commonly recognized norm that no advocate of cultural relativism would be able to reject? In arguing specifically for women's legitimate human rights based on their dignity as human persons, both cultural and moral relativism appear to be antithetical, because, as human rights activists have often remarked, blatant violations of woman's dignity cannot be stopped by an appeal to cultural or moral variability in human behavior. However, in the context of the ongoing debate about the hidden political agenda of international human rights and the need to convince Muslim communities to support the moral universality of human rights, it is more advisable if the protection of women's dignity as human persons were to be approached from the Mu'tazilite theological perspective of moral agency of autonomous human beings endowed with equal capabilities to advance their ends in life. I wish to explore this teleology through a controversial Qur'anic verse that has implications for Muslim women's rights in the private and public domains. Remarkably, the passage of the Qur'an that speaks about a man's guardianship over a woman uses male and female capabilities as a measuring stick to assess claims and duties as well as the excellence of one over the other in the context of a marriage. There is nothing in the verse to suggest biological, that is natural, and hence, immutable inequality between a man and a woman, to which Islamic juridical tradition seems to be inclined in its unfair rulings against women; rather, as I shall demonstrate, all that the passage seems to convey is related to a functional capacity or incapacity that empowers one or the other spouse to assume a role of guardianship in a family. The resolution of this problem of interpretation of a specific verse of the Qur'an has much wider implications for advancing Muslim women's human rights, at least within the more immediate familial situation. There are hundreds of unreported cases of human rights violations that Muslim women suffer in the domestic environment, whose justifications are rooted in traditional patriarchal practices and the religiously concocted superiority of man over woman.

Guardianship (*Qiwāma*) of a Woman

The question whether a woman needs a guardian or manager to protect her interests has assumed a central stage in the debate about the compatibility of Islam and democracy, on the one hand, and Muslim cultural values and human rights norms in Muslim societies on the other. A number of studies, in both Arabic and Persian, have offered lengthy discussions about the verse of the Qur'an that declares in no uncertain terms, "Men are the managers [*qawwām*] of the affairs of women for that God has preferred in bounty one of them over another" (Q. 4:35).[29] In another passage, the Qur'an states denotatively that men have a "degree" above women when dealing with divorce settlements: "Women have such honorable rights as obligations, but their men have a degree [*daraja*] above them" (Q. 2:228). What has God preferred for man in bounty over a woman? What does "a degree" connote in the context of marital life? Is this preferment or degree above women connected with human biology, with ramifications for the permanent social status and superiority of a man over a woman, or is it simply related to the function of providing sustenance and other related familial obligations?[30]

Various Muslim scholars, traditionalist as well as modernist, have endeavored to respond to these questions in view of their intellectual and ideological inclinations. Traditionalist scholarship has adhered to long-held views in historical Islam about the cultural valuation of a woman, using scriptural sources for finding, determining, and constructing obligations specific to women that emanate from the Qur'anic reference to *qiwāma* of men. Much of this scholarship lacks epistemic rigor and integrity, which renders its findings apologetic and lacking normative force in the changed circumstances of contemporary societies. Surely women's issues today include situations where the inherited tradition provides no insight, guidance, or precedent for relevant judicial decisions. Since traditional scholarship remained suspicious of extrarevelatory sources like human reason in independently assessing the contemporary situation to derive new rulings about cases that confronted educated and working women, the normative quality of rational analysis was not admitted in matters that dealt with a radically different social and political standing for women. Hence, an epistemological movement to decide whether human reason would be restored to its original function to become a substantial source for discovering the purposes of the revelation and their applicability in dealing with man–woman relationships was circumvented by the self-proclaimed determinacy of past rulings in the juridical corpus.

Modernist scholarship, on the other hand, had a reformist agenda of challenging and limiting the determinacy and objectivity of the traditionalist decisions in the matter of juridical rulings dealing with women's empowerment through modern education and accruing financial independence that made the *qiwāma* issue irrelevant. For this scholarship, rights attached to women primarily by virtue of their presumed nature and membership in the human community as individuals. Relational aspects of man–woman relationships in the traditional patriarchal cultural context were reduced to secondary considerations in comparison to the inalienable rights of a woman as an individual member of the human community. Accordingly, the epistemic position of this scholarship was to theorize and argue for creating a rights regime under the Sharī'a on the basis of a foundational conception of natural rights that accrue to individuals, including women. The classical Muslim opposition to natural teleology and its dependence upon rational order in traditionalist scholarship were revisited for their relevance to the thesis that challenged the absolute immutability of the inherited tradition. The central argument in modernist scholarship was based on reason's objective and normative authority and its ability to determine both universal and context-sensitive values that advanced women's rights in contemporary Muslim societies.

The most clear voice in traditionalist scholarship was that of seminarians educated in, for example, al-Azhar in Cairo or Ḥawza 'Ilmīya in Najaf. For these seminarians, authentic Islam was what they had learned and what they were expounding. In fact, for these leading traditionalists, the equation between authentic Islam and Azhar or Ḥawza 'Ilmīya was self-evident because these institutions of Islamic learning were the repositories of the scriptural reasoning and positivism that determined religious obligations. Hence, whether it was Muḥammad al-Ghazālī of Egypt or Ayatollah 'Alī Sistānī of Iraq,[31] their evaluation of women's overall role in the Muslim public order or their rights as citizens of a modern nation-state was expressed in terms of its conformity with the divine purposes delineated in the Qur'an and the Tradition. More pertinently, these scholars rejected any suggestion that rationally inferred universal values could challenge the scripturally based, contextually defined role of a woman as a process of accommodation with human rights norms in modern times.

In contrast, modernist scholarship was headed by scholars who were familiar with the seminary curriculum, having studied there at one time or another during their education and then transferred to modern universities to research or teach. Their influence was seminal in the growing awareness of the discrepancies and inequalities in women's domestic and social life. One such figure was undoubtedly Ayatollah Murtaḍā Muṭahharī of Iran, who, in his analysis of women's issues, combined traditional methodology and appreciation of modern conditions in which women found themselves struggling between the forces of modernization and traditionalism.[32]

However, fluctuating between the two trends is a reform movement headed by reform-minded scholars, such as Muḥammad Shahrūr[33] or Naṣr Ḥāmid Abū Zayd,[34] who are calling for fresh hermeneutics of the historical tradition in keeping with the social and political needs of modern citizens in a nation-state. Both these scholars, for instance, have challenged the representatives of traditional jurisprudence who support the status quo in the matter of men's traditionally established capabilities to act as guardians over women's affairs. In terms of the power structure in the Muslim community, it is worth keeping in mind that the traditional scholars represent the authority of the seminaries and their overall influence over the Muslim populace. Therefore, without the participation of the traditionalists in this search for compatibility between Islam and democratic politics, it is doubtful if the modernists can advance anything beyond formal academic expositions.

Turning to the question of the concept of guardianship or governance of man over woman, we should revisit the passage of the Qur'an that functions as a major documentation for curbing a woman's empowerment more directly in domestic life, but also indirectly in public life:

> Men are the *managers*[35] *of the affairs of women* for that God has preferred in bounty one of them over another, and for that they have expended of their property. Righteous women are therefore obedient, guarding [the honor of the household during the] absence [of their husband] as God commands [them] to guard. Those women, who are the cause of fear because of their disobedience, counsel them, [and if they still continue to disobey then] separate them from their beds, and beat them. But if they obey you then do not seek to impose any punishment on them. Indeed, God is the Most Exalted and Most High. (emphasis added) (Q. 4:34)

The controversial interpretation of the phrase indicating guardianship has been largely based upon the lexical-cultural sense of the word *qawwām*, meaning "govern, be mindful, undertake maintenance" and other related senses that suggest exercising some kind of discretion in managing someone's affairs.[36] However, *qawwām* also conveys someone who goes out of his way to perform a task. In relation to a woman, this person is said to manage, to conduct, to order, to regulate, to superintend (*qayyim*) the affairs of the woman.[37] In other words, the term does not convey the exercise of discretion without also indicating the total dedication of *qawwām* to the protection of the interests of the woman.

The authority invested in men fits well with the tribal norms of seventh-century Arabia in which, as a rule, a husband acted as his wife's caretaker or superintendent (*qayyim al-mar'a*). However, the Qur'anic nuance underscores man's responsibility for governance or maintenance of the entire household under his care, whose head is actually a woman, who, despite her major role in maintaining the family in the precincts of a home life, remains vulnerable and in need of protection and care in the harsh social conditions for women in that time and place in general.[38]

This cultural-lexical evaluation has deeply affected Qur'anic exegesis, which clearly reveals that Muslim commentators read the particular verse in its culturally conditioned signification, providing them with normative ammunition to corroborate total empowerment of man over woman based on some kind of biological and psychological differences. The factor of men being the providers in the family was certainly a social function based on man's capacity to take up the task of producing wealth that he could expend for the upkeep of his family. Although there is nothing in the verse to suggest that such a capacity to provide for the family was given only to men, the function of earning and providing was determined by patriarchal cultural values. More pertinently, the division of labor in seventh-century Arabia did not convey social deficiency; rather, it endorsed the prevailing cultural practice. And yet all classical commentaries on the Qur'an, almost unanimously, take this social deficiency as a permanent trait of a woman, who is totally dependent for her survival on man in the order of nature. Moreover, they take God's preferment of "one of them over another" in bounty to mean that God has endowed men with knowledge, religious faith, intellect, and discretionary authority over women.[39]

However, the apparent sense of the verse suggests nothing of that sort. And yet there is no reference to a woman's capacity to learn and become economically independent anywhere in the exegetical literature. The reason, in my opinion, appears to be the attitude of the male-dominated culture that refused to extend equal capacity to woman for her potential ability to assume guardianship in the household. In other words, Muslim jurists refused to read the verse for its obvious message when it spoke of the discretion of one over the other in the matter of social functions each performed based on what men expended for the family, and not necessarily because of biological differences.

To be sure, the Qur'an uses the *qiwāma*, guardianship or management on the basis of various naturally endowed capacities, which, as humans grow and learn, empowers a man or a woman to assume control over affairs for the good of all in the relationship. The Qur'an does not support any discrimination founded upon claims of superiority of one gender over the other, since such a message would have further institutionalized Arab tribal cultural norms in the newly formed religious community of believers, men and women, whose only source of a claim to excellence was their moral and spiritual consciousness (*taqwā*). Even the reference to "expending from their property" needs to be read as a statement of fact rather than a normative state in which women are to assume an economically dependent role, with no capacity to assert their independent personhood at all. Nonetheless, there were Muslim exegetes, like Jalāl al-Dīn al-Suyūṭī (d. 911/1505), for instance, who attributed to the Prophet a tradition that advises Muslims to avoid being governed by women, because "women are deficient in intellect and in religion; their testimony is half of the testimony [of a man], which proves the deficiency of their intellect; and they menstruate because of which they cannot pray. This proves the deficiency of their religion."[40] A number of reformist scholars have rejected such traditions as being unsound.[41] But the culture preserved such a prejudicial attitude toward women, depriving them of opportunities to advance economically as well as politically as men's equals in capacities and dignity. The culture also determined the solutions when disputes arose that threatened the sanctity of family life. Undoubtedly, if one were to accept the prescriptive measures that the passage provides for the resolution of a dispute, it would seem to lead to almost total enslavement of a woman if she engages in aggressive behavior. What is the Qur'an trying to do by proposing physical punishment as a last resort?

The term *nushūz* signifies interhuman aggression and severance of relationship as a result of neglect in the matter of guardianship that is founded upon mutual love and compassion. In this sense, *nushūz* is a show of power and domination by way of depriving the other party of any say in decisions affecting interpersonal justice. It is not, as some exegetes have contended, related to neglect in establishing human–God relationships through regular religious practice or failure to uphold moral virtues in one's conduct.[42] Hence, the passage under consideration describes a situation that occurs in the family when man assumes guardianship in the household due to his capabilities, where a woman could be a wife, sister, daughter, or mother, whose interests he must protect. The assumption of various solutions, meticulously graded by the verse, to the problem of aggression is thus determined by a crisis caused by the act of *nushūz*.

Nonetheless, guardianship is assumed on the basis of qualification rather than gender. A specific situation in the family demands a specific capability to deal with the crisis, by either a man or a woman. It is a woman's empowerment with education and an independent source of income that provides her with the same opportunities that a man enjoys in asserting his rights as a guardian, beginning in the privacy of the home and extending to the public arena. This is made clear in subsequent verses of the same chapter, where if a woman fears rebelliousness or aversion (the same term, *nushūz*, is used to describe his conduct) in her husband, she can seek a resolution by referring the case to the arbiters in the community (Q. 4:129), who should look into the case to remove causes of injustice or maltreatment. The Qur'an underscores the need for a woman to have similar recourse to justice, keeping within the boundaries of male-dominated Arab tribal culture, which specifies a different approach when a woman has to deal with a man's aggressive behavior.

In the final analysis, the solutions that are offered in the Qur'an are culture specific and not normative for a timeless application and, therefore, cannot be used as paradigmatic in deriving judicial decisions that recur throughout human history.

Concluding Remarks

In my concluding remarks, I want to suggest that in cross-cultural application of human rights norms in regards to women's empowerment in traditional societies, it is the language of capabilities, rather than "human rights" directly, that can open real venues for improving women's human rights in Muslim societies. The modern language of human rights is confrontational and insensitive to traditional resources to further women's rights as humans first. The first praise for Muslim society's openness is judged in terms of whether the women in that culture appear like their sisters in the West. As soon as women in those societies appear covered in their headscarves or other forms of covering, our cries of human rights violations become part of media and academic sensationalism. Instead of searching for other yardsticks to measure their empowerment and even work toward their enhancement, we begin to use cultural and moral relativism to justify aggression against women in those cultures. I find justifications and tolerance based on relativism self-defeatist and ultimately accountable for continued violence against women. A shift in our approach to the moral universality of human rights is necessary if we are seriously to confront the male chauvinism that claims normative application in Muslim treatment of the other half of humanity—women. As I shall demonstrate in the next chapter, issues related to women's empowerment to undertake decisions that relate to their own well-being depend on their education and their own assertion of their intellectual and other capacities to make the right decisions without social and psychological pressures applied by communal and group identities. Ultimately, Islamic public theology will need to respond to divine justice as it extends to cover the woman as God's agent to undertake the establishment of a just social order on earth.

5

Individual and Society

Claims and Responsibilities

Modern human rights discourse is thoroughly individualistic even when its secularist universalistic ideology, with its emphasis on global civil society, requires an element of global solidarity to invigorate a sense of human connectedness and common human destiny. Although human rights are worth only as much as the worth of individual human beings, it is unwarranted to assume that by their emphasis on individual human worth as the sole criterion for assessing accruing rights, every doctrine of human rights regards the individual as the primary locus at the expense of some collective entity. It is, moreover, obvious that moral sensibilities and evaluation are approved in the context of collective existence and mutual recognition rather than in the isolation of the internalized world of each individual. The universalization of secular liberal individualism tends to devalue communitarian identities founded upon collective constraints and sanctions that provide a necessary social environment for practical connections between individuals and groups. To obscure the very pattern of their connection is detrimental to the development of individualist assumptions of moral autonomy, which actually depend upon the individual's ability to function as a member of society. Without ignoring the tensions that are part of social existence caught up by contradictory patterns of social agency, human rights discourse can ill afford to absolutize individual moral agency by freeing the individual from the collective restraints that are needed for the smooth functioning of political order.

Issues of human rights are faced with contradictions in terms of their concern to valuation of diverse religious and communal identities, commitments, and desiderata. In many ways, religious universal discourse competes with contemporary secular human rights universalism because historically it was first and foremost where arguments for human dignity and worth were articulated in terms of human entitlements as part of their natural constitution. Paradoxically, it is also from within religious traditions that noninclusive and relativist idioms found their way into religiously based legal systems. It is not an exaggeration to state that the most formidable challenge to the universality of international human rights emanates from religiously formulated relativistic and locally sensitive approaches to human rights. Nonetheless, it is important to recognize the fact that long before the UN Declaration argued for the universality of human rights, religious communities had to reconcile the universality of their claim within the particularity of a specific language (Arabic, for example), culture, and ethical idiom that took claims and responsibilities in human relations as the critical core of their collective and individual identities. Each religious community, like any other transcultural and transnational community, in its own manner had to settle contradictory injunctions that pointed at times to inclusive universal language of the revelation, and at other times to an exclusive particular communal system that defined the group's adherence and identity as the bearer of the historical message.

Consequently, the ramifications of ethical absolutism and the dynamics of local particularism were part and parcel of religious idiom long before modern secular language began to address the issue of universal human rights in the context of a world community made up of different nations and cultures in the postwar era of the late 1940s. Here we are face to face with claims and counterclaims of universal rights originating in Western secular discourse, and how this discourse is refracted in different civilizational discourse informed by religious commitments and responsibilities. The purpose of this chapter is to begin a discussion of the different readings of rights in Islamic tradition as well as of the universal applicability of Western definitions of rights by taking our inquiry into the assumptions of religious and rights-based political discourse.

The rights-based discourse is not a religious one, though the ethical claims it makes are universal in nature and share with religion an evaluation of innate human worth. Indeed, the modern secular and democratic idea of rights sits in a very complicated and contradictory relation to its own religious heritage.[1] While rooted, on the one hand, in the traditions of sectarian Protestantism, it is equally rooted in modern natural law tradition.[2] The process and progress of secularization is critical because to a great extent most Western ideas of universal human rights rest on a secular view of the individual and of the relations between such individuals in a secularized public sphere. The idea of individuals as bearers of something called rights presupposes a very particular understanding and reading of the self essentially as a self-regulating agent. The modern idea of the autonomous self along with "a new idea of the ethical and moral no longer rooted in a transcendent and other-worldly sphere but in the immanent this-worldly workings of reason"[3] envisions social actors as self-contained matrixes of desires who direct their own appetites, desires, passions, and interests. The problem with this way of looking at the morally self-regulating individual is the social reality of human existence and the ways in which that existence needs to be made meaningful through social ties and relations with "morally autonomous and agentic individuals."[4]

This view of the autonomous individual as a self-regulating agent is founded upon a certain moral philosophy and politics. The metaphysical foundation on which this idea is constructed goes back to the anthropomorphic notions in the Genesis account of human creation in the image of God, whereas the politics it purportedly advances is the politics of liberal democracy—politics of a principled articulation of rights over any shared definition of social good and the public sphere that seeks to marginalize religious commitments. This is the core problem in the acceptance of religious claims as having legitimate place in the public forum. The UN Declaration is based on so-called public versus private distinctions that would place religious commitments and grounds for action in a sphere isolated from that of public discourse and public choice. At stake is the place of various religious considerations in both public discussions about human rights, ranging from individual Muslims on religious grounds publicly condemning such evil acts as homosexuality to collective Muslim denial of women's right to marry outside the community in accordance with the religious duties in the Sharīʿa. A public discourse that, according to John Rawls, claims to have an integrity of its own and views religious claims as having no place in the public sphere raises important questions for Muslim group rights advocates: Under what circumstances should the Muslim community abide by the neutrality requirements of the Universal Declaration of Human Rights, which demands they hold the religiously grounded character of their claims regarding proper public conduct and government decision making in privacy?

A demand to abide by a secularly conceived religious and metaphysical neutrality requirement for public discourse founded on the premise of universal reason actually excludes publicly making moral and metaphysical claims bearing on political choices in terms understandable only in the context of Islamic revelatory guidance embedded in the Qur'an and the Tradition.

Traditional Muslim leaders have a problem with a position that rejects the rights of people to decide political questions by what they regard as the best reasons rooted in a transcendent sphere of Islamic revelation. The issue of proper public discourse and choice is of concern for all religious communities who must share a public forum with other religious groups, without insisting on the idea of whole truth connected with their own truth claims. In this regard, the declaration of 1948 may be seen as an extension to the world stage of a neutrality requirement that seeks to disestablish religious considerations so that the secular character of public discourse and public policy is not overshadowed by any religious comprehensive doctrine. Hence, modern secular human rights language, when it speaks about freedom of thought and expression, freedom from arbitrary arrest and torture, freedom of movement and assembly, the right to work for fair wages, protection of the family, and adequate standards of living, education, and health care that the international documents extended at different times in the course of the nineteenth and twentieth centuries, abides by the neutrality requirement in which the individual bearer of rights appears as a citizen with equal political, civil, and social rights rather than as a member of a traditional religious community.

Religion, to be sure, is not oriented around the autonomous dictates of the self-regarding and rights-bearing consciousness. Rather, it seeks to define the self as constituted by the experience of transcendence. Whether the concrete rights of citizenship, which are the products of positive law, can in fact be extrapolated onto the international arena through international covenants in such a manner is of course a critical issue in advocating a position of universal human rights.[5]

It is here that the religious perspective of Muslim traditionalists becomes critical to explore. The Islamic universal discourse conceives of a spiritually and morally autonomous individual capable of attaining salvation outside the nexus of the community-oriented Sharī'a, with its emphasis on an integrated system of law and morality. The Sharī'a did not make a distinction between external acts and internal states because it did not regard the public and the private as unrelated in the totality of individual salvation. Nevertheless, in the absence of ecclesiastical authority mediating between God and humanity in all those acts that one performs as part of one's direct relationship to God, the Sharī'a redefined the communal context to include only interhuman relationships. In this manner, Islamic universal discourse sought to define itself by legitimizing individual autonomy within its religiously based collective order by leaving individuals free to negotiate their spiritual destiny without state interference, while requiring them to abide by the public order that involved the play of reciprocity and autonomy upon which a regime of rights is based.

Religious sensibilities, however, are firmly founded upon a language of duties and responsibilities, which may give the impression that they sit inadequately with any conception of human or individual rights.

That a distinction in sensibilities exists between religious and secular discourse in the matter of human rights cannot be denied. The definition of the individual as a rights-bearing citizen—a concept that is absent in Islamic legal discourse—is of a different nature than the definition of the inviolable self (*nafs dhī ḥurma*) within Islamic legal idiom. At the same time, it is important to emphasize that the secular and religious estimations of the individual do not trump one another. The emphasis on the individual bound by obligations (*mukallaf*) in the Sharīʿa does not necessarily negate the notion of individual rights, nor does the notion of individual human rights necessarily invalidate religious commitments and responsibilities in the context of communal existence. In fact, it is important to underscore plurality in the estimation of human personhood and its relation to the community. Indeed, this plurality exists not only in a particular religious tradition like Islam, but also within different interpretations of secularism about the individual's relation to religious commitments and community and to the overarching secularized public sphere in the modern nation-state. It is for this reason that it may prove useful to inquire into Islamic idiom for a new or different way of framing the terms of human valuation and worth, one that may well allow a mediation between universal and particular desiderata not always given to the categorization of rights.

In the context of Islamic communitarian ethics, it is relevant to raise a fundamental question that the traditionalist scholars have been asking in the context of modern human rights discourse: By virtue of being human, does a person have rights independent of any community he or she may be a member of? An underlying concern in this question is a challenge that all those who want to preserve their communal ties through the system of reciprocity and responsibilities are also committed to the obligations of human rights and their promotion at the individual as well as collective levels. The issue of individual human rights and collective obligations, therefore, assumes a critical stage when Islamic tradition is required to respond to the reality of ethical pluralism in the context of a modern state, on the one hand, and redefine the boundaries of individual conscience and human agency in determining religious and ethical obligations and responsibilities in the context of faith community, on the other. The major problem that faces Muslim leadership in endorsing human rights norms is the secular tone of human rights discourse, which demands that all public discourse and choice be guided by a practical agnosticism, that is, by acting as if God did not exist. In other words, such discourse seems to imply that Islam should limit itself to the private realm separate from the public one, and abandon its role in influencing all public choices that are not in harmony with a democratic constitutional framework.[6]

Earlier I introduced the notion of a neutrality requirement which demands that Muslims should marginalize religious commitments in the public forum to avoid entanglement with public discourse and public choice that affects all individuals, whether religious or not. In other words, they must recognize group boundaries in the public sphere, without insisting that others agree with them on the basis of their religious reasons, which necessarily apply to only those who have declared their commitment to abide by their dicta. Thus far, the attitude of hostility, intolerance, and militancy against those who reject this group identity has been the main source of human rights violations of men and women in Muslim societies. Is there something in the public theology of Islam that can mitigate this hostile attitude by clearly demonstrating the classical heritage that recognizes the existence of a private realm separate from the public one to allow for ethical pluralism to determine interhuman relationships without diminishing the role of religious commitments in developing what John Rawls calls a social democratic constitutional polity?

Decoding Islamic Secularity

If traditionalist Muslim scholars were to reconsider their opposition to the Universal Declaration of Human Rights as an international document that has Western bias and that is intended to engender moral indifference in the communal context of individual rights and responsibilities in Muslim societies, then the major step would be to disestablish the secular character of public discourse and public policy that, for all practical purposes, requires not just the absence of religious establishment that exercises control over public choices, but also aggressively acts and speaks in public as if God or religion did not exist. In other words, total exclusion of public reference to religious grounds in support of secular social structure, even when such references are publicly defended in secular terms (as privatized discourse), would be construed as a conversation stopper in Muslim traditionalist culture today. Muslim reformist discourse has, to some extent, pursued the secular agenda by raising a number of objections to the intrusion of Islamic juridical and religious claims into the public forum. These objections range from specific concerns regarding particular traditional Muslim interpretations that affirm sexism by defending the leadership of men in religious institutions and the family, to special irrelevance associated with religious discourse that has led to religious polarization and that threatens civil peace among different groups in the community.

In this chapter, I want to explore the Islamic tradition's relationship to universal morality and political claims, and to argue how one might plausibly appreciate the nature of the public forum to determine what Muslim leaders must consider improper intrusion of religious claims of Muslims into the public forum and public policy that affect all citizens in a modern nation-state. This I will do by exploring a range of considerations drawn from Islamic tradition and the manner in which historically Muslim religious commitments became functionally attuned to the public forum in being primarily oriented to proper governance in which the right to individual worship and belief became part of the religious ethos of Islam. My argument is built upon the classical Muslim legal theory that clearly circumvented any human intrusion in the realm of the individual's spiritual relation to God, leaving it in the private domain of human social existence. This I argue despite the fact that Islam treated the private and the public realms as an integrated whole. The legal tradition, as discussed in chapter 2, recognized functional secularity with separate jurisdictions for the individual's relation to God and to other humans and society, leaving the plausibility of construing the public forum and its discourse as separate from the private domain of the individual's connection with transcendence without clerical control.

It is important to reiterate the secularity that Islam acknowledges as a default arrangement; this allows for the emergence of a civil structure that is not overburdened by its comprehensive doctrines. From its inception, the Muslim polity had to deal with cultural and religious diversity in society even when the political authority was exercised by Muslims. Muslim scholars had to grapple with the issue of the meaning of what the Muslims call *niẓām ʿurfī*—loosely translated as "customary social order" or even "secular system" without denying God or religion a say in its overall functioning. The Sharīʿa had laid down the basis for organization within the community by distributing the tasks in two categories of individual (*farḍ ʿayn*) and collective duties (*farḍ kifāya*). Individual duties were those duties for the performance of which each individual was personally responsible whether others performed them or not. Most of those acts that were performed as part of one's relation to God came under this category. In contrast, most of the duties that one performed in relation to other individuals were regarded as necessary to maintain public order. The principle of secularity in the sense of an absence of religious control over public discourse, individual choice, and community life, such as would obtain in a limited democracy, was formed on the basis of the relation of the community to nonadherents. Under this principle the sectarian character of religious claims was exchanged for social stability through supporting a multi-faith polity. Hence, the adherents of other religions were allowed to continue in their own religious allegiance, as protected subjects, as long as their form of public life was not too blatantly inconsistent with the public order that recognized the general good of all as defined by Islamic values (not very different from the Rawlsian defense of the social democratic constitutional framework). Thus only those who had personally undertaken the obligations of Islam were expected to live in accordance with the teachings of Islam in their personal lives.

This functional secularity of Islamic tradition provides me with the opportunity to press for the universality of individual human rights in the context of community life as long as the separate jurisdictions for individual relationships with transcendence and interpersonal relations, as projected in the Islamic juridical tradition, are kept in focus. Here the public theology of Islam regarding the moral worth and agency of every human person, self-subsistent and independent from revelation, forms the cornerstone of the integrated and yet distinct private individual conscience and the communal Sharī'a as a bedrock of a good Muslim life. This doctrine supports the internalized moral authority of human conscience; but it generates the sense of responsibility toward others as an important step for an individual in the pursuit of perfection within the orders and institutions of the community. The relationship between individuals in the community provides the terms of group membership that take into consideration social definitions of community in such a way that community does not function as the antithesis of individual interests and concerns. Rather, community strengthens a sense of solidarity that demands individual acts of worship to translate into new meanings to provide motivations for men and women for the development of an ideal social order reflecting this-worldly and other-worldly prosperity.

To speak about Islamic functional secularity derived from public theology raises an important epistemological question: Whose version of Islam supports the phenomenological integrity of an inclusive public forum, leaving the privately and individually constituted conscience to determine its spiritual destiny without intrusion of any secular or religious authority? I do not intend to gloss over the diversity that exists among Muslim scholars about the special claims of Islamic revelation on Islam's adherents, societies, and those states that claim to be founded upon Islamic political values. To determine what Muslims must hold to consider themselves legitimately tolerant about the special claims of the Islamic tradition on individuals, societies, and public order, it is important to recognize the diversity of Muslim religious appropriations for public discourse. For the purposes of this chapter, I will identify three variable categories of Islamic tradition that appear to be prevalent in the community at large.

First, Islam as a civilization and its influence as a culture throughout the regions of the world where it spread as a religious tradition. As one of the most highly successful civilizations and major global cultural traditions, Islam is acknowledged as an influential component of a political order founded upon justice and inclusive spirituality. As a world-embracing tradition, it inspires and sustains a public theology based on concern for others. It continues to motivate moral conduct through its normatively founded emphasis on equality in creation, thereby establishing norms for the universal human cultural heritage. As a significant force in shaping the presuppositions of universal world civilization and as a cultural tradition that has shaped and adjusted its own moral understandings in different social and political environments, this Islam seeks guidance from its own history. Consequently, it can critically evaluate its own heritage in regard to the rights of religious minorities and the place of women in society, being guided by its own experience in history and general progress in moral reflection. This genre of Islam seeks to avoid raising historical contingencies to the status of authoritatively normative models and accepts the role of time and place in interpretive relativism as part of general progress toward relevant appropriation of Islamic beliefs and practices.[7] Indeed, by stepping back from many of the traditional cultural prohibitions (empowerment of women in general, including the licitness of their assuming public roles, and other related issues), as well as by not insisting on literal adherence to traditional Islamic notions (the doctrine of predetermination, submission to authoritarian rulers for the sake of avoiding the greater evil of dissension and chaos), this form of Islam tends to reduce the judicial and the dogmatic to the mystical (different forms and orders of Sufi affiliations and communal celebrations), to cultural public rituals (fasting for Ramadan and other festive public celebrations), and to well-staged public rituals (Friday and Festival worship attended by rulers and public officials and, now, the annual pilgrimage to Mecca, as a show of Muslim unity and power in the divided world of nation-states).

Second, Islam as a religion and philosophy for humankind. Islam, in this sense, is acknowledged as possessing the fullness of God's revelation to humankind, offering unique insight into the importance of God's merciful justice and concern for humanity. Though the revelation is particularistic and addressed to a specific community in a specific language, the grounds for moral conduct and substantive moral discernment are available to all human beings through their natural constitution created by the almighty and all-compassionate God. Since a good moral life is taken to be a sufficient condition for attaining this-worldly and otherworldly prosperity (*falāḥīya*), Islam does not regard itself as the only repository of human salvation, and, in this sense, it cannot make exclusivist claims (e.g., the claim that Islam is the privileged way to the divine truth and salvation). Furthermore, because ethical knowledge is grounded in human nature informed by intuitive reason, Islamic morality shares moral sensibilities with all other human beings equally endowed with that divinely ordained nature (*fiṭra*). Islamic morality develops its moral principles guided by conventional wisdom and moral insight discerned by living with others in society. Strictly speaking, this form of Islam has no peculiarly Islamic morality, only a special ground or motivation for moral conduct disclosed through revelation (e.g., "instituting the good and preventing the evil" and the reward and punishment for acting against the divinely ordained natural constitution).[8]

The underlying thesis of this genre of Islam is that because the rationality of Islamic ethics is held to be the same rationality shared by moral secular viewpoints, this Islam shares in the general secular progress in moral insights that advance religious insights as being compatible with public reason. Since this genre of Islam affords centrality to the overlapping consensus in the matter of moral commitments that not only affect communal bonds but also advance intercommunal relations in the public forum, the moral premises and rules of evidence are culturally inclusive and capable of advancing received moral commitments for the public good.

Third, Islam as the unique and exclusive experience of the Truth. This genre of Islam is popular among Muslim seminarians. Islam, according to this account, is the only complete revelation of God to humankind. Islam offers not only a special motivation for moral conduct, but the full content of the religious life which, if properly lived, could lead to salvation. In order to be saved, one needs the right belief, which should precede right conduct. Living a good moral life for virtue's sake is recognized as insufficient for salvation, in that salvation requires obedience to God's revealed guidance. Human prosperity in this world and the one to come is achieved by bringing the world to affirm what is disclosed by revealed reason, not merely that disclosed by secular reason acting independently of divine guidance. Moral progress is achieved insofar as secular morality comes to conform to religious morality (e.g., by instituting the good and preventing the evil as required by the Sharī'a). This account of Islam is exemplified by what I have identified in this work as traditional Islam.

This traditional Islamic perspective appreciates that moral theological truth is the result of neither sensory empirical evidence nor discursive reason. Truth as a rightly ordered relationship with the transcendent God is beyond discursive rationality. As a result, its traditional commitments cannot be brought into question by supposed moral theological progress grounded in developments in philosophical and metaphysical reflection.[9] Finally, this traditional form of Islam recognizes the external forms of religious practices—the rituals—as secure and sufficient means to affect salvation without any need to relate them to moral progress of the individual or the community.

These three categories are not in any sense exhaustive. They simply enable the reader to understand the source of religious conflicts in the Muslim world when it comes to limiting or delimiting religious discourse in Muslim societies. When it comes to neutrality requirements for public discourse, it is the third genre, the traditional perspective, that poses the most significant threat to the public forum that aspires to bind persons apart from any religious commitments. More to the point, in the context of this study, in order to advance the human rights regime in Muslim societies there is a need to sit in dialogue with the kind of Islam that regards religious considerations as critical in shaping the public forum and its discourse. The dominant culture of human rights advocacy is that of secular liberal agnosticism, which is marked by an affirmation of the priority of liberty as a value, as well as by an affirmation of equality of opportunity as a central societal goal. In the public forum, as Rawls argues, reasons, considerations, and interests must be articulated in general secular terms involving no claims to special knowledge (supernatural revelation, for instance) or transcendent considerations like God's will in the Sharīʿa, so that, as discussed in chapter 4, the demand for women's human rights may not be viewed as a deviation from God's established tradition.

The aggressively secular public order that requires all spheres of life, private and public, to exclude public reference to religious grounds not only asserts control over discourse in the public forum, but also aspires to neutralize religious discourse by recasting its substance into moral commitments materially equivalent to those of secular morality so that it will no longer pose a particularist threat to the universalist aspirations of the secular agnostic morality. This project, as Morsink has shown in the context of the writing of the Universal Declaration of Human Rights, has deep roots in the Enlightenment's commitment to setting aside ecclesiastical power and irrational religious particularity.[10] It is important to keep the context of the demand for public reason for building an overlapping consensus in the public sphere. Obviously, it cannot achieve that consensus in a religiously pluralistic society without transforming religious discourse into an expression of appropriate reciprocal human relations, morally normative through inculcating in persons citizenship that ought to give rational explications to each other for their chosen course of action.[11]

Accordingly, the goal of secularity in Islamic tradition is to broaden the scope of traditionally exclusive claims of a privileged status and access to moral and metaphysical truth. In this sense, Islamic revelation regards religion, morality, and community as working in unison to advance an individual to recognize that through creation morality becomes grounded in universal intuitive reason geared to reflect discursively to access reasons for one's beliefs and actions. From its inception, as discussed in chapter 3 on the Islamic theory of natural law, Islam shaped its public discourse by grounding its morality in critical rationality that sought a correlation between revelation-based and rational premises to forge an important doctrine that religious and secular reasons are not at odds when it comes to determining the public good. Unlike Christians, who as citizens in modern liberal societies must separate themselves according to the demands of secular rationality not grounded in Christian tradition, Muslims could and did articulate their public discourse with reference to reciprocal religious and secular reasoning as citizens.[12]

Universality of Human Rights and Group Rights

In a number of cases, ideas of the universality of human rights have run aground on the particularity of local traditions and practices. In many contemporary moral and political debates, the influence of Enlightenment secular rationality continues unabated, requiring of modern societies that claims made in the public forum be fully grounded in reasons comprehensible to all. Consequently, claims based on a specific religious doctrine requiring a privileged grace, revelation, or cultural insight, if not grounded in empirical experience open to all, are excluded from the public discourse in conformity with the requirements of valid reasoning. However, the question arises whether such an exclusion of religious reasons from the public sphere solves the problem of the arbitrariness of secular moral rationality. All through human history one can observe that morality for any group of people is simply that which its moral community, whether religious or secular, endorses. Taking the modern Muslim juristic discourse in the context of militant and violent expressions of religiosity among extremist groups, one can observe with much dismay the dynamics of religious justifications gone awry. Some Muslim preachers, for instance, have endorsed and provided justifications for carrying out the morally and religiously forbidden act of suicidal bombing of civilians, without any regard to the ethical issues related to individual and group rights to security and safety.[13]

It is difficult, if not impossible, to provide a rational foundation or justification for one group's particular views as a means of coming to terms with moral diversity. The debates in France over the wearing of the headscarf in government-funded schools, or in Milton Keynes in England over separate schools for boys and girls for Muslim communities, reveal the collision course in the public assessment of what is a universally reasonable rational foundation that can speak to all communities. Moreover, these events bring to light the complexities between individual freedoms and group rights in Western liberal democracies. More pertinently, in many countries in the Middle East, including so-called "secular" Turkey, certain religious practices, like wearing the headscarf, have become a symbolic rejection of Western cultural domination of the Muslim world. More than often the younger women, in many cases daughters of an earlier generation of accommodating and secularizing elites, have embraced the headscarf as a protest against the marginalized sources of native cultural institutions and consumerist homogenization of culture and lifestyle represented by Western ideas and values. Indeed, it is not all that clear that the ideas of individual rights or the distinction between private and public domains have the same resonances and significations in other cultures as they do in the West. Appeals to public rationality have, in many cases, turned out to be appeals to secular Western forms and ways of life asserted to hold universal convictions of most contemporary, educated men and women, without any reference to their religious commitments and responsibilities.[14] It goes without saying that the argument about universal moral rationality is made not from a timeless understanding of rationality, but rather from a particular understanding of proper, common governance embedded in a dominant appropriation and confirmation as normative and universal.

The French law banning "ostentatious" religious symbols, including Muslim headscarves in public schools, underscores the need to take a fresh look at the so-called universal public discourse based on political liberalism that claims to base its evaluation of the social and political influence of religion in general, and lately of Islam in particular, on whether it could support and lead to a "political conception of justice that we hope can gain the support of an overlapping consensus of reasonable religious, philosophical, and moral doctrines in a society regulated by it."[15] Particularly problematic for international human rights law are religiously based Muslim states that condition their acceptance of the Universal Declaration of Human Rights on compatibility with the human rights norms with the group identity preserved in the Sharīʻa. It calls for reforming communal institutions, even if their members are committed to living peaceably with those who peaceably affirm opposite moral visions. The fair terms of social cooperation between citizens characterized as free and equal yet divided by profound doctrinal diversity requires that all citizens are afforded measures ensuring adequate means to make effective use of their freedoms without encroaching upon similar rights of others. The case of denying "ostentatious" display of one's religious commitment in a public forum raises a serious foundational difficulty that it legitimates the use of state manipulation and coercion in order to ensure that persons are free not as they wish to be free, but as this particular conception of liberty holds they ought to be free.

Secular liberal democracies, not unlike some Muslim countries, present a serious threat with respect to guaranteeing the individual freedom of religion and freedom to express religiosity in the public sphere.[16] The headscarf controversy in France revealed the inability of France's liberal secular constitution to promote religious tolerance and pluralism. As Xiaorong Li has shown with much-needed sensitivity to human rights issues connected with individuals as well as minorities, liberal secular democracies need to pay attention to competing norms based on the priority of pluralism and tolerance.[17] The claims of secular moral rationality reach into all public speech and private associations. This totalizing character is advanced backhandedly in a notion of the reasonableness of secular liberal culture,[18] which heavily incorporates particular forms of social democratic ideals. In terms of these ideals, all social structures must conform to them by thoroughly reshaping their political goals without introducing doctrinal concerns in the public forum.

It must be acknowledged that certain actions that appear in the West as discriminatory and oppressive are viewed in a very different way by groups and communities in their own cultural contexts. Individual religious or cultural practices with moral ramifications are approbated in a communal consensus. The tensions between collective and individual interests have been overstated in liberal secular evaluations of individual freedom from collective constraints and sanctions. What is true for the public sphere is true for the community and for the individual social actor. Human rights face a lack of clarity and ability to mediate and denote moral values that are open to cultural relativism. The dichotomization of individualist and collectivist positions without defining the matrix of their connection in actual social existence has led to the blatant violation of human dignity of both individuals and minority groups by their governments.[19] In a number of countries around the world where ethnic, cultural, and linguistic groups are struggling to defend their freedoms against state power, the critical question for human rights advocates is how to mediate between the rights of individuals and the rights of groups within the broad framework of international human rights laws. While it is not difficult to condemn, for example, honor killings without any hesitation, as a violation of universal human rights, issues of family relations, marriage, divorce, education, and the legal status of the extended family demand more nuanced analysis of religious and cultural expectations in different communities.

The problem of contradictory injunctions is not difficult to ascertain between a purported standard of universal human rights norms and the diversity of human communities. At the same time, it is important to assert that these contradictions do not always result from a misrepresentation of local traditions, as some Muslim states are prone to claim. Real contradictions and tensions remain that are not always reconcilable. It is also a fact that sometimes making universal claims leads to denigration of particular beliefs and local practices. With the globalization of information and the increasingly interconnected nature of different peoples, the notoriety and relevance of these issues for the protection of human rights only grows from day to day. No culture lives in isolation within the boundaries of the nation-state. Global communication and global commerce implicate all peoples in the social relations of some far-flung regions of the world through commitments and responsibilities generated by the fact of our common humanity.

The Hegemonic Global Discourse in Human Rights

While the controversy over the "ostentatious" display of one's personal religious decision in the matter of headscarves looms large in its ramifications for a number of human rights articles in the Declaration, another critical and even more serious issue connected with women remains unresolved at the global cultural level. This involves the total well-being of those women who undergo genital alteration as part of their cultural and gender-related identities. Let me be clear from the outset that the issue of female circumcision has nothing to do with Islamic religious teachings, although some spurious traditions have been used in providing justificatory documentation for the practice. I raise the issue of female circumcision in this chapter to underscore the importance of recognizing the cultural autonomy of the groups who engage in this practice, which appears to Western observers as objectionable because it violates a woman's dignity and personhood and potentially endangers her health. The case of female circumcision presents one of the most transparent examples of the ways in which cultural globalization becomes the source of the distortion and stifling of local cultures that do not conform with the dominant liberal new world order that actually subsidizes the production of local cultures in its own image. While one cannot ignore such abominable practices as honor killing or widow burning as gross violations of a woman's personhood in some parts of the world, the case of female circumcision and its various forms requires a more nuanced understanding of the ways in which the global project of liberalism needs to be approached and critiqued. The underlying problem in this issue appears to be the universal rhetoric of human rights norms that seek adjudication and application of the norms across cultures without giving local cultures voices to challenge cultural globalization, whose rules have been fixed by wealthy nations of the North. According to Richard A. Shweder, the emerging rules of the cultural correctness game in connection with genital alteration have been fixed by the first world without fully accounting for "[t]he freedoms and constraints associated with the human search for meaning on an international scale and the conditions under which locally produced ideas, ideals and practices are created, perpetuated, exported or reproduced around the world."[20]

It is by now obvious that the single-standard approach, which is the foundational rhetoric of the Declaration, is not shared by those countries where such practices are part of the social or religious identification process of individuals in their collective life.[21] Advocating any policy that condemns the practice and calls for banning it because it violates women's human rights oversimplifies the issues connected with the abominable practice that may or may not serve any meaningful religious or social-economic purpose today. The international campaign headed by Western nations and those who receive both moral and financial support among local leaders and nongovernmental organizations to eradicate the practice is based on this oversimplified view of the practice as "an intolerably harmful cultural practice" or "an obvious and impermissible violation of basic human rights, or both."[22] The actual harm that results from the practice needs to be investigated within the broad positive or negative cultural role it claims to be performing, so that a cross-culturally persuasive idiom can be coined to deal with the empowerment of individual women to protect their right to accept or refuse to submit to the procedure.[23] The critical question that needs to be addressed for international adjudication in any such practice is the issue of whether tolerating a practice, in its acceptable forms, clearly violates the human dignity of a woman and her basic rights.[24]

The Autonomous Individual and Community

The issues connected with the cultural conflict in assessing the practice of genital alterations in different regions of the world raise the relationship, on the one hand, between universalism and cultural relativism, and on the other, between individual autonomy and communitarian ethics. One of the major problems facing the instruments of the human rights movement in Muslim societies is the debate about the absolute or relative character of certain individual rights and the overarching values upheld in the community (for instance, the right to impose communal moral standards). The problem becomes even more intensified when certain communal policies are viewed as nonconsensual in the sense that in the absence of democratic politics no individual participated in reaching that consensus. Group moral particularism favors pluralism for determining the rightness of an action (e.g., adoption of a headscarf, from a group's moral and religious perspective, versus a right to ban it from another group's evaluation of the practice) in a large number of issues in the public forum where one is faced with more than one morally relevant factor when assessing the adoption of a certain course of action. Accordingly, group rights advocates consider more factors than simply a general moral principle (individual claims to freedom of expression, gender equality, or cultural pluralism) as relevant in assessing a course of action. Moreover, it is important for the group to inquire whether a particular location in culture and history is the only source of authority for any claim for the group to insist upon individual conformity with what appears to be a violation of individual freedom guaranteed in the Declaration.

The universalism of human rights discourse founded upon every individual being entitled to certain rights simply by virtue of membership in the human community is in tension or conflict with the moral particularism of group rights that is opposed to making judgments guided by principles alone. To be sure, the declaration retained its foundational authenticity by adopting the natural rights thesis about the autonomy of individuals capable of exercising rational choice that included a capacity for moral discernment. Regardless of the historical problem connected with the origins of natural rights theories and their connection with distinctively Western civilization,[25] according to a number of human rights advocates, they engender a belief in the innate dignity of human persons that deserves to be protected from arbitrary incursion by the state or other coercive association.[26] The assertion of natural rights presupposed the autonomy of individuals capable of exercising rational choice. Hence, the rights rhetoric adopted in the declaration points to an individualistic rather than communitarian society. The protection of the autonomous individual from arbitrary encroachment by the state or other coercive association like a religious community, for example, was critical in the 1940s when the drafters of the international document opted for "the rights of man" to replace the phrase "natural rights," which fell into disfavor in part because of its link to the concept of natural law and its metaphysical foundation. Such an individual-centered discourse about the concept of rights is construed in many Muslim countries as disruptive of traditional social structures, which, ironically, also lead to authoritarian politics.[27]

The idea that there is some kind of inherent opposition between individual rights and group identity formation and subsequent claims to cultural pluralism cannot be sustained in view of the individual's connection with the group. The basic human rights norm that the universalism of the Declaration is geared toward—namely, the protection of individual rights "undefined by role and unconditional on status and circumstance"—in no way disregards the individual's familial and group connections. In fact, individual rights are legitimate claims or entitlements in the context of interpersonal reciprocity and responsibility. Consequently, the very process of group and family formation and the entire symbolic and expressive side of culture that rest on them (for instance, adoption of the headscarf connected with the relevant tradition that regards it as necessary for group dynamics), might be well-justified by reference to some set of collective human existence (right to freedom of association, freedom of religion, freedom of expression). It is this exercise of group rights that is in direct conflict with individual autonomy when a dominant group might refuse to allow a member of a minority to display group identity (e.g., wearing a headscarf) in the public sphere due to changing circumstances—the condition that is considered as an affront to the larger society and engenders provocative reaction, necessitating the minority to adopt prudential avoidance of asserting one's group identity in public. If human rights is an entitlement that derives not from status or circumstance, then individuality must be asserted at all times without any reference to any particular tradition or group that decides or elects to honor the things called rights. However, the group rights argument that the principle of equality of opportunity for citizens to exercise their rights, for instance, requires taking the pluralism argument seriously. Without equal respect for cultural traditions and religious affiliations embedded in group rights, the existing multiculturalism within the nation-states as well as internationally would be difficult to sustain.[28] There is hardly a region of the world in which there is no religious, cultural, or ethnic minority claiming respect and the rights of equality enjoyed by the majority. Nevertheless, taking the example of some extreme forms of cultural practices tolerated by the group that contribute to discrimination and mistreatment of women in honor killings or widow burning, their accommodation under pluralism claimed by the group, however small and limited in its influence, would certainly perpetuate inequality and serious violation of human rights.[29]

Although I do not agree with those who maintain that it is ontologically impossible to speak about objective inalienable rights that accrue to every one of us by the mere fact of our being created as human beings, I do concede that there is no single transhistorical or extracultural authority for the derivation of our moral sensibilities in the variable social and cultural contexts in which we live. As I have shown in chapter 3, cultural differences and cultural relativism are part of the meaningful moral realism in the Qur'an. The emphasis of religion with its particularist discourse on religious commitments and justifications for social action contests extreme forms of individualism that aim at setting an individual loose from communal, familial, and other social connections, thereby questioning the UN Declaration's stated goal of protecting individual rights against the claims of the group. Rights must have some locus, whether individual or group, so that human rights can be assigned to it. However, some group rights advocates, claiming to protect the legitimate rights of a people, have overlooked the problem of the denial of human rights to individuals, even within the group that claims to fight for the rights of each member of the collective body. In contemporary global politics, group rights is one of the four areas of international controversy over internationally recognized human rights. The concept of the individual human being as the primary locus of assigning human rights challenges the ideal of community that sees the individual, rights, and other social options as defined by group membership.

Sympathy for all human persons and a struggle against their abuse in any form has been part of this global commitment to uphold human dignity as the sole criterion for rights. Secularism sees society as transcending community in the way the universal transcends the particular. Accordingly, community is not a rational construct. It has imperceptible historical roots extending back to antiquity.[30] The essential feature of such communities is that one's presence in them is not a matter of choice, that is, one does not decide at a particular time to join such a community, even hypothetically. Human relationships in such communities are constituted more along the lines of status than contract, status inevitably being a matter of kinship.[31] Contractual societies, in contrast, are rational constructs that transcend the particularistic dimension of communities constituted by revelation. The subordination of different faith communities to the secularly contracted society has been regarded as an indispensable facet of democratic governance, which is based on inclusive and equal membership of all citizens regardless of their religious affiliation in their respective faith communities.[32]

Insufficiency of Autonomy for the Promotion of Rights

The Declaration presupposes universal morality by privileging an individual human ability to determine the rightness of one's action. However, with the paradigm shift that recognizes, in however limited a way, the reemerging centrality of community-oriented religious discourse in the public sphere, the secularist stress on human rights discourse can also unwittingly lead to the marginalization of faith communities and thus push them toward militancy, aggression, and separatism. Accordingly, the sociological distinction between a community and a society does not fully resonate with the Islamic paradigm of a religious-political society with its cosmic dimension that can be contrasted and compared with the secular model on the one hand, and the traditional religious community on the other. The essential feature of a Muslim community is that although it is based on religious affiliation derived from revelation, it functions as a comprehensive political society, presupposing the natural and legally constructed entitlements of those who live under its domination. Because of this all-encompassing ambition, historically, Islamic political society from its inception had to come to terms with functional secularity. This secularity signified a clear distinction between religious and political jurisdictions in its administration to accommodate religious pluralism and multicultural social reality within its dominions. In a unique formulation, the Islamic paradigm of a community was able to constitute the secular out of its own tradition of revelation, making it possible for future generations to postulate democratic governance based on the interdependence of the spiritual and the temporal to construct an inclusive political society. Nonetheless, it consciously preserved its unique particularity by claiming some kind of divine entitlement to lead and dominate other communities that lived within its territorial boundaries.

This exclusivist dimension of religious claims and the power they bestowed on the political authority to control dissension had undesirable impacts on individual Muslims' rights to negotiate their spiritual destiny without interference. A person could freely enter but could not leave the community in case of disagreement. Once a person entered the political community he or she was bound by its creed and practice, and leaving it was construed in theological terms of abandonment of one's relationship with divinely the ordained political order, which could become a source of threat to the community's security and well-being. This lack of individual freedom to determine one's religious affiliation is the source of tension because it signifies a rupture between the individual human person and the communal spirit of Islam.

Collective group rights and individual human rights seem to be at odds because of the restrictions imposed by the community on individual members in their relationship with those outside the community. In extreme cases, individuals have been coerced against their will to abide by the decisions of community leaders, which is clearly in violation of human dignity. In the Muslim collective consciousness, there has been a struggle to maintain the integrity of the community by downplaying dissenting voices of individual members and their right to determine the course of action in conditions that require serious moral assessment. There is a strong presumption in the Qur'an in favor of individual rights in certain areas of Muslim political life, even when their exercise threatens the integrity of familial or communal life (Q. 4:135). There are times when a group needs to go through transformation to rid itself of its objectionable attitudes and practices. If the free exercise of the human rights of its members can accelerate that process, then it will be the autonomous decision of the membership to force the necessary change. The decision on the part of Muslim women, for instance, to challenge the culturally sanctioned practice of female genital modification in some parts of Muslim world is such an exercise of individual human rights as a means to exercise individual autonomy to reject something that is deemed by that person as undesirable or harmful.

My argument is built on the prevalent attitude among traditional and militant religious leaders that can be labeled as community-centered religiosity in Islam. The Qur'anic evidence underscores the importance of the community for individuals' spiritual and moral development. But it also asserts the individuality of each human person in its conception of human–God relationships. However, as I want to demonstrate, the Qur'anic emphasis on human individual integrity and capacity to respond to the moral challenge of the Qur'an to create a just polity was overshadowed by the post-Qur'anic community's emphasis on collective identity under the political authority of the caliph or the sultan, to whom obedience was a religious obligation without any reciprocal recognition of individual rights under that authority. This tradition-based doctrine of unquestioning obedience to the ruler, just or unjust, without the right of the people to disagree or dissent, is one of the most insidious doctrines that suffocates any democratic politics based on an individual's right to dissent and assert his or her inalienable human right to conscientious objection. I do not intend to suggest that the adoption of the late-twentieth-century ideology of individualism, embodied in beliefs that people can control their own destiny, is the solution to this ethical dilemma in the face of oppressive existence of Muslim peoples. The power of community-centered theology is so pervasive that Muslim religious authorities have institutionalized status inequalities and religious disabilities to allow for legitimate disagreement to occur without cruel sanctions.

To be sure, community-centered societies exact punishment for nonconformity that violates fundamental human rights. The Islamic law of apostasy upholds capital punishment, despite the fact that the Qur'an with its doctrine of religious diversity does not endorse it. This difference between the Qur'an and post-Qur'anic tradition needs some elaboration. Let me reiterate my earlier argument in clear terms that the Qur'an favors individual rights in political life, which makes the absolute obedience to political authority in Muslim political thought an aberration of the Qur'anic conception of human dignity and integrity as a free moral agent.

Let me, then, turn to the Qur'an to identify its emphasis on the individuality of human personality, keeping in focus the tension between free human agency, with a self-subsistent moral cognition, and the theology of determinism, with its denial of human capacity to make right moral decisions without revelation and the authority that is behind its interpretive enterprise.

The Qur'an does not teach that humanity has fallen through the commission of original sin. But it constantly warns human beings about the egocentric corruption (*istikbār*) that can weaken the determination to carry out divine purposes for humankind. Human pride can infect and corrupt undertakings in politics, scholarship, everyday conduct, and theology. The last is the most sinful aspect of egocentric corruption because it is done in the name of God. Pride in matters of religion corrupts the message as well as the adherent beyond reform. The devastating effect of this kind of corruption in an individual has social implications: such people impair their natural relationship with God, which functions as a constitutive principle for all social relationships among the creatures of God. The Qur'an reminds humankind that had it not been for their creation by God through a single soul, through whom He created the first human couple, the very source of human relations to one another, people would not have realized the greatest good of establishing interpersonal justice in their relations:

> Humankind, be aware of your duties to your Lord, who created you of a single soul, and from it created its mate, and from the pair of them scattered abroad many men and women; and be aware of your duties to God [through whose relationship] you demand one of another, and the wombs [that relate you]; surely God ever watches over you. (Q. 4:1–2)

The passage clearly establishes the mutuality and reciprocity in human relationships founded upon "the wombs" that relate human beings to one another and create in them the awareness of their duties to God, who demands justice in interpersonal relationships.

Who Determines the Common Good?

The debate about the common good has its origin in ideas about the highest end of human existence on the earth, whether it can be realized only through communal cooperation for the collective good, or through widely different and even irreconcilable individual interests. The debate also has its origin in the interface between communitarian and individual claims and obligations, in which overemphasis on one over the other might lead to violations of individual human rights or the collective good. Rights are a social practice that creates systems of obligations between individuals and groups to prevent atomistic egoism and balances competing claims of individuals and communities.[33] Communities see individual rights within the framework of group membership, whereas a secular-liberal vision of human rights, by contrast, sees group affiliations as largely irrelevant to the rights and opportunities that ought to be available to individuals. Individuals must be free to exercise rights, such as freedom of expression, belief, and assembly, in the context of specifically collective activities where the community must respect individual autonomy, whether that autonomy is exercised in private or in public or alone or in association with others.

Traditional religious authorities reject liberal notions of religious pluralism or democracy that empower individuals in asserting their rights to make their own decisions regarding religious and moral issues that are seen as nonconducive to preserving collective traditional values in public space. They have, accordingly, relentlessly attacked some forms of ethical pluralism, which, they believe, relativizes their claim to be the sole moral-religious authorities to provide authoritative judicial decisions connected with the public domain. What if, they ask, institutionalization of this kind of pluralism leads to questionable moral conduct in Muslim society? What role, if any, remains for revelation if divinely ordained ethical norms are reduced to any opinions that can be legitimately made part of public policy through a democratic process? More fundamentally, what is the utility of adhering to democracy if its emphasis on consensus building leads to the adoption of public policies that would result in the disintegration of Muslim familial and societal ethics?

These concerns do not in themselves appear frivolous when the point of reference in this kind of polemical discourse is the situation of individual moral conduct in liberal societies. Do Muslims want to import the problems that accompany visions of liberal human rights that are excessively individualistic and that promote moral relativism? In other words, the requirement of nondiscrimination that calls for toleration and equal protection of all individual moral-political decisions, even when disapproved by the community, lacks cultural legitimacy in the Muslim world. The international human rights—protective regime requires the collective body to adopt neutrality with respect to the exercise of human rights. Equal concern and respect is required for all political beliefs to avoid imposing disabilities on individuals based on disapproved behavior associated with the community.

The secular prescription of liberal democracies seems to suggest that religious toleration can be achieved only when the idea of freedom of conscience is institutionalized in the form of a basic individual right to worship freely, to propagate one's religion, to change one's religion, or even to renounce religion altogether. In other words, the principle of toleration is equated with the idea of individual freedom of conscience. Furthermore, secular moral rationality restricts the role of conscience to the domain of private faith, which is clearly demarcated from the public realm—hence the moral reduction of religion to morality. Whereas one has the freedom to choose between competing doctrines and pursue one's belief in private religious institutions, one is linked in common citizenry in public state institutions. The true human community is that of all persons bound implicitly by the constraints of rightly ordered rationality of the political structures. This is the secularist foundation of a public order in which, in pursuit of freedom of conscience, all considerations drawn from belief in God or other sacred authority in one's private life are excluded from the administration of public life.[34,35]

Islamic Paradigm of Group Rights

By now it is obvious that in order to advance the legitimacy of international human rights documents in the Muslim world, restricting religious discourse from the public forum will prove to be unproductive. In order to negotiate this critical legitimacy through foundational resources in Islamic public theology, I need to search for a logical linkage between individual and communal morality for the peaceable interaction of persons in associations and communities. Social space is meant to serve individual and communal interests in such a way that people can achieve social equilibrium through consensual politics rather than misguided morality or a perverse social order. In other words, religious considerations in their own terms can be advanced in public policies that affect the common good of all without any distinction. These considerations provide criteria to judge the implausibility of secular morality to form society into one community united around a particular conception and detailed exposition of justice, especially one that requires, among other things, the moral and political reformation of peaceable individuals, communities, and associations.

The Declaration is faced with the failure of secular moral foundationalism. Because of this failure, morality has fragmented into a plurality of perspectives so that no single authoritative and satisfactory secular moral understanding can be established as canonical by sound rational judgment. This state of affairs has had mostly negative implications for a reasonable understanding of the universalism of the declaration in Muslim societies. Muslim traditionalists have no hesitation in denying the declaration a legitimate voice in the Muslim public forum. Within a limited democracy in a number of Muslim countries, religious commitments can properly guide the decisions of citizens and political leaders to uphold the inherent human dignity and moral agency of all peoples of different faiths and ethnicity living within the state. However, compliance with a neutrality requirement that seeks to constrain expressing public claims and choices based on religious premises is problematical from a traditional Muslim perspective. Traditional Muslims have no reason to comply with a particular notion of public reason that demands religious claims be advanced in the pluralistic rationality of the public forum. Their refusal to comply with the neutrality requirement is based on the observation that just as there is no one universal religion, there is no transhistorical or extracultural authoritative source for moral obligations. Given the plurality of secular moral rationalities and meanings of reasonableness, there is bound to be a lack of clarity in secular accounts of morality, not unlike those that distinguish religious accounts from secular. In comparison, religious accounts based on acknowledgment of transcendence and realistic heteronomy have the plausibility of building moral consensus in advancing a united source in God for fragmented dimensions of morality—the source of universal norms of human rights. Traditionalist Muslim scholars have good religious reasons that speak to both secular and religious commitments for not only rejecting but vigorously resisting the totalizing demands of democratic politics to abandon cohesive familial and communal relationships in favor of extreme or corrosive individualism.[36]

More than any other group, it is the traditionalists who have resisted the Declaration's articles that deal with individual autonomy at the expense of collective Muslim identity and social cohesion. They see the document as morally disengaged from any enduring metaphysical framework, leaving humanity to struggle with ambiguities and uncertainties in the sea of conflicting intuitions regarding everything around them. It is important to draw attention to the intrusive collective Islamic discourse on moral intuitions, sentiments, hunches, and moral sensibilities in the public sphere, which at times surpasses secular moral rationality in clarity and influence. Muslim social-political commitments and participation in the public forum are based on a set of fundamental beliefs about the direction of human history and the potential for change in the human condition through the acknowledgment of the principle of unity (*tawḥīd*) of God and unity of the human community. The Muslim creed links this world and the next in such a way that faith becomes the essential medium for the comprehension of the norm that guides the collective life of socially responsible selves. Moreover, the socially binding character of the belief in transcendence transforms the act of commitment to a faith into a vision for the creation of a just social order. With common roots in the creed, the branches of revealed truth in the form of life conduct begin to form a single organism—a normatively conceived community—the *umma*.

Islam, as a systematic religion that propounds a set of beliefs and practices, embodies a public dimension in which the integration of the private and public spheres is grounded in the contract between two parties: the Muslims who emigrated from Mecca to Medina under the Prophet's guidance and the Medinan tribes. The political society that emerged through this contractual agreement did not originate so much from a formal acknowledgment of the Prophet's political leadership, but it resulted inevitably from his prophetic function. It integrated the tribal mechanisms of organization and decision making into a formal acknowledgment of belief in one God, on whose behalf Muḥammad, the Prophet of God, was speaking. The new community of the faithful did not simply transcend tribal society in its principle of organization, which was essentially founded upon kinship; it constructed the *umma* on the principle of equality among the believers. In the absence of a mediating religious institution like a church to represent God's claims, the community felt justified in insisting upon individual responsibility in constructing and maintaining an ethical order as a collective response to the Prophet's call of obedience.

The essential characteristic of the early community under the Prophet was its acceptance of not merely the moral demands of the revelation, but also the political leadership of Muḥammad himself. The historical experience of the community conformed to the Qur'an's requirement that leadership under the Prophet link the private individual conscience to the concrete relationships of the collective order. This linkage between a transcendent universality embedded in the human conscience and the particularity of interpersonal relationships of the community provided Muslims an opportunity to build the new social order demanded by God. The development of the individual's conscience was tied to social behavior. The Qur'an also established a new model of the communal order based on the autonomous individual agent newly freed from the past Arab solidarities of kinship and clan. And yet it was a community of faithful that formed the political society. It was exclusive in its religious impulse and collective in its communal outlook, in which group considerations took precedence over all other considerations. Individual rights were not a priority compared to other social policy considerations. As a matter of fact, the seeds of intolerance to political freedoms were sown in the classical age when the emerging political society was faced with internal dissent and had to respond by imposing severe punishments on dissenting members of the community, who were marginalized and socially excluded if not executed.

This negative transformation from the Qur'anic recognition of autonomous individual moral agency and the free exercise of religion to stifling communal control began as soon as the Prophet died in 632. As the initial Qur'anic model of political society moved from tribal to settled and agrarian cultures, the fusion of the religious and the political, which is structurally appropriate and indeed unavoidable in tribal cultures, created severe problems for the early Muslim empire. Muslims inherited some of their solutions to the problems of the interdependency of the religious and political realms from both the Byzantine and the Sassanian empires. Under both these imperial powers, some sort of differentiation of religious and political spheres was recognized as essential. This distinction did not eliminate the tensions between the spiritual and temporal realms but enabled the state to create a complex mechanism for resolving the inevitable power struggle between them. The state under the caliph experienced similar tensions and stood more as a mundane imperial power, no longer based directly on the Islamic vision of egalitarian spirituality and just social order. It was supported internally as well as externally by a particular complex of military and physical power that was partially supported, in turn, by the religious establishment.[37]

The de facto differentiation between the religious and the political was never accepted as fully legitimate. Muslim political thinkers from Māwardī (d. 1058) through Ghazālī (d. 1111) to Ibn Taymīya (d. 1328) increasingly tended to legitimate any political regime that would guarantee a modicum of protection to Muslim institutions by requiring people to obey them.[38] Political authority remained suspect not only to rural activists, who from time to time engaged in armed insurrection to replace a ruler with a more acceptable candidate, but also to urban ulema, who viewed political authority as a necessary evil to avoid political turmoil. In this situation, the state and the political realm in the Islamic world failed to develop an inner coherence and integrity. The state as a legitimate realm of thought and action, with its indispensable role for the citizen, failed to emerge. The religious establishment headed by the ulema played a major role in politically desensitizing the community through a theology of total submission to the rulers for the sake of maintaining the unity founded upon the tradition. The politically desensitized Muslim community, even though lacking any effective means of changing the unjust government, continued to express the only legitimate political self-consciousness in the society, and the role of adult Muslim believers, not that of citizens, was the only inclusive political role. The notion of citizenship—with its concomitant values of membership and participation in collective life, which played so important a role in the political development of the modern nation-state in Western Europe and North America[39]—was nearly absent in the Muslim world until it came into contact with European colonialism.[40]

The proposals offered by the religious elements in the Muslim community since the end of the last century are summed up as government according to the Qur'an and the Tradition (*sunna*). But what this might mean in particular social and historical situations has depended on each group's retrieval and interpretation of these two sources. The Qur'an is clear enough, but it was not an adequate guide to the day-to-day contingencies of autonomy and mutuality within the boundaries of modern nation-states. The crux of the problem lay in applying political terms of reference in these two foundational sources to the changed realities of a modern nation-state. Moreover, in the context of the secular international order, it was important to redefine the political mission of particularistic implications of the Islamic tradition. The context of the nation-state had imposed inevitable modification to a universalistic, comprehensive Islamic vision for a society of transnational and transcultural Muslims.

Buried under the traditional interpretations of Islamic revelation—the pretext of the established practice of the pious elders (*salaf*)—there lies the Qur'anic vision of individual dignity, personal liberty, and freedom from arbitrary coercion. That all Muslims ought to be treated on an essentially equal basis was clearly established through the Prophet's own treatment of his followers. The policy of discriminatory treatment of the non-Muslim populations under Muslim political dominance is traceable neither to the Qur'an nor the early community. Yet classical Muslim jurisprudence that deals with "conquered and subjugated peoples" and their legal status under Muslim political dominance explicitly dictates that non-Muslims cannot have the same rights, obligations, and liberties as Muslims. Hence, the traditional rulings provide no help in resolving the problems raised by modern political thinking about citizenship.

The value of the Islamic tradition as a resource for policy in the modern world still awaits intelligent articulation. The Islamic impulse toward a just society, which has expressed itself in every Islamic century, resonates powerfully with the needs of modern society. But the formalization of that ethical imperative in the vast body of the Sharīʿa, though it has succeeded in providing a rallying point for the unity of the community through the ages, has grown increasingly inflexible in the face of the major problems now facing Muslim peoples. Unfortunately, in the social and political context within which Islamic jurisprudence developed, the Qur'anic provisions about civil society were ignored; it was the post-Qur'anic precedents that became effective in the formulation of rulings dealing with non-Muslims in a Muslim state. The rethinking of this tradition must emanate from within the Muslim community and must proceed with unremitting honesty and integrity.

The Qur'an's vision for the Muslim community was founded on a new locus of social solidarity that replaced distinctions based on tribal allegiance. Each individual was now endowed with personal dignity and liberty as part of his or her *fitra*, standing in direct relationship with God, the Creator, the Master of the Day of Judgment. This unmediated relationship, this covenant between God and humanity, suggested a new autonomy and agency of individuals sharing a set of beliefs and ideological commitments to the transcendent power and authority of God:

> And when thy Lord took from the Children of Adam, from their loins, their seed, and made them, testify touching themselves, "Am I not your Lord?" They said, "Yes, we testify"—lest you should say on the Day of Resurrection, "As for us, we were heedless of this." (Q. 7:172)

This is the covenant regarding the nature (*fiṭra*) with which God created humanity, and the connection with transcendence that all humans are endowed with, which is presented as a proof of God's Lordship, of humanity's acceptance of that Lordship, and of its obedience to the divine plan for human beings.[41]

The *fiṭra*, then, is the Qur'an's model of individual human responsibility and shared moral commitment with which a Muslim society is to be established. The model also affords a glimpse into the Qur'anic notion of universal human identity, both social and individual, constantly engaged in a struggle to locate the self in the sphere of existence and of just relationships with other human beings. The struggle for achieving fundamental equality of all human beings before God, regardless of their creed or race, is part of the dynamic of the *fiṭra*. The function of the *fiṭra* is to provide moral direction to individual and social activity by interrelating this world and the next in such a way that human religiosity finds expression in the perfection of public order and institutions. The Qur'anic vision of an ideal order is not based on the separation of the private and public; rather, it is an integrated path that requires the perfection of both to render human struggle in this world soteriologically efficacious. In the integrated version of personal and public life, the Qur'an insists on individual freedom of conscience as the cornerstone of existence and faith as they relate to intra- and intercommunal life. Without the focus on autonomous individual conscience located in the *fiṭra*, it is difficult to gauge the strong impetus that the Qur'an provided to the social and institutional transformation from a tribal, kinship-based society to the emergence of a cosmopolitan community in which the nature of social and individual identity and meaning were determined by shared moral commitments (*al-ma'rūf*).

As pointed out earlier, the Qur'anic terms for social existence must be defined by the profound secularity of the *fiṭra*. By secularity of the *fiṭra*, I mean the this-worldliness of human nature in which, by its very creation, human *fiṭra* recognizes its limitations in matters that enhance religious life without becoming entangled in claims of the superiority of one path over the other except in objectifiable moral action. Accordingly, the *fiṭra* sits in judgment to determine the moral value of wordly human action but avoids judging the rightness or wrongness of human faith. And, although *fiṭra* has the capacity to relate and integrate individual responsibility with spiritual and moral awareness (*taqwā*), its divinely ordained mandate is to engage in ethical purification through moral awareness.[42]

The Qur'anic moral order was founded upon the moral behavior of each individual, who carries within himself or herself the potential for prosperity as well as corruption. And, although faith was the defining term of the normative order and of participation therein, in matters of coexistence among several faith communities it was personal morality, founded upon the dictum of "competing with one another in good works," that defined the ultimate human community. The Qur'an interweaves religious and civil responsibilities into an integrated pattern of human interaction and socialization upon which it built its unique version of a civil society.

Christianity developed the inherent split between the sacred and secular in a monastic ideal of radical withdrawal from the world, particularly the familial and political world, which was quite alien to the Hebrew Bible's way of thinking. Islam under Muḥammad made an extraordinary leap forward in social complexity and political capacity. When the political society that took shape under the Prophet was extended by the early caliphs to provide the organizing principle for a world empire, the result was, for its time and place, remarkably modern in the stress on individual commitment, involvement, and participation in shaping the destiny of the community. The effort of modern Muslims to depict the early community as a prototype of egalitarian participant nationalism is by no means an entirely unhistorical ideological fabrication.[43]

From Individual Integrity to Community-Centered Salvation

Let me now turn to the theology of community-centered salvation and its impact upon the development of the political and social rights of Muslim peoples. The main purpose of this theology was to neutralize the sense of outrage that people felt toward corrupt Muslim rulers and shift individual attention from demands of their reform or removal to an autonomous ideal community under the Qur'an and the Tradition. The process was gradual, but it was carefully crafted by the ulema, who, although in agreement with the public sentiment against the ruling dynasties, found regime change and the ensuing political turmoil far more dangerous to the survival of the community. This was the genesis of transformation of the Qur'anic emphasis on individual integrity and morality to a deceptive sense of salvation through membership in the community. This shift from individual to collective salvation could not have come about without inculcating an unquestioning submission to absolute political authority, the Imam, with whom, according to the Qur'an, the people will come in God's presence to be judged collectively.

The Qur'an spoke about both individual and collective final judgment when God will call people with their leader (*imām*):

> On the day when We shall call all human beings with their leader (*imām*), and whoso is given his record in his right hand—those shall read their record, and they shall not be wronged a single date-thread. (Q. 17:72)

However, community-centered salvation also required the ulema to centralize salvation by limiting it to only one of the several communities that had sprung up under various political leaders and Imams. In the absence of an ecclesiastical body who could speak on behalf of the entire community, Muslim jurists sought to gain the support of the rulers to uphold one school of legal thought as the official theology of the state, whose nominal head was the symbolic caliphate devoid of any real power. This process centralized disparate groups under the title of People of Community and Tradition (*ahl al-sunna wa al-jamā'a*), whose main spokespersons were the jurists under the patronage of the rulers, who depended on the jurists to provide them with religious legitimacy to exercise political authority over the community. Minority groups that refused to join the main community were either marginalized or forced to go underground. This laid the foundation of internal hostilities and intolerance toward dissension within the Muslim community. The history of Baghdad in the ninth and tenth centuries is replete with instances of intracommunal hostilities between the followers of different rites and schools of thought. Today, Sunnī-Shī'ite sectarianism and the violence generated by both sides' exclusive claims are very much entrenched in this centralized communal piety that has proven to be quite intolerant to minority claims to salvation.

There are two concepts at the heart of the theoretical and practical formulations about Islamic order that provide incontrovertible evidence about the political shift from individual to community-centered rights and responsibilities for creating and maintaining a just order on earth. Both these dimensions are important to understand the Islamic framework as well as ideological changes that have taken place in the Muslim world today. In Islamic order, which is inclusive of the private and the public, these two concepts are composed of the theoretical creed and political philosophy.

As a member of the community, an individual cannot claim obedience as his right. It is actually his duty. In contrast, obedience is the right of God, his Prophet, and those who are invested with authority. However, if obedience is the right of these authorities because of this investiture, then due to the fact that individuals in the community live under their governance it becomes a duty on them, a duty they cannot avoid to start with. As for disagreement, it is part of his or her right in the group that is formed around a well-defined creed and specific practice. But these two founding concepts, that is, obedience and disagreement, cannot be applied without restriction, since everything is implemented in accord with certain prerequisites, restrictions, and conditions.[44]

Islamic society emanates from an indisputable foundation, which is that the ruler's restraining power is an inevitable condition for the establishment of this society. Ghazālī, speaking about the absolute necessity of political power to manage human affairs, maintained that religious public order cannot be achieved without secular public order, which needs an *imām* (leader) who is obeyed (*al-imām al-muṭā'*).[45] Before Ghazālī, this opinion was already formulated in the juridical tradition where the necessity of appointing an *imām* who is obeyed was well established. To be sure, assertion of the importance of religious order was the first condition in such a society, but without political backing it was on its own sufficient. Forceful political power, hence, guaranteed the social-political legitimacy relying on the religious order for its rightness and its success. Nonetheless, this could not be accomplished except by means of just politics, which were formulated by Muslim thinkers in their works on the principles of governance,[46] and governance in accord with the Sharī'a based on the following verse:

> God commands you to deliver trusts back to their owners; and when you judge between the people, that you judge with justice. Good is the admonition God gives you; God is All-hearing, All-seeing. O believers, obey God, and obey the Messenger and those in authority among you. If you should quarrel on anything, refer it to God and the Messenger, if you believe in God and the Last Day; that is better, and fairer in the issue. (Q. 4:58–59)

Muslim commentators do not have a problem in the matter of obedience to God and the Prophet, since it is clear that the execution of God's commands and prohibitions is dependent upon obedience to the Prophetic practice. However, they have raised questions about the identity of and obedience to those "invested with authority." Who are they? While that question has entangled the political history of the Muslim empire, the other fundamental question that has occupied the jurists is the extent of the obedience to this third category. Is this obedience to those invested with authority obligatory under all circumstances and times? In other words, is there a right for a Muslim to dissent from this obedience and defy the authority of those invested with authority, and thereby endanger the unity of the community and its perpetuity under such leaders? If the rejection of obedience is legitimate, in what sense it is so?

Anas b. Mālik, one of the early and prominent associates of the Prophet, relates a tradition in which the Prophet advises Muslims regarding their rulers: "Listen and obey, even if a black slave with shaggy head rules over you!" In another tradition, the Prophet is reported to have said: "The one who obeys me obeys God; and the one who disobeys me disobeys God. The one who obeys the ruler (*amīr*) obeys me, and the one who disobeys the ruler disobeys me."[47] There are numerous traditions like these in which obedience to the ruler is linked to obedience to God and the Prophet, hence legitimating this political act through religious justification.[48]

The fact is that limitation on the absolute authority of the rulers was applied only in the situation of strife among the community members, whereas obedience was required in conformity with one's ability to obey at all times. Nevertheless, some traditions cautioned against claims that justified the duty of obedience to those in authority, while divesting the people of the right to dissent, thereby necessitating the estrangement of the ruled from the ruler in the event of the ruler demanding obedience in matters that led to the disobedience of God's laws. Obedience to the ruler was obligatory and effective as long as he did not command disobedience to God's laws, because there was no obedience in that matter. However, the prevailing state of affairs among the Sunnis from early times was to counsel the rulers on the one hand, and to discourage armed insurrection leading to civil strife on the other. By issuing a verdict against the people's right to depose a ruler even if he is wicked, Muslim jurists rejected the right to rebel against the ruler.[49]

This trend of silencing the individual's rights as part of one's religious commitment has continued in modern times. Instead of demanding reform of the ruler to comply with democratic politics, the religious establishment has ignored particular moral commitments in favor of authoritarian communal politics. Among the leading contemporary Sunni scholars, Muḥammad Saʿīd Ramaḍān al-Būṭī has reasserted the classical juridical vision regarding the ruler and the ruled without critically analyzing the rights language that is at stake in this political discourse:

> The Imam is the guardian over all matters that affect the generality of Muslims. It is for this reason that he is the guardian of all those who do not have a guardian. Therefore, his discretions in their affairs is conditional upon the assessment of the public good; that is, they do not become effective unless its public interest aspect becomes apparent. However, God has imposed a duty on the people to obey him with a view to this exercise of authority (*wilāya*) which he enjoys through investment, and which stands validated as long as he keeps in mind the good of the people and endeavors to implement it wherever necessary. In other words, obedience to him is not because of his domination (*siyāda*) which he enjoys over them; rather it is exclusively because of his efforts in implementing the people's general welfare and the people making it possible for him for ordering the good of the people through this investiture.[50]

The public theology that advocates obedience to the rulers, among both ancient and contemporary Muslim leaders, maintains obedience and prohibits armed insurrection as two important political strategies. In their communal life, Muslims must adhere to the public order validated by Islamic juridical tradition as part of their religious obligation. The right of any individual to oppose such power is undesirable, in spite of the fact that there is an explicit ruling prohibiting obedience to the government in the event of such obedience leading to disobedience of God. Yet this does not mean approval or endorsement of the wicked. As a matter of fact, denying the right to engage in armed insurrection did not mean negation of other forms of protest or passive resistance. Historical accounts dealing with Muslim political experience present a number of events of passive resistance, which resembles peaceful civil disobedience. There are situations of silence or reticence that in themselves publicize disobedience to the rulers. Passive resistance took many forms, including the refusal to work for these unjust governments, or visiting those in power, or reconciling oneself to persevere under their banner, or avoiding civil strife, or leaving the announcement of their opposition to these unjust rulers for the Day of Judgment. These attitudes and stances were matched with attitudes of those who are described by Ghazālī as "relentless in their religion" (*al-mutaṣallabīn fī al-dīn*) who in the political history of Islam represented "opposition power" that struggled against the hostile government and strived to attack it with weapons or secret revolutionary organizations. They justified their insurrection by means of particular claims or through traditions of the

Prophet in the vein of the ascetic Muslim leader in the eighth century, Ḥasan al-Baṣrī (d. 728): "The best martyr of my community will be a man who stands up to an unjust ruler and commands him to do good and forbids him from doing evil, and the ruler kills him for that. Such a person is the martyr (*al-shahīd*). His station in the paradise will be between Ḥamza and Jaʿfar [the Prophet's uncles who were killed in the battlefield]."[51]

This well-known dissenting force in history did not become obsolete with the end of the classical age of Islam. It has emerged once again in the modern period among militant Muslim movements. These movements have taken the duty of preventing evil to its extreme, not limiting it to tongue and heart; rather, they have taken it to the use of force as it had become in the early period, following the advice regarding the duty of preventing evil that says: "Anyone among you who sees evil should change it with his hands, that is, by force; if he cannot, then with his tongue; and if still he cannot, then with his heart. This is the weakest expression of the faith."[52] This did not shackle coerced obedience or passive disobedience and prevent civil strife and seclusion. It simply maintained limits over revolution and armed insurrection.

To summarize: obedience to God, the Prophet, and those invested with authority is obligatory. There is a difference of opinion on its limits and actual manifestation in society. This is captured in those traditions that describe the legitimacy of the power that is used by the government to coerce obedience. However, any person who is compelled to submit to this authority is conceived as the possessor of rights—some natural and some legal. As for an individual's natural rights, they are related to capacity (*al-istiṭāʿa*), since if obedience to God, the Prophet, and those invested with authority is the goal of religious commitment and responsibility, then this can be attained as long as that individual has the capacity to obey. Naturally, this capacity is potentially responsible for the totality of principles and rules that enable a person to bring about the fulfillment of the duty of obedience. In this connection, investigation of other aspects of Islamic religious-ethical thought is indispensable. These include the question of justice; the principle that rejects the imposition of obligation beyond one's capacity; the condition that the government or the ruler or the one invested with authority are bound to obey God and the Prophet, that is, the ordinances of the Sharīʿa; and so on. Since these conditions cannot be fulfilled, repudiation of obedience, insurrection, or armed resistance become legitimate solutions, and implementation of human rights becomes possible. This means that lack of commitment on the part of the ruler or the government to implement God's rights and the rights of people or citizens, as treated in the details of the books dealing with the principles of governance and social management, leads directly to the right of an individual to dissent and to oppose, as a legal-moral necessity.

Obviously, as the principle of correlation demands, if obedience is treated as a duty then its opposite—that is, dissent—must be regarded as a right. However, community-centered theology does not treat dissent as any kind of intellectual disagreement. It treats it as a social and political threat to the well-being of the entire community. Its religious integrity is elusive, since it is treated as a moral-civil offense with sanctions that clearly violate individuals' human rights to free exercise of religion. This is one of the fundamental problems in the classical tradition, where dissent is treated as an evil act requiring restraint by political authority. This problem also extends to apostasy, which, if treated as a purely religious offense, according to the Qur'an, does not merit capital punishment. Human courts have no jurisdiction over such cases, which strictly fall under the human–God relationship. But, if this expression of personal freedom in choosing one's religious community becomes translated as a political act of repudiation of one's communal affiliation, then the punishment for it clearly leads to a human rights violation. I will come back to the problem of treating apostasy as a civil offense in the following chapter on freedom of religion.

Concluding Remarks

In the Islamic tradition group rights are based on the notion of religious duty to obey God, the Prophet, and those invested with authority. Obedience to the rulers is conceived as a major source of communal unity and its integrity as a religious body. Individual rights are consequently subsumed under the ideological concerns of the preservation of the political unity of the community. Such ideological considerations lead to unavoidable differences in evaluations about human conditions that are sometimes responsible for coercion and repressive politics in the Muslim world. Authoritarian politics in Muslim societies are at the root of disagreements based on variable interpretations of Islamic revelation about individual moral agency in the context of collective restraints in place in Muslim societies. These restraints, as interpreted by the ulema with their commitment to "group salvation," require individual members to assess their own claims to human rights in the interest of group rights as part of their faith, which requires them to conform to the divine commandments.

The tensions between religious group commitments and desiderata, and secular human rights, with its emphasis on individualism, are real. An exclusive particular communal system that forged the group's identity as the bearer of the religious truth in a different social-political order is in direct conflict with the universal human rights discourse. The most formidable challenge to the universality of international human rights stems from this exclusively formulated relativistic approach to human rights. Muslim groups remain the staunchest advocates of group rights and voice their concern about the self-centered individualism of the secular human rights document that is insensitive to Islamic familial and societal values. By concentrating on group solidarity that smacks of some kind of "tribalism" in the name of Islamic "unity," they have unwittingly endorsed authoritarian politics in Muslim societies. The politics of religiously justified "obedience" to those "invested with authority" for the sake of imagined "unity" has occurred at the expense of the full development of democratic constitutionalism that supports the human rights of all citizens as equal right-bearers regardless of gender, race or creedal differences. The rights-based discourse offers an opportunity to the traditionalists in the Muslim world to engage Islam's complicated and contradictory relation to the principle of the inherency of human dignity and individual moral agency. Without a very particular understanding and reading of the Islamic heritage of the modern idea of the autonomous self, properly anchored in a transcendent and otherworldly sphere but essentially of this-worldly interests and aspirations, it will be challenging to sit in conversation with the secular advocates of a morally self-regulating individual freed from the collective restraints needed for the smooth functioning of public order.

6

Freedom of Religion and Conscience

The Foundation of a Pluralistic World Order

As I begin to conclude this study, I need to clarify my position as an insider and outsider academician. As an insider to Islamic tradition, I face specific challenges to my inherited perspectives and allegiances. The major challenge for me is to step outside my own community to explore other vocabularies and how notions of value are understood by other communities. In my initial research on the topic of freedom of religion and conscience in my earlier work, *The Islamic Roots of Democratic Pluralism* (2001), I found that I was confined to and even trapped in familiar and conventional concepts of the Islamic juridical tradition, unable to expand the horizons of the possible and desirable interpretation that was sometimes implicit and at other times explicit in the Islamic revelation. As an ethicist I sought relevance to, rather than radical departure from, the normative Islamic tradition. I endeavored to seek the approval of the community reassuring it about the significance of Islamic tradition rather than challenging its gross misunderstanding of the pluralistic impulse of the Islamic revelation. Under the burden of my ties with the Muslim religious establishment and the gratitude I owed to my teachers in the seminaries in Iraq and Iran, I constantly struggled with these debts, which seemed to demand compromise of my ethical stance when it came to offering honest criticism and proposing alternative readings of the scriptural sources. I was faced with the risk of becoming insufficiently and improperly impartial to my ethical responsibility to make an incontrovertible case for the freedom of religion in the Qur'an.

Without the recognition of religious pluralism as a principle of mutual recognition and respect among faith communities, and without affirming the identification of religious morality with moral rationality of public discourse, I believe that the community of nation-states is faced with endless violence and radical extremism propelled by an uncompromising theological stance in the matter of exclusive religious truth and perspectival rather than objective morality.[1] Whereas I have throughout this work taken up the challenge of endorsing the universal morality that undergirds the Universal Declaration of Human Rights and have sought to demonstrate that Islamic theological ethics holds enormous potential to support the foundational principles of universal moral law, the problematic of exclusivist theology that undermines this universality remains to be unpacked. In my assessment, both moral relativism, in the sense of subjective and perspectival morality that suffocates universal moral principles, and exclusionary theology, can undo any progress toward world peace with justice.

Having observed and participated in some of the international forums to construct bridges of understanding between and within different faith communities, I can assert without any reservations that the impending danger to a human rights regime will come from both moral relativist arguments and exclusionary theological doctrines. On the one hand, moral relativist arguments are self-defeatist, in the sense that the moment cultural relativism enters human rights discourse, they unwittingly endorse human rights violations as acceptable in the context of their own particular cultural valuation of human dignity. As I have shown in several places in this study, Muslim societies have suffered from certain social and cultural practices that have been justified on relative cultural grounds: "We are different!" The faith communities, on the other hand, regard secular human rights discourse as yet another ploy to exclude peoples of faith in formulating the terms of inclusive, universal moral discourse. More important, they disapprove of the secular demand to speak about a reasonable pluralism of those comprehensive religious and moral doctrines that are consistent with the requirements of a social democratic understanding of public order. In fact, the traditionalists among them regard religious pluralism as incompatible with the uniqueness of their exclusive experience of truth. More poignantly, they reject any religious understanding of universal morality without first recognizing that a necessary condition for the acceptance of such common moral terrain is possible through its disclosure by the revelation from God that sets the terms of the correlation between the premises of religious and secular reasons for human moral growth.

For the last thirty-five years I have observed the emergence of interfaith dialogues, and have even participated in some of them, as a way of forging intercommunal understanding and tolerance of the differences that exist between world religions. These differences, even as they appear irreconcilable, are an indispensable part of each community's unique collective identity. No community, however enlightened, is willing to abandon its unique religious identity and its claim to salvation. Interfaith dialogue, in my opinion, has essentially remained political-academic without much impact on ordinary believers' negative perceptions about the religious other. In the post-911 political-religious climate as if to underscore its irrelevance to traditional Christians or Muslims, who recognize no grounds to comply with neutrality requirements based on the idea that there can be several kinds of religion leading to one true God,—the dialogue has been formally appropriated for political and diplomatic ends among some nations, with religious or secular constitutions. The real goal of the dialogue, namely, of bringing peoples of different faiths to "a common word" among them remains far from being fulfilled. "A Common Word" is the Qur'anic phrase that calls "peoples of the Book" to unite in the worship of One God as "a word common between us and you, so that we serve none other but God, and that we associate not aught with Him, and do not some of us take others as Lords, apart from God" (Q. 3:64). Iran and Saudi Arabia come to mind immediately as examples of the countries that claim such a dialogue as part of their international efforts to promote tolerance of other religions. Ironically, besides their formal participation in some officially organized dialogues that have continued to take place under different international sponsorships, their record of human rights violations in the matter of free exercise of religion, and their patterns of discrimination, intolerance, and persecution remain to be improved.

The universal morality and the inherency of human dignity that empowers individual human persons to exercise the right to freedom of thought, conscience, and religion has not received full recognition in the traditionalist scholarship on freedom of religion in the UN Declaration. In some recent works on Islam and human rights, some Muslim jurists have begun to address and reconsider the juridical perspectives on apostasy and the right of a Muslim to sever his or her relationship with the community by converting to another religion. Some of the recent rulings in the matter of apostasy have critically undertaken to reexamine the precedents that provided the justificatory documentation for the harsh treatment meted out to apostates in the Sharī'a. Since the death penalty is deduced on the basis of the traditions rather than the text of the Qur'an, where one's rejection of Islamic faith after having accepted it is regarded as a sin against God, these scholars have ruled against it and have consequently regarded the issue as beyond the jurisdiction of the Muslim state.[2] Among the leading jurists in Iran, for instance, Ayatollah Muntaẓirī has upheld the right to freedom of religion and change of religious allegiance.[3] However, the majority of the jurists in the Muslim world continue to affirm the traditional rulings in this matter and, at least theoretically, maintain the validity of the classical formulations regarding apostasy.[4]

Areas of Conflict between Human Rights Norms and Islam

The requirement to abide by religious and metaphysical neutrality in the public sphere is at the heart of all public claims regarding consensual politics to ensure constitutional democratic governance. Such a requirement excludes making moral and metaphysical claims bearing on political choices in terms of specific religious doctrines and commitments that in principle cannot be affirmed by all citizens, irrespective of their religious beliefs. The theoretical presumption of the Declaration, to be sure, is constructed in terms of the neutrality requirement in the public domain so that human rights norms find their cross-cultural application in the secular mode of morality without any reference to revelation or religion. This presumption about the normative universality attached to the Declaration is rejected by Muslim traditionalists, who assert the right of individuals and groups to voice their religious commitments in the public sphere. The latter aspect of traditionalist public theology is also a major source for deep-seated suspicion of modernity and its adverse ramifications for the sacredness of the revealed texts that function as the foundation of traditional legitimacy. When revelation-based political systems such as Islamic governments in Iran or Saudi Arabia are asked to evaluate their compliance with the Universal Declaration of Human Rights and the secular norms that undergird it, they discern an oblique threat to their faith-based social-political system that must comply with democratic politics. By doing so, they believe, they will end up denying a public role for Islamic norms. In the seminarian assessment in Muslim centers of traditional learning, modernity and democracy are construed as major threats to the Islamic revelation and the Sharīʻa-based governments it supports.

Taking the case of freedom of religion, for example, one can detect three major areas of differences related to international human rights norms of freedom of religion and the Islamic juridical tradition in the context of diverse Muslim cultures: first, freedom of the individual to choose a religion other than Islam, of which he or she is a member; second, the relationship between Muslim political authority and religious belief and whether the state has the right to enforce religious beliefs and considerations; and third, the irreconcilable claims of the exclusive and final Islamic truth and its implications for intercommunal and international public order. From an Islamic juridical perspective, the first area of difference dealing with conversion leads to ascriptions of apostasy, heresy, and promotion of religion or belief and proselytism that impact negatively upon community-centered salvation in Islam. The Islamic laws of apostasy are totally at odds with human rights articles and their insistence upon every human being having the right to freedom of thought, conscience, and religion, which includes the right to change religion or belief. The second area of difference raises the implications of the state—religion relationship for the rights of religious minorities in Islamic states where a Muslim majority claims a privileged relationship with the state, and where the state and religion are intertwined to create a national religion with special considerations in imposing its values in the public square. The third area of difference between Islamic tradition and universal human rights standards is associated with the relationships among different faith communities when Islamic doctrines of superiority and exclusivity impinge upon the essentially pluralist nature of modern nation-states and their commitment to international human rights standards based on neutrality in matters of religion and belief.

In Islamic tradition, there is a tension over whether human beings are endowed with the natural capacity to choose and act or whether all their actions are predetermined by God. The basic argument in relation to the freedom of religion in Islamic revelation and pluralism, in the specific meaning of various spiritual paths to divine truth, is that the revealed texts capture the real experience of the early community struggling to regulate the relation between tolerance and the exclusive truth claim that provided the people with their unique identity among communities of faithful. The guidelines that appeared for promoting religious tolerance and freedom of religion in the classical texts remain to this day part of the justificatory documentation for interfaith relations. There are differing, and often conflicting, interpretations of these normative documents that address the question of religious diversity, disbelief, and its negative and even damaging consequences for the spiritual and moral well-being of humanity. It is worth keeping in mind that the essential element in the above-cited three areas of disagreement between Islamic tradition and international human rights is exclusionary theology and its implications for the freedom of religion article (Article 18 of the Declaration), which promotes the individual's autonomy to determine their spiritual destiny without any interference from the religious or political establishment. To put it differently, pluralism as a distinct feature of the multifaith and multicultural global community is at odds with the traditionalist community's sense of the uniqueness and superiority of its religious tradition and its community-centered salvation that refuses to grant individual believers autonomy and freedom to determine personal faith. From the traditionalist point of view, what appears to be a predicament for religious-minded people is that while the Declaration supports the individual right to believe what one wishes regarding the implementation of divinely ordained norms and values, it does not endorse the freedom of one's decision to act upon one's convictions. This contradiction is not so much in Article 18 as it is in its implementation within those states with a Muslim majority. According to these religious scholars, while the Declaration, on the one hand, upholds the freedom to believe and to manifest one's belief in practice, on the other, it evaluates religiously inspired political activity negatively, perhaps even as incompatible with democratic governance. However, what has been overlooked in this critical assessment of the Declaration is the possibility of an attempt to rethink the Sharī'a in order to bring it in line with universal norms of human rights and to account meticulously for extra-revelatory sources of international law that are based on a secular estimation of religious pluralism as a principle of coexistence and cooperation among various inter- and intrafaith communities. Muslim religious discourse on the subject of pluralism indicates that there is a vehement rejection of any notion that would take away the unique claim of Islam to be the only religion that is acceptable to God. In fact, both the Arabic *ta'addudīya* and the Persian *takaththur-garāyī* for pluralism are treated as foreign impositions on Muslim religious thought and, hence, are treated as lacking internal cultural legitimacy. But in fact many Western scholars of human rights, as I have shown, demonstrate the presence of religious arguments and convictions in the history of the rise of human rights. Indeed, at the foundational level and, more particularly, in affording the international document cultural legitimacy in Muslim societies, religious discourse is not only licit but indispensable for developing an appreciation of various forms of justificatory reasoning prevalent in global society in which a human rights regime must guarantee the rights to free exercise of religion.

In comparison to traditionalist exclusionary theology, Muslims with a modern education, who see their faith in cultural terms as an important source of their identity, have shown little resistance to complying with appropriate public discourse that does not deny the integrity of their religious identity and yet complies with the nonsectarian rationality that undergirds the freedom of religion article in the Declaration. Nevertheless, as my fieldwork suggests, even among educated Muslims there is no wholehearted acceptance of the culturally dominant secular morality of the West, which they believe undergirds the Declaration. The major problem at the international level, as I perceive it at this time, is the lack of conversation between traditionalist Muslim scholars and human rights advocates. The latter's strategy, to impose an aggressive human rights discourse that reduces faith commitments to the private domain and denies faith claims a legitimate voice in the public forum, inevitably backfires with the Declaration's outright rejection by Muslims as culturally insensitive to Muslim social values.

The aftermath of 9/11 has certainly put Islam on the defensive. The assessment of Islam's ability to forge peaceful coexistence is under greater scrutiny today in view of the rising tide of religious extremism and militancy in many sectors of Muslim societies that suffer social and political injustice. It is no longer possible to convince the international community that the public role of religion is desirable in building bridges between communities. And yet, the influence of faith communities in advancing human well-being and human flourishing, even if this advancement is robustly grounded in exclusive beliefs, cannot be ignored as politically infeasible. Although religions have traditionally inspired strongly particularistic loyalties with a domineering attitude toward both adherents and outsiders, the world order today needs to overcome this dominating feature of religion by encouraging a healthy diversity and pluralism within and among religious communities. Can this be achieved by disestablishing religion? Can disestablishment be realized without thoroughly privatizing religion and imposing secular neutrality on it?

My readings in the present militantly radical Islamic movements force me to be cautious in suggesting the secularization of Islamic tradition with its comprehensive doctrines that claim relevant application in all spheres of human society, both spiritual and temporal. Such a proposition to limit the role of religion to a private domain has the potential of its going underground and becoming the breeding ground for the radicalism and reactionary politics of Muslim extremism. In the Muslim world, modernist discourse is associated with an agnostic secular culture that defines the public forum and its discourse. It is culturally illegitimate to speak about the form of secularism that not only asserts hegemony over discourse in the public forum but also aspires to transform Islam into its image and likeness.

From its inception, Islam as a source for the spiritual and temporal life of its community has been directly involved in setting the purpose of government and regulating interhuman relationships in society. At the present time, with the weakening of the state's overall influence in directing the moral and political life of its citizens, Islam has once again stepped in to assume its critical role in providing the guidelines for an ideal public order. However, under its traditionalist interpreters, historical Islam lacks the conceptual framework to develop a modern notion of citizenship. Historical Islamic tradition has grown to be notoriously exclusive in its theology and discriminatory in its juridical tradition. Whereas the Qur'an treats the diversity of religions as a divinely ordained system, and the unification of all humanity under one confessional tradition as beyond any human power, the Islamic juridical tradition empowers Muslim governments to impose restrictions and discriminate against non-Muslim minorities by reducing them to second-class citizens.

The fundamental problem in establishing freedom of religion in Islamic tradition has been a lack of serious conceptual analysis to distinguish the strictly religious from the political. Muslim jurists were, more or less, aware of the two separate spheres of human activity in the realm of spiritual and temporal existence. Accordingly, they distinguished separate jurisdictions in formulating the spiritual in distinction from the temporal in Islamic jurisprudence. The human–God relationship, as part of strictly spiritual relevance, remains permanently beyond the reach of human institutions, including political power; in contrast, human–human relationships retain their secular relevance under the legal and consensual structure that must be accepted as part of one's reciprocal responsibility in all human institutions. This separation of jurisdictions in the Sharī'a could have served as the foundation of freedom of religion and conscience, which was beyond any human institutional control. Recovering this other path is what I have tried to urge in this book.

Traditionalist Engagement with Pluralism

In the last chapter I identified three variable categories of Islamic tradition that continue to exercise influence and shape the public forum and its discourse in Muslim societies. Essentially, Islam as a world-embracing tradition inspires and sustains a civilization based on a civil religion that embraces pluralistic ideas and concern for those who are not adherents of its creed and practice. This kind of Islamic understanding provides moral grounds that enable the faith community to establish relations with other communities. The second kind of Islam, which many modern Muslims find relevant to their situation of ever-shrinking national and cultural boundaries and the emergence of global universalism at many levels of their material and cultural relations with larger human communities, is guided by conventional wisdom and moral insights provided by one's participation in a plurality of communities under the dictum "Live and let live." The third kind of religious discourse encapsulates the unique and exclusive experience of Islamic truth that is based on the fundamental doctrine that human prosperity in this world and the next is restricted to adherents of the Islamic revelation. This kind of religious discourse does not take interfaith dialogue as an intellectual and sincere endeavor to understand the religious other as one's equal. Rather, it is taken as an opportunity to convert the "misguided other" to one's own tradition. Hence, it is viewed as a missionary work, not very different from Christian evangelical efforts to save the "pagan other."

This traditionalist Muslim discourse challenges the usefulness of interfaith dialogue, which is viewed with much suspicion and trepidation as nothing more than a compromise of one's own religious claims under foreign domination. However, its progress on the path of, at least, intellectual appreciation of other humans' faith is very much dependent upon internal dialogue among different schools of thought and sects among Muslims. More than the exclusive claims against other faiths, it is the internal understanding of the pluralistic theology of religions in Islam that awaits intelligent articulation with phenomenological integrity.

The phenomenological integrity of Islamic public theology is dependent upon the acknowledgment of the differences between traditional and modern perspectives on human nature, society, and the world at large. Such an analysis can illuminate the ways in which scriptural resources were retrieved and manipulated to justify one interpretation or another that impacted the reality of religious diversity in terms of interfaith relations or freedom of religion in Muslim societies. Both modernists and religiously oriented intellectuals fail to emphasize the fact that, in large measure, social and political history influences how people read and understand the revealed texts. Remarkably, different periods of Muslim history have generated different interpretations of the Qur'an in consonance with the social and political conditions that faced the community. During the heyday of the Muslim empire's political ascendancy, some Qur'anic passages were evoked to determine a tolerant attitude toward other faiths, and religious minorities enjoyed, relatively speaking, better treatment at the hands of Muslim administrations. In contrast, in the age of European political dominance over Muslim regions, the Qur'an and the Tradition have been searched and interpreted to provide justifications for armed resistance against non-Muslim powers and their representatives, and intolerance toward non-Muslim populations living among Muslims. This lack of awareness regarding the historicism of the normative sources in traditionalist Muslim scholarship leads to many misunderstandings and unjustified accusations about Muslims and their scriptures among non-Muslim powers. Such a historical retrieval of the revealed texts in traditional scholarship has become the major source of fears and concerns in the West that can easily be, and often is, transmuted into hatred and violence.

Recognition of religious pluralism within a community of the faithful may be challenging, but it promises to advance the practical principle of inclusiveness in which the existence of competing claims to religious truth need not precipitate conflict within religiously and culturally varied societies. In fact, although people always need to anchor themselves in one community so that they can forge long-term relations, in order to grow spiritually and morally they may not be confined to any one community in order to benefit or effect change in themselves or others based on the standards of another. Moreover, recognition of inclusive truth claims in other communities should encourage the development of a sense of multiple and unique possibilities for enriching the human quest for spiritual and moral well-being through participation in a plurality of communities, "the relation of which should be pictured as a series of partially overlapping circles, not as a series of wholly concentric circles."[5]

Religious pluralism, it is worth emphasizing, is not peculiar to the modern world of increasing interdependence brought about by the phenomenal technological advancement that has changed the way we think about the other. All religious communities have required the faithful to search for peaceful ways of dealing with comparable and competing claims of exclusive salvation in other faith traditions. In dealing with pluralism, Islamic tradition had actually found expression in the pluralistic world of religions, which it acknowledged and evaluated critically but never rejected as simply false. The major task confronting the early Muslim community was to secure an identity for its followers within the God-centered worldview on which different groups had claims. The community provided necessary instruments of integration and authenticity without denying other religious groups their due share in God-centered religious identity. The Muslim polity was founded on some form of inclusiveness in the public sphere to deal with the broad range of problems arising from the encounter of Muslims with non-Muslims living together. These historical and scripture-based precedents should lead contemporary Muslim societies to institutionalize pluralism without having to succumb to secularizing Islam and severing its connection to the transcendence founded upon God-centered pluralism. More pertinently, it should lead them to affirm the right of all human beings to freedom of religion and conscience.

The ability to accept or reject faith and to pursue an ethical life presupposes the existence of an innate capacity that can guide a person to a desired goal. This innate capacity is part of human nature—the *fiṭra*—with which God shapes humanity (Q. 91:7–10). This innate capacity encompasses the faculty of moral reasoning. Conscience in the Qur'an is connected with the source of ethical knowledge because its point of reference is human nature and its inherent ability to shape laws of conduct. Conscience, then, is a God-given ability to judge values and obligations. In this sense, conscience is a necessary locus of universal moral guidance. God has endowed human beings with the necessary cognition and volition in their nature to further their comprehension of moral truths. Moreover, the distinction between evil and good is ingrained in the human personality as a form of a prerevelatory, natural guidance with which God has favored human beings. It is through this natural guidance that human beings are expected to develop the ability to perform and judge their actions and to choose that which will lead them to prosperity without any fear of external sanctions, immediate or eschatological.

Guidance from God is an exaltation of the individual conscience as opposed to forcible, collective conformism; hence, the responsibility for the salvation of each Muslim lies in his or her own hands rather than in any religious authority. God provides a general direction, a spiritual predisposition that can guard against spiritual and moral peril (if a person hearkens to its warnings); this natural guidance is further strengthened through prophetic revelation. The Qur'an repeatedly shows the path to salvation to emphasize the fact that this form of guidance is universal and available to all who aspire to become godly and prosperous.

If the function of religious guidance through revelation is to provide precepts and examples to all men and women in worshipping God and in dealing justly with their fellow humans, then it presupposes an individual responsibility that flows from an inward stance, a "natural faith" that lies at the heart of any religious and moral commitment.[6] The Qur'an differentiates between formal submission to the sacred authority—which could become mere utterance of the formula of faith without any real commitment to uphold God's commands—and the faith born of the voluntary consent of conscience, free of external coercion, developing from a keen spiritual and moral awareness and motivation.[7] The faith that enters the "heart" (another term for "conscience" in the Qur'an) is the result of a choice innately available to all human beings, which is then strengthened and assisted by revelation. In this sense, faith is freely and directly negotiated between God and human beings and cannot be compelled. This is an extremely important observation about individual autonomy in matters of faith. The Qur'anic utterance "No compulsion is there in religion" (Q. 2:256) seems to be saying that a person cannot be deprived of civil rights on account of a religious conviction, no matter how distasteful it might be to the dominant faith community.[8]

In support of freedom of religion in the early days of Islam, the commentators relate a story of a Muslim belonging to the tribe of Sālim b. 'Awf of Medina, whose two sons had embraced Christianity before Islam was preached. When the sons came to visit their father in Medina, their aggrieved father asked them to convert to Islam. The two refused to do so. The father brought them before the Prophet and asked him to intervene in the controversy.

It was precisely on this occasion, according to these commentators, that the "no compulsion" verse was revealed, and the father, apparently on the advice of the Prophet, left his two sons alone. And yet, the classical exegetes endorsed the view that tolerance in the matter of religion was to be afforded only to the people of the Book and that others were to be coerced into converting to Islam.[9]

Free exercise of religion and belief is an inalienable right of all human persons. The cornerstone of religious pluralism is the verse "No compulsion is there in religion." Since no authority can coerce an individual to believe or accept a particular faith, human beings are free to negotiate their personal faith and its consequential connection to a community to which that faith commitment relates the individual. Whereas in matters of private faith the position of the Qur'an is noninterventionist; that is, human authority in any form needs to defer to individuals acting on their own internal convictions; in the public projection of that faith, the Qur'anic stance is based on coexistence among faith communities, even if one among them enjoys a majority in terms of membership and political power. Without denying the uniqueness of its own message, the dominant community needs to leave the public space noncoercive and cognizant of other communities' rights to follow their religious practices without any impediment. In this particular sense, religious discourse needs to recast its spirituality into moral commitments materially equivalent to those of secular morality so that it can participate in the universalistic aspirations of the public order to establish justice for all regardless of their creed, gender, or color. Such an inclusive religious discourse is grounded in religiously inspired rationality and projects normative application through seeking to promote how persons of different religious commitments ought to live together by providing common public and religious reasons for their adopted course of moral action in the public sphere. It is in no sense a thoroughgoing reduction of religion to morality, as Immanuel Kant perhaps attempted in the context of Christianity.[10]

Dealing with Religious Exclusivism

Although at one level Qur'anic rationality can capture secular universality and produce an inclusive public theology to solve the problem of diversity of human faiths in the public sphere, at another level the same theology can breed exclusivist claims that can completely destabilize social and political cohesion. The problem, as I have identified in this book, is the difficulty connected with the affirmation of any particular moral position, whether secular or religious, as the single universal morality secured through sound rational argument. The subjectivity of any moral perspective is conditioned by the particular subject's circumstances, commitments, and assumptions, including his or her particular moral framework, with the result that the disputants will inevitably speak past each other, thus creating an irresolvable moral quandary at the international level. Unless people share life experiences framed by the same moral and metaphysical assumptions, it is impossible to discover common moral premises and rules of moral evidence to solve problems of social and political injustices around the globe. Competing moral visions in international communities need to endorse the normativity of a particular understanding of reasonableness of revelation-based rationality in order to deal with fundamental freedoms, including the freedom of religion, to promote universal human rights norms.

At this juncture, I need to come back to my earlier observation that exclusive claims about Islam or any other religion remain a strong and adamant part of one's religious identity. My field experience suggests to me that even men and women with a modern education, at one time or another, reveal this exclusivist tendency and its natural accompaniment, that is, intolerance if not outright bigotry. Here a critical evaluation of some revisionist-pluralist presumptions that stifle the acknowledgment of profound disagreements or affirmation of the truth of one's own beliefs and practices has implications for the progression of the notion of pluralism among Muslims. Traditionally, Muslims developed a theory about Islam's self-sufficiency in relation to other religions and regarded Islam as possessing the religious and moral truth required by all humanity until the end of time. The Qur'an spoke of Muḥammad as "the seal of the prophets," who confirmed the revelations to previous prophets where they were sound and corrected them if they had been corrupted. This doctrine also implied that there would be no other prophet after Muḥammad, so that he was God's final word to humanity. This theology was the foundation of Muslim exclusiveness. The finality of the Islamic revelation, in addition to the corporate solidarity founded upon the sacred Sharīʿa and Muslim rule, formed the resilient self-assurance with which Muslims considered the exclusive truth they possess, over against the abrogation or supersession of other traditions like Christianity and Judaism.[11] In light of this theology, to be sure, Muslim religious opposition to international human rights stems from the fear that endorsement of the UN Declaration would deny them their exclusive claim to religious and moral truth—the important sources of community-centered salvation. In supporting freedom of religion and conscience, human rights advocates seem to be saying to all faith communities that in order to prevent discord, enmity, and violence, they need to stress the commonalities of the world's major religions and avoid the temptation of maintaining that their religion possesses absolute truth to the exclusion of other faiths.

There is much in this pluralist presumption for interreligious dialogue that is realistic and conducive to outwardly better relations between dialogue participants. The proposal that the practitioners of different religions must be encouraged to accept the historicity and cultural specificity of their traditions to engage in searching for a common orientation to the divine to strike some kind of parity in their endeavors of relating properly to it is sound and practicable. However, it is not realistic to expect that people in dialogue will not adhere to exclusive views about their religious beliefs. In view of entrenched self-righteous attitudes among adherents of major religious traditions, it is not irrational or immoral for these staunch believers to think of their religion as the only source of human salvation. Exclusionary attitudes certainly deserve closer scrutiny in light of my own reservations about our ability to transcend intercommunal theological claims and counterclaims to convince faith communities that their exclusivist theologies are irrational and must be abandoned for the good of all humanity.[12]

Exclusivists who believe that certain doctrines of their religion are true and that what is incompatible with them is false are actually engaged in religious truth exclusivism founded upon sufficient familiarity with other religious traditions. They acknowledge in all sincerity that although these other traditions can generate genuine piety and dedication, they have doctrines that do not necessarily generate confidence in their truthfulness. In contrast, there can be exclusivists who, as part of their soteriological exclusivism, deny the ability of any religion other than their own to guarantee salvation. In other words, the other tradition is rejected simply because it does not teach the creed they believe in. Such a soteriological exclusivism remains popular among large sectors of the Muslim community around the globe. However, in recent years, truth claim exclusivism connected with the Muslim religious leadership, which has condemned relativizing the divine truth of Islam into multiple truths, has in some important ways downplayed the popular soteriological exclusivism to allow religious inclusiveness to emerge as an important ingredient of international relations policy.[13]

In our common world and at the present time, when our physical and mental isolation is at an end, the development of humanity from a religiously endorsed uniqueness of faith commitments that breed exclusivity and intolerance to an equally religiously prompted mutual respect and harmony founded on shared moral connections, rests on a retrieval and interpretation of appropriate Qur'anic passages. It is not necessary that religious exclusivism among Muslims or, for that matter, among any other religious group will grow into hatred for those with whom one fundamentally disagrees. Doubtless the challenge for the Muslim religious establishment is to find ways of channeling the disagreements to develop respect for one another's exclusivist truth claims while still believing that one is right and the other is wrong.

The Challenge of Mutual Respect

Some religious groups in the Muslim community have not hesitated to commit inhuman acts toward peoples of other faiths with whom they disagree, whether doctrinally or politically. Although it is not difficult to find political or economic reasons to explain (but not excuse) discriminatory behavior toward non-Muslim minorities, religious intolerance seems to be the root cause of human rights violations. Even in the case of intrafaith violations of human rights, as observed in the Sunni-Shīʿite sectarian carnage in Iraq, Afghanistan, or Pakistan in the aftermath of the American invasion, religious sources regarded as authoritative by both communities remain the main legitimizing source for endless violent clashes between the two communities. No international effort has succeeded in downplaying the religious histories and their ramifications in perpetrating violations of the fundamental right to freedom of religion. While it is true that communal religious histories that recount the victimization of the minority by the dominant majority cannot be rewritten to generate a variant form of reconciliatory collective memory, religious leadership with its exclusionary theology has been uninterested in bringing diverse communities together on a pluralist platform that can be extracted from the revealed texts of Islamic tradition. In my meeting with Iraqi religious leaders in 2003 in Amman, Jordan, there was no sign of reconciliation between Sunni and Shīʿite delegates, or consensus between the Muslim and Christian leaders that a change of attitude is the key if tolerance is to be built and discrimination eliminated. The prominent Sunni Iraqi leaders bemoaned the lost political power that had been concentrated in the hands of the Sunni minority under Saddam Hussein. The Shīʿite leadership reiterated its community's victimization by Saddam's government and saw very little advantage for its majority community to accept power-sharing arrangements that were being negotiated by the international power brokers. In the midst of all the arguments and counterarguments, the rights of the people to life and security were being threatened and violated in all these countries by militant Muslims supporting one or the other claim to truth and victimization. It is depressing to note that the religious leadership on both the Sunni and Shīʿite sides, whether in Iraq or Afghanistan, were totally indifferent to the moral consequences of relativizing human dignity through exclusive interpretations of the sanctity of life of fellow believers or other human beings. Religious revival in its nationalistic and militant forms can be cited as the main cause for the majority of human rights violations in these regions.

To add to these violations of human rights in the matter of freedom of religion on the ground, now, with the help of Internet technology, interreligious and intrafaith warfare is being conducted in cyberspace. The interreligious battles are no longer local; they have become global and are being fiercely waged by the so-called Soldiers of God. More than ever before, cyberspace is faced with the spread of intolerant and immoral messages about one religious group or another, dampening any hope for salvaging the deterioration of equitable relationships between communities based on recognition of the inherency of human dignity and mutual respect due to all humans. No religion is immune from such abuse by its own followers. The Abrahamic faiths, with their political vision for humanity, have more than ever become a weapon for encouraging discrimination and violation of basic human dignity. Online religious information, instead of functioning as a source of increasing mutual understanding and articulating a common vision for the global community under universal morality, has amplified intentional misinformation about the religious or cultural other and has led to mutual condemnation of peoples of faith. In view of the growing potential in modern-day religious revivals for discrimination and violence against those with whom one disagrees, who can one turn to for retrieving authoritative moral-religious resources to instill mutual respect among diverse religious and ethnic groups that make up the modern citizenry?

Traditionalist Muslim scholars and their large following among the masses remain the most conscious of directing Islamic public order in Muslim majority societies, with a clear understanding that political governance can attain legitimacy by committing itself to implementing the Sharīʿa. In this conscious commitment to founding a public order based on the divinely ordained Sharīʿa, Islam has been accurately described as a faith in the public realm.[14] In comparison to the performance of religious-moral duties, laid down in minute detail in the Sharīʿa, the official creed plays a secondary role in orienting the faithful to this goal. It is relevant to note that communal identity among Muslims is even today, therefore, defined less in terms of a person's adherence to a particular doctrinal position than in terms of his or her loyalty to one of the officially recognized rites of the Sharīʿa.[15]

Religious pluralism as a sociological fact, as far as the Sharīʿa was concerned, was not simply a matter of accommodation with competing exclusive claims over religious truth in the private domain of an individual's faith, where it had to begin anyway. It was and remains inherently a matter of public policy in which a Muslim government had to acknowledge and protect the God-given right of each and every person to determine his or her spiritual destiny without coercion. The recognition of freedom of religion in all matters related to human moral and spiritual life is the cornerstone of the Qur'anic notion of religious pluralism, at the level of interreligious as well as intrareligious relations.[16] In other words, the Qur'an lays down the foundation of theological pluralism that takes the equivalence and equal rights of human beings as a divinely ordained system. The statement that "the people are one community" in the Qur'an indicates that while this sense of unity among diverse peoples needs to be acknowledged theologically as part of God's activity, it is attainable in the sphere of ethics and its function in sustaining just relationships between peoples of diverse faith traditions.

However, the political ascendancy of Muslim rulers had far-reaching consequences for the ways in which the Qur'anic teachings about pluralism were side-stepped in favor of discriminatory rulings in the Sharīʿa to gain control over conquered peoples. The active engagement of contemporary militant leaders with these discriminatory rulings in the juridical corpus to seek political solutions to the problems faced by Muslims living under their autocratic rulers points to the ongoing tension that exists between the Qur'anic principles of justice and fair treatment of non-Muslims and the political demands of maintaining Muslim public order. There is little doubt that in the Muslim world the struggle is for the shape of public culture, for the style of life that is visible in the public square. Respect for the dignity of all humans is a key element in the principle of coexistence among peoples of diverse faiths and cultures, and yet the denial of extending that equal dignity to all humans, regardless of their color, creed, or sex is at the heart of violations of human rights in these societies.

Religious systems have traditionally claimed absolute devotion and an exclusive salvation history for themselves. Even within a single faith community it was by no means always conceded that the direction taken by dissenting schools of thought, for instance, the Shīʿite in the larger context of the majority Sunni community, could lead to authentic salvation.[17] Some classical Muslim scholars of the Qur'an attempted to separate the salvation history of the Muslim community from other Abrahamic faiths by attesting to the superseding validity of the Islamic revelation over Christianity and Judaism.[18] In an attempt to demand unquestioning acceptance of the new faith, Muslim theologians had to devise terminological as well as methodological stratagems to circumscribe those verses of the Qur'an that tended to underscore its ecumenical thrust by extending salvific authenticity and adequacy to other monotheistic traditions.

One of the methods of circumscribing the terms of a toleration verse was to claim its "abrogation" (*naskh*) by another verse that spoke of combating disbelief. There are a number of classical works dealing with abrogation in the Qur'an in which Muslim commentators discuss verses that are regarded as abrogated. However, modern scholarship, undertaken by some prominent Muslim jurists, has proved with incontrovertible documentation that of the 137 verses listed as abrogated, in reality not even one of them has been abrogated.[19] In jurisprudence as well as the commentaries of the Qur'an, there are references to a number of laws enacted in the early days of the community that were abrogated. Nonetheless, there is a controversy over whether any Qur'anic ordinances were abrogated at all—whether by other Qur'anic verses, as reported sometimes in the form of a prophetic tradition, or as established through a consensus reached by the jurists, as is historically evidenced. Muslim legal scholars agree that a claim to abrogation of an ordinance cannot be regarded as authentic if the documentation is based on a weak tradition reported. The major problem facing modern scholars is to accept the judgment of past scholars about the abrogated verses that deal with interfaith relations.[20] As a result, they have maintained that the chronologically later verse that speaks about initiating hostilities with the disbelievers abrogates the tolerant ruling of the earlier one. This attitude is rooted either in poor judgment or in a loose application of the concept of abrogation in its lexical sense. The lexical sense of the concept conveys the meaning of "transformation," "substitution," or "elimination" of the conditions that require repeal of the earlier ruling. When this lexical sense assumes a technical sense, then abrogation becomes interpreted as "supersession," thereby eliminating any claim by other Abrahamic traditions to validity. Obviously, this interpretive move is unwarranted when one considers those verses of the Qur'an that speak about other religions and their saving capacity.

The apparent contradiction between some passages of the Qur'an that recognized other monotheistic communities as worthy of salvation through adherence to their own traditions, and other verses declaring Islam as the only source of salvation, had to be resolved to provide a viable system of peaceful coexistence with the communities. Qur'anic pluralism was expressed by promising salvation to, at least, "whoso believes in God and the Last Day" among "those of Jewry, and the Christians, and those Sabaeans" (Q. 2:62). In contrast, Islamic absolutism asserted in no uncertain terms that "whoso desires another religion than Islam, it shall not be accepted of him; in the next world he shall be among the losers" (Q. 3:85). Hence, the resolution of the nonpluralistic, absolute claim on the one hand with the recognition of a pluralist principle in salvation, on the other, had enormous implications for the community's relations with other communities in general, and the people of the Book in particular.

The principle of chronology provided theologians with the notion of supersession or abrogation to expound various stages of revelation throughout history. According to this principle, essentially the same revelation was delivered piecemeal, the later revelation completing and thereby abrogating the previous ones. What was overlooked in this connection was the fact that the Qur'an introduces the idea of abrogation in connection with legal injunctions revealed in particular verses in which one aspect of legal requirements may be said to have abrogated or superseded another verse. Consequently, invoking abrogation in connection with Islam's attitude toward the earlier Abrahamic traditions was, to say the least, inconsistent. Even those classical exegetes like Muḥammad b. Jarīr al-Ṭabarī (d. 923), who had supported the principle of chronology to argue for the exclusive salvific efficacy of Islam and its role as the abrogator of the previous monotheistic traditions, could not fail to notice the incongruity of extending the notion of abrogation to the divine promise of rewarding those who believe in God and the Last Day, and work righteousness (Q. 2:62). In fact, Ṭabarī regards such abrogation as incompatible with the concept of divine justice.[21] Nevertheless, those who accepted the notion of supersession of the pre-Qur'anic revelations depended on a tradition reported in many early commentaries on the verse that states that no other religion than Islam would be acceptable to God. The tradition purports to establish that the verse, which was revealed subsequent to the verse that spoke about the salvific efficacy of other monotheisms, actually abrogated God's promise to those who acted righteously outside Islam. Ibn Kathīr (d. 1373) has no hesitation in maintaining that based on the verse nothing other than Islam was acceptable to God after Muḥammad was sent. Although he does not appeal to the concept of abrogation as evidence, his conclusions obviously point to the idea of supersession when he states the salvific state of those who preceded Muhammad's declaration of his mission. Ibn Kathīr maintains that the followers of previous guidance and their submission to a rightly guided life guaranteed their way to salvation only before Islamic revelation emerged.[22]

Evidently, the notion of abrogation of the previous revelation was not universally maintained even by those exegetes who otherwise required, at least in theory, other monotheists to abide by the new Sharī'a of Muḥammad. It is difficult to gauge the level of Christian influence over Muslim debates about the supersession of the previous revelation. It is not far-fetched to suggest that debates about Islam superseding Christianity and Judaism, despite the explicit absence of any reference to it in the Qur'an, must have entered Muslim circles through the most thoroughgoing Christian debates about Christianity having superseded Judaism, more particularly when Christians claimed to be the legitimate heirs to the same Hebrew Bible that was the source of Jewish law. The Muslim community, with its independent source of ethical and religious prescriptions, the Arabic Qur'an, in addition to its control over the power structure that defined its relationship with others, was in little need of establishing its independence from the previous monotheistic traditions, with which it never severed its theological connection through Abrahamic salvation history.[23]

The exigencies of modern living, which has allowed multicultural and multifaith societies to live side by side, have inevitably made the rationalist theological position regarding free human agency in determining its spiritual destiny a most desirable theology to cultivate peaceful coexistence among Muslim peoples. This theology maintains that human beings are endowed with adequate cognition and volition to pursue their spiritual destiny through the revealed message of God. Thus, Rashīd Riḍā (d. 1935), reflecting the rationalist theology of his teacher, a prominent Muslim modernist, Muḥammad 'Abduh (d. 1905), maintains that human responsibility to God is proportionate to the level of his exposure to God's purpose, about which he is apprised through either revelation or reason. The purpose of revelation is to clarify and elucidate matters that are known through the human intellect. Basic beliefs like the existence of God and the Last Day are necessarily known through it. Prophets come to confirm what is already intuitive to the human intellect. Accordingly, there is an essential unity in the beliefs of "the people of divine religions [*ahl al-adyān al-ilāhīya*]" who have been exposed to the divine guidance as well as having an innate disposition to believe in God and the Last Day, and do good works.[24] Moreover, God's promise applies to all who have this divine religion, regardless of formal religious affiliation, for God's justice does not allow favoring one group while ill-treating another. For all peoples who believe in a prophet and in the revelation particular to them, "their wages await them with their Lord, and no fear shall there be on them, neither shall they sorrow" (Q. 2:62). Rashīd Riḍā does not stipulate belief in the prophethood of Muḥammad for the Jews and Christians desiring to be saved, and hence, he implicitly maintains the salvific validity of both the Jewish and Christian revelations.[25]

Among the Shī'ite commentators, 'Allāma Ṭabāṭabā'ī (d. 1982), following well-established Shī'ite opinion from the classical age, rejected the notion of abrogation of the divine promise in Q. 2:62. In fact, he does not support the supersession of pre-Qur'anic revelations even when he regards them as distorted and corrupted by their followers. Nevertheless, he regards the ordinances of the Qur'an as abrogating the laws extracted from the two earlier scriptures. Evidently he confines abrogation to its juridical meaning, where it signifies repeal of an earlier ordinance by a fresh ruling because of its inapplicability in changed circumstances. In connection with those passages that supported the ecumenical thrust of the Qur'an, like verse 2:62, he rebuffed the opinion held by some Muslims that God promises salvation to particular groups because they bear certain names; on the contrary, anyone who holds true belief and acts righteously is entitled to God's reward and protection from punishment, as promised in Q. 6:88: "God has promised those of them who believe and do good, forgiveness and a great reward."[26]

Modern commentators like the Sunni Rashīd Riḍā and the Shī'ite 'Allāma Ṭabāṭabā'ī represent the unmistakable Qur'anic spirit of God-centered identity for humanity in which the external form of religion is demoted in importance when compared to the inward witness of the divine that defies any exclusive and restrictive identification. In fact, religious pluralism is seen by the Qur'an as fulfilling some divine purpose for humanity. That purpose is the creation of an ethical public order, for the attainment of which, before even sending the prophets and the revelation, God created an innate disposition in human beings capable of distinguishing good from evil. This divine gift requires humanity, regardless of its affiliation to particular religious paths, to live with each other and work toward justice and peace in the world.

Concluding Remarks

The process of cultural self-identification in the Muslim community was carried on through shared religious beliefs, practices, and attitudes. The religious commitment to a community-oriented belief system necessarily led to the formulation of an exclusivist theology in which all pre-Qur'anic revelations were considered superseded. Politically, this theology was not neutral; it led to the negation of pluralism, overshadowing the ethical mission of creating a just society founded upon the universal obligation to call people to good and forbid evil. The community was tempted and did succumb to the abandonment of the common ethical element in Abrahamic monotheism, which demanded attention to the concerns, needs, and capabilities of all people irrespective of their particular religious affiliation.

The predicament of conflicting claims to exclusive salvation had to be resolved if the Muslim community was to prove its universal excellence as an ethical and spiritual paradigm. In the words of the Qur'an, in order to be the best community "ever brought forth to human beings," the historical community had to undertake to institute good and prevent evil so that faith in God could become objectified in an inclusive attitude toward all peoples of different faiths. The best community had the moral responsibility of working toward the creation of a just society in which peoples of different religions would coexist in peace and harmony. This was the divinely ordained future for humanity.

The Qur'anic universe is moral. Human beings are by nature moral beings, that is, capable of knowing right from wrong, good from evil, and acting accordingly. In order to protect this nature in its original form, it is fortified with faith. Accordingly, the criteria for the best community are both ethical and religious: ethical in instituting good and preventing evil, and religious in responding to God's guidance. Inasmuch as the fulfillment of other-regarding ethical obligations justifies and even requires institutional structures like government agencies that can use reasonable force to ensure justice and fairness in all interpersonal human situations, the self-regarding duty of faith is founded upon a noninterventionist approach.

At this juncture, the best community faces its greatest challenge: how it can create an inclusive political society if the guiding principle of its collective identity as a confessional community is strictly founded upon shared religious doctrine. How about the Qur'an's repeated reminder that if God had willed, "whoever is in the earth would have believed, all of them, all together," and that people cannot be constrained "until they are believers" (Q. 10:99)? Does this not contradict the emphasis on a comprehensive shared religious doctrine in a political society? Given the logic of divine wisdom in endowing humans with the freedom to believe, it is inconceivable that the foundation of this just society in the best community be based on an exclusionary notion of mandatory uniformity in human religiosity.

The Qur'an severely criticizes the exclusive claims of the pre-Qur'anic communities, which led to hostilities among them and destruction of life, including the lives of God's prophets, who were unjustly killed while calling people to serve God's purposes. In fact, to alleviate the negative impact of such behavior, the Qur'an went back to the very source of the monotheistic tradition, namely, "submission to the Divine Will." Essentially and fundamentally, it is the acceptance of the same Creator that determines the spiritual equality of the followers of diverse religious traditions. Nevertheless, this God-centered pluralism of the Qur'an was in tension with the historical, relative experience of the new political society, which regarded its own system as the best. This exclusionary conceptualization of historical Islam proved to be both a point of departure for the early community, affording it a specific identity as a Muslim community, and the beginning of an internal dialogue within the Muslim community about the Qur'anic commandment to create an inclusive, just public order under divine revelation. The importance given to the moral duty to institute good and prevent evil indicates the way the Qur'an conceived of ethics as the basis for interreligious cooperation, in a religiously oriented civil society, with equally shared responsibility for the moral well-being of the people.

The juridical thesis that Islam does not make a distinction between the religious and the political requires revision in light of what has been argued in this book. God–human relations are founded upon individual autonomy and moral agency regulated by a sense of accountability to God alone for any acts of omission or commission. Interhuman relations, in contrast, are founded upon an individual and collective social-political life, with personal responsibility and social accountability as the means of attaining justice and fairness in human relations. This latter category of interhuman relations has customarily provided Muslim governments with a principle of functional secularity that allows them to regulate all matters pertaining to interpersonal justice. The same principle rules out the authority of Muslim governments to regulate religious matters except when the free exercise of religion for any individual is in danger. The foundation of a civil society in Islam is based on equality in creation in which the privilege of citizenry attaches equally to Muslim and non-Muslim, entailing inclusive political, civil, and social membership in the community.

Functional secularity was well entrenched in the political thinking of the early community. A number of Arab tribes that had submitted to the Prophet Muḥammad felt themselves free of any further obligation when the Prophet died, and they refused to send any further taxes to Medina. They viewed their relation to the public order under the Prophet as null and void because of the death of the party to the contract. But some men had a more integrated conception of the Islamic polity and of the community Muḥammad had created. Islam was not merely a matter of each individual obeying God; it was a compact in which all Muslims and non-Muslims were bound to one another as well. This compact did not cease with the Prophet's death; the pattern of life he had instituted could be continued under the leadership of those who had been closest to him. Anyone who separated from the core of the Muslims at Medina was in fact backing out of the Islamic polity; they were traitors to the cause of God for which Muḥammad and his followers had so long been fighting. That cause was still to be fought for and demanded a single chief to whom all would be loyal. The successors to Muḥammad are credited with persuading the Muslims of Medina to adopt this daring interpretation of a latent political membership as distinct from a religious membership. It is remarkable that when one studies the religious sermons that were delivered by the early Muslim leaders on Fridays or other religious holy days, there are hardly any comments about getting rid of the non-Muslims as a threat to Islamic public order. Their treatment of their subjects is illustrated by their inclusive rather than exclusive political order. Moreover, the remarkable example provided by the Prophet in the story about a Muslim belonging to the tribe of Sālim b. ʻAwf of Medina, whose two sons had embraced Christianity before Islam was preached, clearly sets the tone of the future relationship between a Muslim state and its religious minorities.

My total endeavor in this book has been to capture such moments in the early history of Islam and in the impeccable example of Islam's founder, the Prophet Muḥammad, to underscore my unflinching support for the Universal Declaration of Human Rights based on the inherent human dignity and moral ability to negotiate its spiritual destiny without the interference of the state. The Prophet's non-interventionist policy in the matter of the enforcement of religious faith was based on the confidence generated by the Qur'an regarding the universal moral intuitive ability of all human beings who needed to work together to make this world an ideal place for all human beings to live in harmony and peace.

Notes

CHAPTER I

1. For traditionalist Muslim scholars, the term *pluralism*, in its Persian and Arabic (*takththur-garā'ī* or *ta'addudīya*, respectively) rendering, which smacked of Western liberalism, was more problematic than *democracy*. *Pluralism* suggested "decentralized truth-claim," which led to belief in the relativity of the exclusive claim of Islamic revelation, rendering it one among many claims of truth. For Muslim seminarians, for whom pluralism, whether religious or moral, was unacceptable as part of their exclusive claim to the truth of Islam, the critical question was: How can there be many truths when the only truth was what Islam had proclaimed? Moreover, how can one maintain that final revelation from God for Muslims is relative to other similar truth claims maintained, for instance, by Jews and Christians?

2. Roger Ruston, *Human Rights and the Image of God* (London: SCM Press, 2004), in his introduction traces the development of Christian-Catholic criticism of the liberal paradigm of human rights since the universal declaration in 1948. While there are some common themes that unite Muslim critics with their Christian counterparts, for Muslims the major problem with the liberal paradigm has been its hostile attitude to religion per se, and its enormous confidence in secularism, which has failed time and again in delivering justice in Muslim countries that adopted its presuppositions for their reconstruction of modern Muslim societies. It is not only Turkey that institutionalized secularism through constitutional politics and is facing internal challenges posed by an Islamic cultural revival; Algeria also stands out as another unmistakable example of colonial secularism enforced from the top, which failed to deliver a democratic political system, justice, and fair distribution of national wealth to its citizens.

3. In his book on human rights, prominent traditionalist scholar of Egypt Muḥammad al-Ghazālī lends qualified support to the international document that must be respected by Muslims because some of its "foundations" are also enunciated in the Qur'an. For Ghazālī, like other traditionalist scholars in the Muslim world, Islam provides the norms that are culturally legitimate and applicable within the Islamic world. As such, an alternative declaration of Islamic human rights is appended to the translation and discussion of the international document. See: *Ḥuqūq al-insān: Bayn ta'ālīm al-islām wa i'lān al-umam al-muttaḥida* (Human Rights: Between the Teachings of Islam and the Declaration of the United Nations) (Alexandria, Egypt: Dār al-Da'wa, 1422/2002). This trend in traditional human rights scholarship has undermined the legitimacy of the universal declaration in Muslim eyes. The only way to lessen the negative influence of this trend is to engage traditional scholars in exploring the metaphysical foundations of the human rights declaration and demonstrate the common moral ground that is shared by world religions in upholding the norms that undergird the international document. By denying any normative foundations for the human rights declaration and insisting upon its secular thrust, the opportunity to stimulate conversation with the actual representatives of Islamic tradition is lost.

4. Johannes Morsink, *The Universal Declaration of Human Rights: Origins, Drafting, and Intent* (Philadelphia: University of Pennsylvania Press, 1999), p. 282.

5. Khaled Abou El Fadl and Abdullahi Ahmed An-Na'im are among the few serious discussants of human rights in the context of Islamic tradition.

6. Muḥammad 'Amāra, *al-Islām wa ḥuqūq al-insān: Ḍarūrāt . . . lā ḥuqūq* (Islam and Human Rights: Necessities . . . Not Rights) (Kuwait: 'Ālam al-Ma'rifa, 1405/1985) criticizes both Muslim fundamentalist and Muslim secular scholarship for having failed to demonstrate human rights within the parameters of Islamic comprehensive doctrines. The secularist scholarship that was produced under the Orientalist masters and that followed the Western cultural and civilizational domination of Muslim minds was guilty of not examining Islamic sources carefully before agreeing with the Western thesis about the inadequacy of Islam and its juridical tradition to issue anything similar to the international declaration of human rights. The Muslim secularists' prescription that one must derive human rights from Western civilization instead of searching for them in Islamic sources, according to 'Amāra, must be totally rejected because it smacks of new Western hegemony over Muslim societies (pp. 9–10).

7. Michael Ignatieff, *Human Rights as Politics and Idolatry* (Princeton, NJ: Princeton University Press, 2001), p. 54.

8. Jeffrey Stout, *Democracy and Tradition* (Princeton, NJ: Princeton University Press, 2004), p. 2, points to two prominent American thinkers on American democracy, namely, John Rawls and Richard Rorty, who want to severely restrict the use of religious reasons in public discussions about politics. Stout takes seriously the concerns of these thinkers and the claims of their opponents. In response to their prescription, which leads to virtual hiding of one's religious reasons lest they are rendered unreasonable by not accepting a freestanding notion of justice as a universal point of reference in political discussion in pluralistic societies, Stout defends the "reasonableness" of religious reasons by focusing on the sharing and hearing of particular reasons in public

discourse and by pointing out that "a person can be a reasonable (socially cooperative) citizen without believing or appealing to a free-standing conception of justice." He notes that Rawls's definition of reasonable as being willing to govern their conduct according to a universally applicable principle "implicitly imputes *unreasonableness* to everyone who opts out of the contractarian project, regardless of the *reasons* they might have for doing so" (p. 67).

9. In this study I have rendered the Arabic term *sunna* with capital "T" in the translation of this technical term (Tradition), which refers to all that is reported as said, done, and silently confirmed by the Prophet. The translation of *ḥadīth* (the vehicle of *sunna*, through which it is reported) is rendered with a lowercase "t" (tradition) or simply *ḥadīth*-report.

10. Several studies of the relationship between Islam and human rights have, understandably, concentrated on the legal component of rights and their compatibility with the international standards provided in the Declaration. See, for instance, studies by Abdullahi Ahmed An-Na'im, Ann Elizabeth Mayer, and others. However, there is a need to shift the debate over compatibility to investigation of the possibility of seeking legitimacy for the declaration through theological-ethical doctrines that could dispel the sinister attitude that prevails among Muslim religious thinkers toward the document's European pedigree. This negative attitude has also served as a powerful weapon for Muslim political authorities to deny the human rights of their own citizens, especially women and minorities. See: Ann Elizabeth Mayer, "Citizenship and Human Rights in Some Muslim States," in *Islam, Modernism and the West: Cultural and Political Relations at the End of the Millennium,* ed. Gema Martin Munoz (London: I. B. Tauris, 1999), pp. 109–121.

11. Max L. Stackhouse, "Human Rights and Public Theology: The Basic Validation of Human Rights," in *Religion and Human Rights: Competing Claims?,* ed. Carrie Gustafson and Peter Juviler (Armonk, NY: M. E. Sharpe, 1999), pp. 12–30, has shown with much evidence that theological principles are indispensable to sustaining the idea of human rights as a universal guide in ethical and juridical argument.

12. Alasdair MacIntyre, "Community, Law, and the Idiom and Rhetoric of Rights," in *Listening* 26(1991), 96–110.

13. Alasdair MacIntyre, *After Virtue* (London: Duckworth, 1981), pp. 64–67.

14. I have examined Islamic ethical and theological notions to demonstrate the Qur'anic principles of social coexistence and civil cooperation founded on common morality that touches all humans, independent of one's faith affiliation, in *The Islamic Roots of Democratic Pluralism* (New York: Oxford University Press, 2000).

15. Mahdī Abū Sa'īdī, *Mabānī-yi ḥuqūq-i bashar* (Tehran: Intishārāt-i Āsiya, 1964), p. 12.

16. See: Donald W. Shriver Jr., foreword, in *Religion and Human Rights: Competing Claims?,* ed. Carrie Gustafson and Peter Juviler (Armonk, NY: M. E. Sharpe, 1984), pp. ix–xii.

17. Conceptually, I have relied upon the insights of J. Shelley, introduction, in Dorothee Solle, *Political Theology* (Philadelphia: Fortress Press, 1974) to explain my adoption of Islamic political theology in the context of human rights theory.

18. These are the Qur'anic notions captured in two important phrases: *al-mustaḍ'af* (the downtrodden, the wronged) and *mufsid fi al-'arḍ* (the one who corrupts the earth, that is, corrupts the public order and makes it uninhabitable). The Qur'an admonishes people who stand by while wrongs are committed and God's earth is corrupted by injustice. In the words of the Qur'an, the downtrodden will be asked what stopped them from emigrating to safer places: "Was not God's earth wide, so that you might have emigrated in it?" (Q. 4:97). These phrases were also part of Ayatollah Khomeini's political theology that saw the ultimate overthrow of the Pahlavi dynasty in 1978–1979.

19. Khaled Abou El Fadl, "A Distinctly Islamic View of Human Rights: Does It Exist and Is It Compatible with the Universal Declaration of Human Rights?" in *Islam and Human Rights: Advancing a US-Muslim Dialogue,* ed. Shirin T. Hunter with Huma Malik (Washington, DC: CSIS Press, 2005), pp. 27–42, touches upon "the moral trajectory" of the Qur'an, which he develops to derive relevant understanding of, for instance, the sanctity of life in human rights discourse. In another scholarly chapter, "Islam and the Challenge of Democratic Commitment," in *Does Human Rights Need God?,* ed. Elizabeth M. Bucar and Barbara Barnett (Grand Rapids, MI: Eerdmans, 2005), pp. 58–103, El Fadl has detailed what I consider to be part of political theology, as outlined in this chapter. El Fadl's thesis that Islam itself is compatible with democratic politics is built upon his meticulous analysis of the legal writings of the classical jurists and their aversion to unrestrained authoritarianism and preference for a government bound by religious law "where human beings do not have unfettered authority over other human beings, and there are limits on the reach to power" (p. 59). This characteristic is certainly compatible with ethical limits on the exercise of unrestrained power which must finally submit to public scrutiny.

20. Citing dissident Muslim intellectuals like Naṣr Abū Zayd or Muḥammad Shaḥrūr, for example, on the discrepancy between the classical interpretations of the Qur'an and the Tradition, and the irrelevance of their doctrines for the development of a human rights regime in Muslim societies does not achieve anything substantial to convince educated Muslim readers, who read the highly politicized secularism of human rights language as nothing more than the imposition of Western values on their culture. Moreover, they see this highly publicized talk about rights as the denial of their right to disagree with the Declaration's liberal, Western, or secularly conceived views about its nonreligious, nonmetaphysical foundations.

21. Max Stackhouse, *Creeds, Society, and Human Rights* (Grand Rapids, MI: Eerdmans, 1984), p. 40 (as quoted and commented on by John Kelsay, *Human Rights and Conflict of Cultures: Western and Islamic Perspectives on Religious Liberty,* co-authored with David Little and Abdulaziz Sachedina (Columbia: University of South Carolina Press, 1988), p. 32.

22. The interview with Ayatollah Bojnūrdī was published as "Ta'āmul wa ta'āruḍ bayn-i fiqh wa ḥuqūq-i bashar," *Farzāne* 3 (1989), 7–13.

23. 'Abd Allāh Javādī Āmolī, *Falsafe-yi ḥuqūq-i bashar,* ed. Sayyid Abū al-Qāsim Ḥusaynī (Qumm: Isrā,' 1375/1996), p. 89.

24. Various articles in the volume *Religion in the Liberal Polity*, ed. Terence Cuneo (Notre Dame, IN: University of Notre Dame Press, 2004) discuss some of the issues raised in this section. See, in particular, the introduction by Terence Cuneo.

25. Such a view of religion and its problematic for the establishment of democracy and implementation of human rights has had a long history in the West. Some two centuries ago, Alexis de Tocqueville in his assessment of the American republic in *Democracy in America* (New York: Harper Collins, 1988) pointed out that the "great problem of our time is the organization and the establishment of democracy in Christian lands" (p. 311). In the nineteenth century it was Christianity that was seen as incompatible with democracy; and today it is Islam that is regarded as the "greatest problem of our time." This extension of an observation in the nineteenth century about Christianity to Islam in the twenty-first century is not merely a coincidence. In the wake of the events of September 11, 2001, Western views about religion's relationship to democracy have hardened to the point that a widely held opinion among a number of prominent American social scientists, encapsulated by Francis Fukuyama, states explicitly, "There seems to be something about Islam or at least fundamentalist versions of Islam that have been dominant in recent years, that makes Muslim societies particularly resistant to modernity" ("History Is Still Going Our Way," *Wall Street Journal,* October 5, 2001).

26. See: Abdulaziz Sachedina, *The Islamic Roots of Democratic Pluralism* (New York: Oxford University Press, 2001).

CHAPTER 2

1. Among Muslim scholars who have critically evaluated the problem of compatibility between Islamic juridical tradition and the declaration, one can mention the name of Mohsen Kadivar, who, with his seminarian and university education, has provided one of the most profound analyses of Islamic laws in the area of its penal system. For details, see his interviews with *Aftāb,* no. 27 (Tir/July, 1382/2003), 54–59; no. 28 (Shahrivar/September, 1382/2003), 106–115.

2. Various articles in the volume *Religion in the Liberal Polity*, ed. Terence Cuneo (Notre Dame, IN: University of Notre Dame Press, 2004), discuss some of the issues raised in this section. See, in particular, the introduction.

3. For a detailed critical evaluation of religion and public reason, see Jeffrey Stout, *Democracy and Tradition* (Princeton, NJ: Princeton University Press, 2004), chapter 2.

4. See Abdulaziz Sachedina, *The Islamic Roots of Democratic Pluralism* (New York: Oxford University Press, 2001).

5. A number of prominent Muslim modernists were interviewed by *Kayhān-i andīshe* (vol. 44, November 1989, pp. 176–182) during the seminar on Human Rights From Western and Islamic Perspectives held in Hamburg, Germany September 20–25, 1989) to seek their response to the main question about the compatibility of democracy with the Islamic government in Iran. It is revealing to note that these interviews were published in full without any censorship. Among those interviewed are: 'Abd al-Karīm Surūsh, Muḥammad Javād Ḥujjatī Kirmānī, Sayyid Muṣṭafā Muḥaqqiq Dāmād, and Abū al-Faḍl 'Izzatī.

6. Stout, *Democracy and Tradition*, chapter 3, relates freedom of religion to freedom of expression in support of his argument to allow religious reasons "for a political conclusion" in the public domain. Muslim traditionalists approach the same freedom with a different twist to freedom of expression related to freedom to act upon one's convictions in the public domain, leading to actual formation of religious governance based on a comprehensive religious doctrine.

7. Nicholas Wolterstorff in his chapter, "Why We Should Reject What Liberalism Tells Us about Speaking and Acting in Public for Religious Reasons," in *Religion and Contemporary Liberalism*, ed. Paul J. Weithman (Notre Dame, IN: University of Notre Dame Press, 1997), pp. 162–181, makes a strong case for the "reasonableness" of acting decisively in accord with one's faith in public because freedom of religion does connote the freedom to engage in religiously inspired activity in the public domain that leads to morally sound political decisions—which then is congruent with public reason. This and other articles in the volume critically evaluate contemporary liberalism and the ways in which it can or cannot appeal to religiously inspired political activity.

8. Ibid., p. 165.

9. Katerina Dalacoura, *Islam, Liberalism, and Human Rights*, rev. ed. (London: I. B. Tauris, 2003), p. 6.

10. Human rights violations suffered by thousands of civilians for being identified as Shīʻa, especially in Afghanistan under the Taliban and in Iraq under Saddam Hussein went unnoticed until mass graves were discovered in those countries after the American invasion. The suffering of the Hazara and other Shīʻite tribes simply because they departed from the majoritarian theology remains to be recorded by conscientious observers of human rights violations. Minorities in general suffer everywhere unless the state institutes policies to protect their human rights. Religious minorities in the Muslim world are no exception to this overall discriminatory theology and inhuman treatment by rulers.

11. Fahmī Jadʻān, "Al-ṭāʻa wa al-ikhtilāf fī ḍawʻ ḥuqūq al-insān fī al-islām," in *Ḥuqūq al-insān fī al-fikr al-ʻarabī*, ed. Salmā Khaḍrā Jayyūsī (Beirut: Markaz Dirāsat al-Waḥdat al-ʻArabīya, 2003), pp. 201–220, makes the case for the revival of Muʻtazilite rationalist theology to support fundamental freedoms like freedom of religion and conscience. See also: Naṣr Ḥāmid Abū Zayd, *Al-ittijāh al-ʻaqlī fi al-tafsīr: dirāsa fī qaḍīya al-majāz fī al-qur'ān ʻinda al-muʻtazila* (Beirut: Dār al-Tanwīr, 1982), which is a study of al-Qāḍī ʻAbd al-Jabbār al-Muʻtazilī's take on intellectual exegesis of the Qur'an in his magnum opus, *Al-Mughnī*.

12. See Walterstorff's critical analysis of Rawls's liberalism on the matter of separation in "Why We Should Reject What Liberalism Tells Us," pp. 166–168.

13. In a number of articles in the volume on human rights in Arabic thought some modernist authors have taken up theological ethics and its implication for human rights. See, for instance, Jadʻān, "Al-ṭāʻa wa al-ikhtilāf," pp. 201–220, and Muḥammad ʻĀbid al-Jābirī, "Mafāhīm al-ḥuqūq wa al-ʻadl fī nuṣūṣ al-ʻarabīya al-islāmīya," in *Ḥuqūq al-insān fī al-fikr al-ʻarabī*, pp. 25–76.

14. In this connection, it is interesting to note that while the majority of Western observers have credited Ayatollah Sayyid ʻAlī Sīstānī of Iraq with "democratic" ideas,

in his personal communication to me in August 1998 he rejected both pluralism and human rights as "un-Islamic." The reformist leaders' voices in Iraq or in Afghanistan have been drowned by such "traditionalist" rhetoric voiced by the likes of Sistānī among the Sunnis.

15. Joseph Schacht, *An Introduction to Islamic Law* (Oxford: Clarendon Press, 1964), pp. 189–190, discusses procedure in Muslim courts, observing: "No action is possible without a claimant. . . . This principle is limited by the competence of the kadi to take action in matters of public welfare. . . . It is not compulsory to apply to the kadi, . . . as long as no party applies to the kadi he takes no notice."

16. Ḥāmid Khalīl, "Al-fard wa sulṭa fī al-fikr al-'arabī al-ḥadīth," in *Ḥuqūq al-insān fī al-fikr al-'arabī*, pp. 891–914, traces the development of the civil and political rights of citizens in modern Arabic thought. This and other articles in this volume begin to tackle the question of human rights language and its compatibility with Islamic historical tradition based on the interpretations of normative texts.

17. Kent Greenawalt, *Religious Convictions and Political Choice* (New York: Oxford University Press, 1988), p. 69.

18. The Sharī'a treated non-Muslim minorities as a special legal category of *ahl al-dhimma*, giving them a status of "protected minorities." And, even when it discriminated against these minorities, their autonomous status as a self-governing community was well-established. On the contrary, there is nothing in the law to guarantee the protection of the life and property of a dissenter within the community. A Shī'ite minority was viewed as a "heretical" group by a Sunni majority in power. The situation changed when a Shī'ite dynasty was in power. However, the sheer majority of the Sunni Muslims ruled out the treatment they meted out to the Shī'ite minorities that lived among them. Muslim sources are replete with reports about the execution of "heretics" (that is, Shī'ite Muslims) who posed a threat to Sunni governments in power and who openly dissented from the official majority view of Islam. M. G. S. Hodgson, *The Venture of Islam*, 3 vols. (Chicago: University of Chicago Press, 1974) at various points brings out the state policy of Muslim rule governing its religious minorities. For instance, see: vol. 1, pp. 242–251, 305–308; vol. 2, pp. 536–539; vol. 3, pp. 33–38. The oppressive treatment of Shī'ites continues to this day in a number of Arab and Muslim countries.

19. The tradition that says: "God created human being in His image [*ṣūratihi*]" has been recorded in one of the most authentic compilations of the Sunni traditions: Muḥammad b. Ismā'īl al-Bukhārī, *Ṣaḥīḥ al-Bukhārī* (Beirut: 'Ālam al-Kutub, 1986), vol. 8:91. However, the interpretation has less to do with theological justifications for human rights than with the nobility conferred on human beings by God's act of creation.

20. John Rawls, "The Priority of Right and Ideas of the Good," in *Philosophy and Public Affairs*, 17(4, 1988), 251–276.

21. Ibid., 260, 265.

22. Adam B. Seligman, *The Idea of Civil Society* (New York: Free Press, 1992), chapters 1 and 2, traces the development of the idea in Europe and the United States. The work is not comparative in any sense and therefore does not deal with similar developments in other societies. But, as pointed out in this work, Muslim societies are

heir to both biblical and Greek ideas of individual, private, and public realms of human activity. Hence, some of the characteristics that are now identified as being consonant with a civil society have been present in all cultures where people had to learn to live in harmony.

23. Michael Walzer, *Thick and Thin: Moral Argument at Home and Abroad* (Notre Dame: University of Notre Dame Press, 1994), pp. x–xi uses "thick" to designate detailed references to "particularist stories" across different cultures, which also possess "a thin and universalist morality" that they share with different peoples and cultures. The thickness and thinness of the moral tradition of particular peoples and cultures also lead us to recognize the maximalist and minimalist meanings, respectively, in that tradition, with a clear understanding that "minimalist meanings are embedded in the maximal morality, expressed in the same idiom, sharing the same . . . orientation" (p. 3). I have introduced "universal" and "particular" guidance in the Islamic tradition in a similar conceptual framework, where the universal provides the minimalist and thin description of the moral principles, while the particular provides the maximalist and thick description of culturally integrated moral language that responds to specific purposes.

24. Abdulaziz Sachedina, "Justifications for Violence in Islam," *War and Its Discontents: Pacifism and Quietism in the Abrahamic Traditions,* ed. J. Patout Burns (Washington, DC: Georgetown University Press, 1996), pp. 122–160.

25. Schacht, *An Introduction to Islamic Law,* pp. 175–176.

26. The instructions given to the governor are widely reported in all major historical works written by Muslim historians. The important principle is part of the following text, translated by William Chittick, *The Shī'ite Anthology* (London: Muhammadi Trust of Great Britain and Northern Ireland, 1980):

> Infuse your heart with mercy, love and kindness for your subjects. Be not in face of them a voracious animal, counting them as easy prey, for they are of two kinds: *either they are your brothers in religion or your equals in creation.* Error catches them unaware, deficiencies overcome them, (evil deeds) are committed by them intentionally and by mistake. So grant them your pardon and your forgiveness to the same extent that you hope God will grant you His pardon and forgiveness. For you are above them, and he who appointed you is above you, and God is above him who appointed you. (p. 69, emphasis added)

CHAPTER 3

1. Muḥammad b. Muḥammad al-Ghazālī, *al-Iqtiṣād fī al-I'tiqād* (Beirut: Dār al-Amāna, 1969), pp. 214–215.

2. Muḥammad al-Ashmāwī, an Egyptian modernist jurist, has demonstrated this in his several critical works on historical Islamic legal tradition and its inability to deal with political and social development.

3. M. G. S. Hodgson, *The Venture of Islam: Conscience and History in a World Civilization* (Chicago: University of Chicago Press, 1974), vol. 3, p. 166.

4. Gene Outka and John P. Reeder Jr., eds., *Prospects for a Common Morality* (Princeton, NJ: Princeton University Press, 1993), pp. 3–4.

5. Sayyid Quṭb, *Fī ẓilāı al-qur'ān* (Beirut: Dār al-Shurūq, 1973), vol. 1:26.

6. Sayyid Muḥammad Ḥusayn al- Ṭabāṭabā'ī, *al-Mīzān fī tafsīr al-qur'ān* (Beirut: Mu'assasa al-A'lamī, 1392/1972), vol. 1:43ff.

7. Edward Lane, *An Arabic-English Lexicon* (Beirut: Librairie du Liban, 1968), part 6, p. 2416.

8. Muḥammad b. 'Umar Fakhr al-Dīn al-Rāzī, *al-Tafsīr al-kabīr* (Cairo: al-Maṭba'a al-Bahīya, 1938), vol. 1:9.

9. Ṭabāṭabā'ī, *al-Mīzān*, vol. 1:43–52.

10. Most of the exegetes of the Qur'an take *al-islām* as the proper noun, meaning the religion that was preached by the Prophet of Islam in the seventh century. However, the contextual aspect of verse Q. 6:125 evidently introduces *al-islām* in the signification of the act of submission as the desired spiritual and moral purpose of God's creation. It is in this sense that all humans and all of nature are inclined to be "muslim," that is, those who have submitted to the will of God.

11. This section captures the main line of thinking in the Mu'tazilite-Shī'ite position in Ṭabāṭabā'ī, *al-Mīzān*, vol. 1:302–303, which explains the submission of the entire order of nature to God's will and the gradual submission of humanity and the resulting levels of faith in God's absolute will without compromising human moral agency and freedom of religion.

12. Ibid., vol. 20:297ff.

13. Lane, *Arabic-English Lexicon*, part 7, p. 2554.

14. Ṭabāṭabā'ī, *al-Mīzān*, vol. 26:356.

15. David Little, "Duties of Station vs. Duties of Conscience: Are There Two Moralities?" in *Private and Public Ethics: Tensions Between Conscience and Institutional Responsibility*, ed. Donald G. Jones (New York: Edwin Mellon Press, 1978), p. 135.

16. The story of Joseph in the Qur'an introduces the metaphor "the soul that incites to evil" (*al-nafs al-'ammara*), the soul that can correct its shortcomings through self-discipline and through God's mercy and forgiveness. See chapter 12, verses 53–54. The reflective function of the soul here is the function of conscience that allows humans to reflect upon their own nature and approve and disapprove its performance in accord with the standard laid down in the "heart"—the mind that sits in judgment.

17. Rāzī, *Tafsīr al-kabīr*, vol. 2:19–22.

18. Major works on dialectical theology written by al-Ash'arī and other prominent theologians in this school emphasize God's sovereignty based on God's absolute will without foundation in the essential nature of things, rejecting moral law as an expression of the divine will.

19. Ṭabāṭaba'ī, *al-Mīzān*, vol. 1:52.

20. George Hourani, *Islamic Rationalism: The Ethics of 'Abd al-Jabbār* (Oxford: Clarendon Press, 1971), p. 3.

21. The Ash'arite exegete Fakhr al-Dīn al-Rāzī, who maintains complete subordination of the human will to the divine will, recognizes two forms of "guidance": first, guidance by means of demonstration (*dalīl*) and proof or evidence (*ḥujja*), both activities of the human rational faculty, which he considers limited; second, guidance through inner purification of the soul and ascetic practices. He does not speak of revelation as a

separate form of guidance; rather, as an Ash'arī, he considers that revelation (i.e., the will of God) superimposes all forms of guidance. See his *Tafsīr al-kabīr*, vol. 1:9ff.

22. To speak about such a possibility in the highly politicized "theology" of international relations is not without problems. Like the development language for which modern Western society provides the model that all peoples in the world must follow, any suggestion of creating a metacultural language of bioethics runs the risk of being suspected as another hegemonic ploy by the Western nations. However, there is a fundamental difference in the way development language is employed to connote Western scientific, technological, and social advancement, and a biomedical vocabulary that essentially captures universal ends of medicine as they relate to human conditions and human happiness and fulfillment across nations. It is not difficult to legitimize bioethical language cross-culturally if we keep in mind the cultural presuppositions of a given region in assessing the generalizability of moral principles and rules.

23. Abdulaziz Sachedina, "Justifications for Violence in Islam," *War and Its Discontents: Pacifism and Quietism in the Abrahamic Traditions*, ed. J. Patout Burns (Washington, DC: Georgetown University Press, 1996), pp. 122–160.

24. Benjamin Braude, "Foundation Myths of the *Millet* System," in *Christians and Jews in the Ottoman Empire: The Functioning of a Plural Society*, ed. Benjamin Braude and Bernard Lewis (New York: Holes & Meier, 1982), p. 69.

25. Will Kymlicka, "Two Models of Pluralism and Tolerance," in *Toleration: An Elusive Virtue*, ed. David Heyd (Princeton, NJ: Princeton University Press, 1996), p. 82.

26. Braude, "Foundation Myths of the *Millet* System," pp. 69–72.

27. For details of the history of the inherence view of human rights based on the concept of the inherent dignity of human beings and its political application in preserving the foundation of "freedom, justice and peace in the world," see: Johannes Morsink, *The Universal Declaration of Human Rights: Origins, Drafting, and Intent* (Philadelphia: University of Pennsylvania Press, 1999), pp. 281ff.

CHAPTER 4

1. See, for instance, Michael J. Perry, *The Idea of Human Rights: Four Inquiries* (New York: Oxford University Press, 1998), pp. 4ff.

2. In addition to Michael Perry's study (and the sources he has used to write this important corrective work on the role of religion in human rights), see Roger Ruston, *Human Rights and the Image of God* (London: SCM Press, 2004), which undertakes to investigate the idea of the image of God in Christian theology to accentuate the role it has played in deriving the fundamental notion of human dignity from which human rights derive.

3. Having spent extended periods of time in Muslim societies in different countries in the last fifty years or so, I can say without hesitation that issues related to women form the basis for moral relativism in the Muslim world, however differently each culture forms the basis for Muslim identities and social functions. Most of the controversial issues connected with the granting of women's human rights can be traced

back to cultural rather than religious norms. Nevertheless, religious teachings, however distorted, are retrieved to provide legitimation to the relativist stance on universal human rights.

4. Deniz Kandiyoti, "Reflections on the Politics of Gender in Muslim Societies: From Nairobi to Beijing," in *Faith and Freedom: Women's Human Rights in the Muslim World*, ed. Mahnaz Afkhami (Syracuse: Syracuse University Press, 1995), pp. 19–32.

5. Martha C. Nussbaum, "Religion and Women's Human Rights," in *Religion and Contemporary Liberalism*, ed. Paul J. Weithman (Notre Dame, IN: University of Notre Dame Press, 1997), pp. 93–137, has, through numerous examples from different parts of the world, shown the level of male-dominated religious discourse founded upon misappropriation of religious beliefs and religious laws based on these doctrines regarding women's social roles to perpetuate violations of women's human rights in major world religious traditions.

6. See, for instance, Abdullahi Ahmad An-Na'im, "The Rights of Women and International Law in the Muslim Context," *Whittier Law Review* 9, no. 3 (1988), 491–556; Rebecca J. Cook, ed., *Human Rights of Women: National and International Perspectives* (Philadelphia: University of Pennsylvania Press, 1994); Deniz Kandiyoti, ed., *Women, Islam and the State* (Philadelphia: Temple University Press, 1991); Guity Nashat, ed., *Women and Revolution in Iran* (Boulder, CO: Westview Press, 1983).

7. Muslim women scholars who have written extensively on the subject of women's human rights and dignity include: Fatima Mernissi, *The Veil and the Male Elite: A Feminist Interpretation of Women's Rights in Islam*, trans. Mary Jo Lakeland (Reading, MA: Addison-Wesley, 1991); Aziza al-Hibri, ed., *Women and Islam* (Oxford: Pergamon Press, 1982); Haleh Afshar, ed., *Women in the Middle East: Perceptions, Realities and Struggles for Liberation* (New York: St. Martin's Press, 1993); Amina Wadud-Mohsen, *Qur'an and Women* (New York: Oxford University Press, 1993).

8. See, for instance, Muḥsin Kadīvar's corrective criticism of the Islamic juridical tradition, which he correctly identifies as "historical Islam." In addition, Muḥammad Mujtahid Shabistarī and other reform thinkers have voiced their criticism of the essentiality attached to the classical juridical formulations.

9. Significantly, although not surprisingly, important Muslim countries with a claim to be the custodians of "authentic Islam," like Saudi Arabia, Iran, Pakistan, and the Sudan, have not ratified the convention. See: United Nations, *Human Development Report 1995* (New York: UN Development Program, 1995), p. 43.

10. See an interview with Ayatollah Bojnūrdī, "Ta'āmul va ta'āruḍ bayn-e fiqh va ḥuqūq-e bashar," *Farzāne* 6 (1997), no. 3, 7–14. Muḥammad Mujtahid Shabistarī has also deemed it necessary to change classical judicial decisions in order to make them compatible with human rights in his *Naqdī bar qarā'at-i rasmī az dīn* (Tehran: Ṭarḥ-i Nov, 2002).

11. Ziba Mir-Hosseini, "The Politics and Hermeneutics of Hijab in Iran: From Confinement to Choice," *Muslim World Journal of Human Rights* 4, no. 1 (2007), Article 2.

12. Dominic McGoldrick, *Human Rights and Religion: The Islamic Headscarf Debate in Europe* (Portland, OR: Hart Publishing, 2006), has investigated the debate on the

headscarf across Europe, which followed the ban in France in 2004, and the implications of such a ban in the context of international human rights norms. The underlying problem appears to be the protection of group rights under the freedom of religion guaranteed to faith communities.

13. The term *'awra* is defined as "the pudendum, or pudenda, of a human being, of a man and of a woman, so called because it is abominable to uncover, and to look at, what is thus termed" (E. W. Lane, *An Arabic-English Lexicon* [Beirut: Librairie du Liban, 1968], 5:2194). In the Sharī'a for man, the *'awra* (indecent to expose) is between the navel and the knee; for a woman, all the person, except the face and hands as far as the wrists. The term also applies to times of the day, as in the Qur'an (24:57), when it is improper for a grown-up child to appear in his or her parent's private chamber.

14. Whether *'awra* includes a woman's voice has been a matter of dispute among Muslim jurists. Some interesting comments on this matter are to be found in Muḥammad al-Ghazālī, *Qaḍāya al-mar'a bayna al-taqlīd al-rākida wa al-wāfida* (Cairo: Dār al-Shurūq, 1992), 164–165. The author represents modernist trends among some traditional Muslim scholars and hence, rejects the view that a woman's voice is also part of the *'awra.*

15. The Qur'an made no attempt to lay down a comprehensive moral system, because it treated morality as "the known" (*al-ma'rūf*). *Al-ma'rūf,* in the meaning of moral behavior in the Qur'an, signifies "goodness," a "good quality or action," "gentleness in any action, or deed," whose goodness is known by reason and by revelation. See Lane, *An Arabic-English Lexicon*, 5:2014.

16. The question of "authorial pretext" or "author's intentions" and contextual significance and their relation to broader context in historical understanding of a text is taken up by Jeffrey Stout in his article, "What Is the Meaning of a Text?" *New Literary History: A Journal of Theory and Interpretation* 14, no. 1 (1982–1983), 1–12.

17. The Qur'an speaks about a light that shines into the heart: "God is the light of heavens and earth. . . . God guides to His light whom He wills" (Q. 24:35). Once this light has shone into the heart, no darkness can ever overcome it.

18. For the translation of the Qur'an, I have depended, throughout this study, on A. J. Arberry, *The Koran Interpreted* (New York: Macmillan, 1955), with some revision to conform with the original Arabic text.

19. Muḥammad b. Jarīr al-Ṭabarī, *Jāmi' al-bayān fī tafsīr al-qur'ān* (Beirut: Dār al-Ma'ārif, 1972), vol. 3:82–83; Abū 'Alī al-Faḍl b. al-Ḥasan al-Ṭabarsī, *Majma' al-bayān fī tafsīr al-qur'ān* (Beirut: Dār Iḥyā' al-Turāth al-'Arab, 1959), vol. 1:398–397.

20. Ṭabarsī, *Majma'*, 1:398.

21. 'Abd Allāh b. 'Umar, *Anwār al-tanzīl wa asrār al-ta'wīl* (Cairo: al-Maba'at al-'Uthmānīya, 1939), 1:64.

22. Among these exegetes is Mulla Fatḥ Allāh Kāshānī, *Minhāj al-ṣādiqīn fī ilzām al mukhālifīn* (Tehran: Kitābfurūshī Islāmīya, 1969), vol. 2:155–156. This is contrary to the classical Shī'ite authorities on Qur'anic exegesis like Muḥammad b. al-Ḥasan al-Ṭūsī, *al-Tibyān fī tafsīr al-qur'ān* (Najaf: al-Maṭba'a al-'Ilmīya, 1957), 2:373–374; Ṭabarsī, *Majma'*, 2:398.

23. The opinion is cited by Kāshānī, *Minhāj al-ṣādiqīn*, vol. 2:157, on the authority of Zamakhsharī, the Mu'tazilite Sunnī theologian exegete.

24. "Istiṭā'a," in *Encyclopedia of Islam* (Leiden: E. J. Brill, 2001), vol. 4:270b. Also, George F. Hourani, *Islamic Rationalism: The Ethics of 'Abd al-Jabbār* (Oxford: Clarendon Press, 1971) in various places takes up the Mu'tazilite and Ash'arite positions on whether the acts of human beings are determined, even by their own motives, or whether human beings have the power or ability (*qudra*) to act or to refrain from acting.

25. Hourani, *Islamic Rationalism*, pp. 37–39, 81–89.

26. Ibid., pp. 56–62, discusses the Ash'arite views in the context of the Mu'tazilite refutation of relating value to the commands and prohibitions of God and their ethical purport.

27. See, for instance, several pertinent studies in *Engaging Cultural Differences: The Multicultural Challenge in Liberal Democracies*, ed. Richard A. Shweder, Martha Minow, and Hazel Rose Markus (New York: Russell Sage Foundation, 2002). In chapter 11, "'What About Female Genital Mutilation?' and Why Understanding Culture Matters in the First Place," pp. 216–251, Shweder convincingly argues for cultural pluralism to underscore the importance of engaging the African culture of female circumcision on its own terms before campaigning against "female genital mutilation" as a human rights violation.

28. A number of studies regarding receptivity to women's human rights in different Muslim societies and cultures indicate that cultural relativism has come to be a dominant conceptual tool to deny women their legitimate claims and entitlements. See, for instance, a penetrating account of Egyptian women's mosque movement and its implications for feminism, liberalism, and Islamic traditionalism, in Saba Mahmoud, *The Politics of Piety: The Islamic Revival and the Feminist Subject* (Princeton, NJ: Princeton University Press, 2004).

29. In Persian, among a number of published works, serious articles on the subject have appeared in *Pajūhish-hāye qur'ān: vije-ye zan dar qur'ān* 7, no. 25–28 (1380/2001). For Arabic works, see the following note.

30. To cite just one example from the commentary that is most often referred to by Sunni Arab Muslims today: Ismā'īl b. Kathīr, famously known as Ibn Kathīr, *Tafsīr al-qur'ān al-'aẓīm* (Beirut: Dār al-Andalūs, 1385/1966), vol. 1:481, in explaining "men are a degree above women" asserts explicitly that this is in the sense that men have excellence over women in creation (*khalq*) and character (*khulq*), in status (*manzila*) and obedience, in being provider and in being managers of their interests and in enjoying excellence in this world and the next. He goes on to cite the verse on God's preferment (Q. 4:35) as evidence for his conclusion. Remarkably, there are no traditions cited as documentation in this regard since the interpretation is derived by his own understanding of the apparent sense of the verses.

31. Muḥammad al-Ghazālī has authored a book on women's issues. See note 14 above. Ayatollah Sistānī, as far as I know, has not written an independent book on rulings dealing with women's issues. However, in my meeting with him in Najaf in August 1998, he clearly rejected modern assertions about the equality of women with men in terms of their abilities and accruing rights and obligations. However, he is

not alone in such denial of the modern realities of women's existence as breadwinners and as bearers of equal rights and dignity.

32. Murtaḍā Muṭahharī wrote a number of articles and a book on various dimensions of a woman's life in family and in society. His most influential work remains on the subject of modesty and continues to be read and disputed in the Iranian seminaries. What is refreshing in his approach to the question of minimum requirements regarding the head covering is a realistic appreciation of modern lifestyle that poses problems for the traditional heritage and which requires rational evaluation to infer the spirit of divine law as it seeks application today. See a summary of his views in a volume specifically dealing with the subject of women in the Qur'an: *Pajūhish-hāye qur'ān: vije-ye zan dar qur'ān* 7, no. 25–28 (1380/2001), 14–29.

33. Muḥammad Shahrūr, a civil engineer by training, is a Syrian Arab who received his training in Russia and Ireland. His writings about fresh readings of the Qur'anic notions of pluralism include a reformist agenda that seeks to promote women's rights in the Muslim world. His writings include: *Naḥwa uṣūl jadīda li al-fiqh al-Islāmī: fiqh al-mar'a: al-waṣīya, al-irth, al-qiwāma, al-ta'addudīya, al-libās* (Damascus, Syria: al-Ahālī li al-Ṭibā'a wa al-Nashr wa al-Tawzī', 2000); *al-Islām wa al-īmān: manẓūmat al-qiyam* (Damascus, Syria: al-Ahālī li al-Ṭibā'a wa al-Nashr wa al-Tawzī', 1996); *Dirāsāt Islāmīya mu'āṣira fī al-dawla wa al-mujtama'* (Damascus, Syria: al-Ahālī li al-Ṭibā'a wa al-Nashr wa al-Tawzī', 1994); *al-Kitāb wa-al-Qur'ān: qirā'a mu'āṣira* (Damascus, Syria: al-Ahālī li al-Ṭibā'a wa al-Nashr wa al-Tawzī', 1990).

34. Naṣr Ḥāmid Abū Zayd is an Egyptian Muslim thinker, whose books include: *al-Khiṭāb al-dīnī: ru'ya naqdīya: naḥwa intāj wa'y 'ilmī bi dalālat al-nuṣūṣ al-dīnīya* (Beirut: Dār al-Muntakhab al-'Arabī li al-Dirāsāt wa al-Nashr wa al-Tawzī', 1992); *al-Khiṭāb wa-al-ta'wīl* (Casablanca, Morocco: al-Markaz al-Thaqāfī al-'Arabī, 2000); *al-Mar'a fī khiṭāb al-'azma* (Cairo: Dār Nuṣūṣ, 1994); *al-Naṣṣ, al-ṣulṭa, al-ḥaqīqa: al-fikr al-dīnī bayna irādat al-ma'rifa wa-irādat al-ḥaymana* (Beirut: al-Markaz al-Thaqāfī al-'Arabī, 1995); *Dawā'ir al-khawf: qirā'a fī khiṭāb al-mar'a* (Casablanca: al-Markaz al-Thaqāfī al-'Arabī, 1999); Nasr Abu Zaid with Esther R. Nelson, *Voice of an Exile: Reflections on Islam* (Westport, CT: Praeger, 2004); *Naqd al-khiṭāb al-dīnī* (Cairo: Sīnā li al-Nashr, 1994); *Mafhūm al-naṣṣ: dirāsa fī 'ulūm al-qur'ān* (Cairo: al-Hay'a al-Miṣriya al-'Āmma li al-Kitāb, 1990); *al-Ittijāh al-aqlī fī al-tafsīr: dirāsa fī qaḍīyat al-majāz fī al-qur'ān 'inda al-mu'tazila* (Beirut: Dār al-Tanwīr li al-Ṭibā'a wa-al-Nashr, 1982).

35. I am using A. J. Arberry's rendering of the word *qawwām* as "manager"—the signification that is fundamental to the concept. However, as indicated by the lexicographers, the term is rich and its usage in Arab culture carries discretionary exercise of authority over someone whose interests need to be protected.

36. Jamāl al-Dīn Muḥammad b. Mukarram Ibn Manẓūr, *Lisān al-'arab* (Beirut: Dār Ṣādir, n.d.), vol. 12:496ff.

37. Rāzī, *Tafsīr al-kabīr*, vol. 10:88. For the richness in lexical signification, see: Lane, *An Arabic-English Lexicon*, vol. 8:2995.

38. See: Muḥammad b. Muḥammad Murtaḍā al-Zabīdī, *Tāj al-'arūs min jawāhir al-qāmūs* (Kuwait: Maṭba'a Ḥukūma al-Kuwayt, 1965–1997), vol. 9, under NASHAZA.

39. Ibn Kathīr, *Tafsīr al-qur'ān*, vol. 2:275 explicitly asserts this cultural understanding of the verse by taking the word *qiwāma* in the meaning of having "custody" over a woman, that is, being empowered to exercise authority over her (*al-ḥākim 'alayhā*) and even to reprimand her if she misbehaves. He then goes on to declare in no uncertain terms that "man is superior to woman, and it is for this reason that the prophethood was limited to men just as the great kingship was." Again, it is remarkable that he does not cite any traditions in support of his interpretation. He simply relates the tradition on the authority of the Prophet in which the Prophet warns his community, "No people will ever be successful if they turn over their affairs to a woman."

40. Jalāl al-Dīn 'Abd al-Raḥmān al-Suyūṭī, *ai-Durr al-manthūr fī tafsīr al-qur'ān bi al-ma'thūr* (Beirut: Dār al-Iḥyā al-Turāth al-'Arabī, 2001), vol. 2:481ff. cites numerous traditions that support the purport of these traditions that are reported on the authority of the early companions.

41. See Abū Zayd's comments on these verses in his article on women's human rights in *Ḥuqūq al-insān fī fikr al-'arabī*, pp. 259ff. It is interesting to note that Ṭabāṭabā'ī, *al-Mīzān*, vol. 5:343ff. discusses at length the connotation of the *qiwāma* verse and avoids citing any of the traditions that are damaging to the overall standing of a woman in Islamic tradition. But he too believes that although men and women are equal in all other aspects and that a woman has a right to advance in all fields of human engagement in modern contexts, men enjoy superior intellectual and physical abilities, which disqualify women from assuming judgeships and military positions. More pertinently, his advice to women is to excel in their domestic performance for the betterment of family and society. See in particular his assessment in light of the *qiwāma* verse.

42. All the commentaries cited in previous notes discuss the matter of aggression denoted in the term *nushūz*. Ibn Kathīr, for instance, takes up the matter and interprets it in the sense of "rising against [*irtifā'*] their husbands." In this sense, "*nāshiza* is a woman who rises against her husband, disobeying him, opposing him, infuriated against him" (vol. 2: 277).

CHAPTER 5

1. Although a UNESCO document of 1949 entitled *Human Rights: Comments and Interpretations. A Symposium edited by UNESCO* (New York: A Wingate, 1949) suggested that the discussion of human rights goes back to the beginnings of philosophy, in both the East and the West, few have endorsed such a contrived assessment of world history as far as rights are concerned. Among Christian scholars, Alisdair MacIntyre has dismissed natural or human rights as mere fictions, an unfortunate invention of modern liberal individualism that should be discarded. See Brian Tierney, *The Idea of Natural Rights* (Grand Rapids, MI: William B. Eedermans, 1997), p. 2, who cites MacIntyre and Alan Gerwith for their views on the document.

2. Richard Tuck, *Natural Rights Theories: Their Origin and Development* (New York: Cambridge University Press, 1979) deals with the development of the language of rights in the classic texts of rights theory, which were developed from the Middle Ages to the end of the seventeenth century in both Catholic and Protestant Europe. See also a

detailed examination of the development of rights language in Tierney, *The Idea of Natural Rights,* especially the first two chapters.

3. Adam B. Seligman, *Modernity's Wager: Authority, the Self, and Transcendence* (Princeton, NJ: Princeton University Press, 2000), p. 116. Chapter 4 has important pointers that show how the self was internalized in modern discourse on individual autonomy and the language of human rights.

4. Seligman, *Modernity's Wager,* p. 116.

5. Ibid. In different contexts, this valuable study takes up the idea of individual and community in the contexts of modern rational choice and reductionist visions of the self, with the concomitant loss of transcendence and the potential loss of any idea of self as moral evaluator within the context of communal approbation.

6. In the words of John Rawls, all public choices must be in harmony with reason that are defensible in terms of a particular social structure that will affirmatively transform the public space to that of a social democratic constitutional framework. His concept of free and equal persons and the idea of a well-ordered society as "a society effectively regulated by a political concept of justice" form the basis of his public sphere. See his *Political Liberalism* (New York: Columbia University Press, 1993), p. 14.

7. Abdolkarim Soroush, *Reason, Freedom, and Democracy in Islam: Essential Writings of Abdolkarim Soroush,* trans. and ed. M. Sadri and A. Sadri (New York: Oxford University Press, 2000), in several places introduces the crisis of epistemology in juridical sciences caused by traditional moralism and dogmatism.

8. Abdulaziz Sachedina, *The Islamic Roots of Democratic Pluralism* (New York: Oxford University Press, 2001).

9. Ebrahim Moosa, *Ghazali: The Poetics of Imagination* (Chapel Hill, NC: University of North Carolina Press, 2005), critically evaluates modern Muslim revivalist attitudes to rational inquiry in the light of classical traditional debate between theological-juridical and philosophical discourses.

10. Johannes Morsink, *The Universal Declaration of Human Rights: Origins, Drafting, and Intent* (Philadelphia: University of Pennsylvania Press, 1999), chapter 8.

11. Gerald F. Gaus, *Justificatory Liberalism: An Essay on Epistemology and Political Theory* (New York: Oxford University Press, 1996), undertakes to delineate the difficulty of providing public justification of a public morality by accounting for epistemologically justified beliefs through a theory of both personal and public justification. In the context of a public forum where interpersonal discussions about what one believes take place, justification dynamics require participants to be prepared to adjust their beliefs as supporting reasons develop and change in accordance with change in belief.

12. John Rawls, "The Idea of Public Reason Revisited," *University of Chicago Law Review* 64 (1997), 769. In another place in this article, Rawls gives the impression that his position is not aggressively secular, even when he advocates that religious reasons and sectarian doctrines should not be invoked to justify legislation in a democratic society. Islamic secularity, on the other hand, makes room for a secular moral rationality because it does not believe that religious reasons in the public space contradict public reasons.

13. Among the more circumspect endorsements of this evil practice is the *fatwā* that appears in, for instance, *Bayyināt*, a weekly bulletin that is published from Beirut, in which a strict contextual condition of combat is set forth to minimize its impact on innocent bystanders. See: *Bayyināt* (Beirut: Maktab al-Thiqāfa wa al-I'lām), 22, no. 207 (January, 2001), 8.

14. Richard A. Shweder, Martha Minow, and Hazel Markus, eds., *Engaging Cultural Differences: The Multicultural Challenge in Liberal Democracies* (New York: Russell Sage Foundation, 2002). In several articles, authors have captured the debate about the place of groups in liberal democracies, around the globe, pointing out the hegemonic Hellenization of world culture, pursued by the first world through the instrumentality of human rights.

15. Rawls, *Political Liberalism*, p. 10.

16. Dominic McGoldrick, *Human Rights and Religion: The Islamic Headscarf Debate in Europe* (Portland, OR: Hart Publishing, 2006), takes up the entire debate from French and European constitutional to international human rights law to reveal the complexity of the dispute over the proposed French ban on ostentatious religious symbols.

17. Xiaorong Li, "What's in a Headscarf?" *Philosophy and Public Policy Quarterly* 24, no. 1/2 (2004), 14–18.

18. Jeffrey Stout, *Democracy and Tradition* (Princeton, NJ: Princeton University Press, 2004), in chapter 3, "Religious Reasons in Political Argument," takes up the way liberal political thought employs "reasonableness" and disqualifies traditional arguments to engage public rationalities in the public sphere.

19. For a balanced position on this dichotomy between individualist and collectivist positions and its implication for individual rights, see: Seligman, *Modernity's Wager*, in various places. The author challenges modern assumptions about individualist moral autonomy freed from collective restraints and its transcendent referent. For this chapter, his discussion in chapter 5, "Tolerance and Tradition," is important in showing with much evidence that individual rights in America did not spring solely from positive law, but had acquired a "transcendent justification unique in the modern world" (p. 127).

20. Richard A. Shweder, "'What about Female Genital Mutilation?' and Why Understanding Culture Matters in the First Place," in *Engaging Cultural Differences*, ed. Richard A. Shweder et al., pp. 216–251, and his forthcoming article, "When Cultures Collide: Which Rights? Whose Tradition of Values? A Critique of the Global Anti-FGM Campaign," takes up the fundamental question of whether rights arguments can be applied to "the normative and socially valued practice of genital modification in East and West African communities."

21. Ibid. Shweder has examined and critiqued in detail the pro- and antifemale genital mutilation (FGM) literature to draw his larger conclusion that one needs to understand the native practice without imposing cultural adjudication from outside so that the prevalent distortion of the practice could be avoided.

22. Ibid. Shweder cites numerous anthropological and medical studies to argue that the global project to eradicate the practice remains ill-informed and biased

against it simply because the project lacks fairness, reciprocity, and equality of the voices in the process of negotiating the impact of female circumcision on either the health or the human rights of the women who have undergone this type of cultural initiation.

23. Although Shweder is correct in his criticism of the popular press that is biased toward those who advocate the eradication of the practice based on the claims that female genital modification is a harmful practice, and produces "objective" evidence from medical field research done under the sponsorship of the Medical Research Council, his cultural analysis falls short of questioning the reasoning that is used to justify the practice. There is surely a difference between male circumcision (which is usually accompanied by brief pain, and which rarely harms health or sexual or reproductive function) and female circumcision, even when both practices seem to fulfill a similar cultural role.

24. Xiaorong Li, "Tolerating the Intolerable: The Case of Female Genital Mutilation," *Philosophy and Public Policy Quarterly* 21, no. 1 (2001), 2–8, takes up the issue of the apparent inconsistency in the domestic and international positions of the U.S. government on the practice. In this particular instance, I share her critique of the cultural relativist position that the practice should be tolerated in those cultures where it is seen as a meaningful procedure in that culture. In addition, the principle of "No harm, no harassment" in Islamic social ethics would seem to rule out the practice in any situation that is conceived as probably harmful to the dignity of a female child. See my chapter, "The Search for Islamic Bioethics Principles," in *Principles of Health Care Ethics*, ed. Richard E. Ashcroft, et al. (West Sussex, UK: John Wiley, 2007), pp. 117–125.

25. Tierney, *The Idea of Natural Rights*, traces this history and the problematic of denying natural rights for the modern development of the concept of human rights.

26. Jack Donnelly, *Universal Human Rights in Theory and Practice* (Ithaca, NY: Cornell University Press, 2003), pp. 89–106, takes up the issue of the universality of the UN declaration in the context of cultural diversity of human communities. Although he emphatically endorses universal values that undergird the practical concerns of the international document in order to protect human dignity, in the conceptual exposition of human rights in the first chapter he fails to confront "the notorious problem of philosophical foundations" of the document, which is, as this study argues, the only intelligent and cross-culturally legitimate mode of addressing the widely discussed issue of the secular (and almost anti–human nature) bias of the Declaration among Muslim and other religious communities.

27. Henry J. Steiner, Philip Alston and Ryan Goodman, eds., *International Human Rights in Context: Law Politics Morals*, 3rd ed. (New York: Oxford University Press, 2008), in section 6, "Rights or Duties as Organizing Concepts," the authors raise several key questions about the rhetoric and concepts of rights in the international context.

28. Jürgen Habermas, "Struggles for Recognition in the Democratic Constitutional State," in *Multiculturalism: Examining the Politics of Recognition*, ed. Amy Gutman (Princeton, NJ: Princeton University Press, 1994), pp. 107–148, takes up the politics of recognition of collective identities in the context of a Eurocentric global society which, under the democratic constitutional states, is geared toward protecting individual rights and marginalizing multicultural forms of life and tradition.

29. In a recent case of a Muslim girl, Aqsa Pervez, in Toronto, Canada (November 2007), whose death was caused by severe head injury caused by her own father for refusing to abide by the Islamic dress code, there was certainly an abuse of parental authority and gross violation of the girl's human rights.

30. For the incisive critique of this liberal thesis, see David Novak, *Covenantal Rights: A Study in Jewish Political Theory* (Princeton, NJ: Princeton University Press, 2000), introduction, which situates humankind in relation to the terms *person* and *community*. Human existence is characterized by a person's participation in a series of communities, each related to the other. A person is never part of only one community. Actually, he or she participates in a plurality of communities in the form of overlapping circles.

31. Sir Henry Sumner Maine, *Ancient Law: Its Connection with the Early History of Society and Its Relation to Modern Ideas*, repr. ed. (New York: Dorset Press, 1986), p. 140, takes up the issue of status in all its forms, which "are coloured by, the powers and privileges anciently residing in the family . . . the movement of the progressive societies has hitherto been a movement *from Status to Contract*."

32. Ronald Inglehart, in his chapter, "Culture and Democracy," in *Culture Matters: How Values Shape Human Progress* (Basic Books, 2000), pp. 80–97, puts forward a defensible thesis about cultural change in developing nations that is closely linked to economic development. It seems that it is not secularization alone that can ultimately bring about the necessary but gradual changes that make democratic governance through institutional development possible in the Muslim world.

33. Donnelly, *Universal Human Rights*, pp. 204ff.

34. John Rawls, "The Priority of Right and Ideas of the Good," *Philosophy and Public Affairs* 17, no. 4, 251–76.

35. Will Kymlicka, "Two Models of Pluralism and Tolerance," in *Toleration: An Elusive Virtue*, ed. David Heyd (Princeton, NJ: Princeton University Press, 1996), pp. 81–105, has critically evaluated the Rawlsian liberal, secular model of religious tolerance based on the twin principles of justice and autonomy. Kymlicka, in agreement with the importance of the individual freedom of conscience as a human right, has shown another model of religious toleration in which a dominant religious community, committed to a particular belief system in its comprehensive political life, could provide a system that would ensure harmonious intercommunal life in a multifaith society. In spite of the fact that Islam recognizes the centrality of autonomous human conscience in negotiating its spiritual destiny, it is the second model proposed by Kymlicka that has historically provided the Muslim state and its legal system means to secure some semblance to modern citizenry.

36. There are numerous Muslim traditionalists who address this traditionalist concern about corrosive individualism that is being imposed from outside by the advocates of liberal democracy. More poignant is their criticism of the neutrality requirement that leads to the silencing of religious criticisms of the Muslim public order. Ultimately, the question for these scholars revolves around the supposed benefit of transforming Muslim societies to what Rawls identifies as "social democratic constitutionalism."

37. Marshall G. S. Hodgson, *The Venture of Islam: Conscience and History in a World Civilization* (Chicago: University of Chicago Press, 1974), vol. 1:218.

38. See Ann K. S. Lambton, *State and Government in Medieval Islam* (Oxford: Oxford University Press, 1981), chapters 6–9.

39. Adam B. Seligman, *The Idea of Civil Society* (New York: Free Press, 1992), chapter 3.

40. Hamed Enayat, *Modern Islamic Political Thought* (Austin: University of Texas Press, 1991), chapter 3.

41. Sayyid Quṭb, *Fī ẓilāl al-qur'ān* (Beirut: Dār al-Shurūq, 1973), vol. 3:1392–1393, regards this as the most unique passage of the Qur'an where the divine lordship is asserted in light of the covenant with the Children of Adam with their Creator until the Day of Judgment. The locus of this covenant is human nature, the *fiṭra*, which runs through the generations to confirm the autonomous human relation to God. Sayyid Muḥammad Ḥusayn al-Ṭabāṭabā'ī, *Al-Mīzān fī tafsīr al-qur'ān* (Beirut: Mu'assasa al-A'lamī, 1392/1972), vol. 8:306–309, regards this verse as a human testimony to its own commitment to fulfill its own need to be perfected. How can human beings go against their own testimony about their need and disbelieve in God's lordship established through the covenant that God took before they were physically created? The covenant also separates each individual from another and makes that individual testify against himself or herself and confess God's lordship. In the following verse human beings are warned: "Lest you say: Our fathers were idolaters aforetime, and we were seed after them. What, wilt Thou then destroy us for the deeds of vain-doers?" (Q. 7:173).

42. Quṭb, *Fī ẓilāl al-qur'ān*, vol. 6:3917, in his commentary on verses 7–10 of chapter 91, explains the theory of human creation with twofold nature: capable of doing good and evil; being guided and misguided; and endowed with the capacity to distinguish between the two. This is a concealed power in human existence which the Qur'an introduces sometimes as inspiration (*ilhām*) and at other times as guidance (*hidāya*). This is concealed in our innermost being in the form of a potential that external factors may arouse from time to time, sharpening and orienting them in this or that direction. However, they cannot create this twofold potential, because it is created in the *fiṭra*. Ṭabāṭabā'ī, *al-Mīzān*, vol. 20:297–299, treats the question of inspiration in the context of ethical epistemology. He regards inspiration as the medium through which God presents knowledge in the form of conception or confirmation and instructs the human soul about its ethical responsibilities. God provides the knowledge of both good and evil related to the same act, such as consuming wealth; for instance, consuming the wealth of an orphan is wrong, and consuming one's own wealth is right. Hence, *ilhām* about the wrongness and the rightness of an act is perfected in practical reason through the divine command regarding "human by nature upright" (Q. 30:30–31).

43. Robert Bellah, "Islamic Tradition and the Problems of Modernization," in *Beyond Belief: Essays on Religion in the Post-Traditional World* (New York: Harper and Row, 1970), p. 150.

44. 'Ali 'Ūmlīl, *Fī shar'īya al-ikhtilāf* (Beirut: Dār al-Ṭibā'a, 1993), takes up the issue of permission to disagree in the matters of creed and practice in Muslim tradition, and

demonstrates that while Muslim leaders tolerated interfaith disagreements and gave the right to Jews and Christians, they did not extend that right to Muslims for fear of intercommunal dissension and disunity.

45. Muḥammad b. Muḥammad al-Ghazālī, *al-Iqtiṣād fī al-I'tiqād* (Beirut: Dār al-Amāna, 1969) pp. 214–215.

46. For instance, 'Alī b. Muḥammad al-Māwardī, *al-Aḥkām al-sulṭānīya wa al-wilāya al-dīnīya* (Kuwait: n.p., 1989), pp. 24ff. takes up the issue of obedience in several places in his work and argues in favor of it being the right of the ruler to exact obedience from the ruled as long as the ruler fulfills his duty toward God and the community.

47. Major compilations of the Sunni traditions mention this particular report. See, for instance, Muslim b. al-Ḥajjāj b. Muslim, *Ṣaḥīḥ muslim* (Beirut: Dār Iḥyā' al-Turāth al-'Arabī, 1972), vol. 6:13; *Ṣaḥīḥ al-bukhārī*, vol. 4:6; Aḥmad b. Muḥammad b. Ḥanbal, *Musnad ibn ḥanbal* (Cairo: Dār al-Ma'ārif, 1392/1972), vol. 2:253.

48. Mālik b. Anas, *al-Muwatta* (Beirut: Mu'assasa al-Risāla, 1993), vol. 1:345–346.

49. A number of juridical opinions not only discourage dissension and demand communal unity through obedience of Muslim rulers, they actually forbid the religiously legitimated right of every individual, male or female, to take a stance against injustices in the so-called Islamic public order. This is part of the right to freedom of religion as shown by Rashīd al-Ghannūshī, *al-Hurriyat al-'āmma fī dawlat al-islāmīya* (Beirut: Markaz Dirāsāt al-Waḥda al-'Arabīya, 1993), pp. 42–46. See also al-Būṭī in note 50.

50. Muḥammad Sa'īd Ramaḍān al-Būṭī, *'Alā ṭarīq al-'awda ilā al-islām: rasm li-manāhij wa ḥall li-mushkilāt* (Beirut: Mu'assasa al-Risāla, 1992), pp. 64–65.

51. Muḥammad b. Muḥammad b. 'Ahmad b. al-'Ikhwa, *Kitāb ma'ālim al-qirba fī aḥkām al-ḥisba*, ed. Muḥammad Maḥmūd Sha'bān, et al. (Cairo: al-Hay'a al-Miṣrīya al-'Āmma li-l-Kitāb, 1976), pp. 67–68.

52. Ibid.

CHAPTER 6

1. Richard A. Posner, *The Problematics of Moral and Legal Theory* (Cambridge, MA: Harvard University Press, 1999), p. 6, maintains that there is no transhistorical or extracultural authoritative source for our moral obligations. A form of moral relativism is dominant in an adaptationist conception of morality, in which "morality is judged nonmorally... by its contribution to the survival, or other ultimate goals, of a society or some group within it." Such a view would ultimately lead to irreconcilable differences among world communities regarding universal moral values that provide human rights norms their validity internationally. I do concede that cultures retrieve and apply these norms in the context of their social-political experience in varied ways; but they cannot afford to negate them as being relative to their humanity. Otherwise it will be impossible to speak about a fundamental right to freedom of conscience and religion.

2. A number of Sunni and Shī'ite jurists have questioned the applicability of the classical rulings about the death penalty, mainly because the Qur'an treats the matter as

strictly between God and human beings and, hence, beyond the jurisdiction of Muslim courts over the offense. In my earlier research I have not only argued against the death penalty as such; I have also questioned the application of the concept in the Islamic juridical corpus because of the absence of a church that can determine the seriousness of the offense. In addition, the problem seems to be the lack of precision in categorizing the offense as religious, since the precedent that provided the paradigm case for the later rulings of capital punishment in early Muslim history was certainly a matter of rebellion against Muslim political order and not against the religion of Islam.

3. For example, Ayatollah Muntaẓirī has ruled against capital punishment in this regard and has criticized the Iranian government for ignoring one of the fundamental articles of the Declaration about freedom of religion.

4. In his article on the rights of religious minorities in the Muslim world, prominent traditionalist Sunni jurist Yūsuf al-Qarāḍāwī, while asserting the rights of minorities to freedom of religion, entirely ignores the right of a Muslim to convert from Islam to another recognized religion like Christianity or Judaism. See "Ḥuqūq al-aqalliyāt ghayr muslima," *al-Tawḥīd* 84 (2006), 13–23; *al-Tawḥīd* 85 (2007), 15–28.

5. David Novak, *Covenantal Rights: A Study in Jewish Political Theory* (Princeton, NJ: Princeton University Press, 2000), pp. 5ff. discusses the relation between person and community and human existence in terms of a person's participation in a series of communities.

6. I have adopted the phrase from Muḥammad b. 'Umar Fakhr al-Dīn al-Rāzī, *Tafsīr al-kabīr* (Cairo: al-Maṭba'a al-Bahīya, 1938), 25:120, where he believes this to be sufficient for the proper affirmation of the unity of God as explained in the revelation.

7. Sayyid Muḥammad Ḥusayn al-Ṭabāṭabā'ī, *Al-Mīzān fī tafsīr al-qur'ān* (Beirut: Mu'assasa al-A'lamī, 1392/1972), 18:328; and Sayyid Quṭb, *Fī ẓilāl al-qur'ān* (Beirut: Dār al-Shurūq, 1973), 6:3349, make a distinction between a deeper commitment through *īmān* and formal submission through *islām*. As Quṭb points out explicitly: "This external *islām* is the one that has not as yet fused with the heart in order to become transformed into a trustworthy and dependable faith." And, although God accepts this *islām* because He is most forgiving and merciful, it is not the expected ideal faith.

8. See, for instance, Quṭb, *Fī ẓilāl al-qur'ān*, 1:291 and Ṭabāṭabā'ī, *al-Mīzān*, 2:342–343, for representative commentaries of the Sunni and Shī'ite thinkers, respectively.

9. Muḥammad b. Jarīr al-Ṭabarī, *Jāmi' al-bayān fī tafsīr al-qur'ān* (Beirut: Dār al-Ma'ārif, 1972), 3:10–12; Rāzī, *Tafsīr*, 4:15–16. For a variety of interpretations of the verse to circumscribe its general meaning, see Mahmoud Ayoub, *The Qur'an and Its Interpreters* (Albany: State University of New York Press, 1984), 1:252–255.

10. Immanuel Kant, *Religion within the Limits of Reason Alone*, trans. Theodore M. Greene and Hoyt H. Hudson (New York: Harper and Row, 1960), p. 98, argues that the real content of religion is that secured by the rational requirements of a universal morality. Morality is identified with rationality, that is, acting on reasons grounded in discursive reflection. Kant's pluralism is underscored by his statement: "There is only *one* (true) *religion;* but there can be *faiths* of several kind."

11. See Kenneth Cragg, "Islam and Other Faiths," in *Theology of Religions: Christianity and Other Religions* (Rome: Editrice Pontificia Universita Gregoriana, 1993), pp. 257–270. Cragg's essentialist and reductionist analysis of the selected passages of the Qur'an is undertaken to assess the possibility of dialogue with Muslims in light of their exclusive claim to religious truth and its finality founded upon the doctrine of supersession. It is worth pointing out that a similar case can be made for the most exclusive theology for Christianity and its relation to other religions.

12. W. T. Dickens, "Frank Conversations: Promoting Peace among the Abrahamic Traditions through Interreligious Dialogue," *Journal of Religious Ethics* 34, no. 3 (2006), 397–420, has critically evaluated John Hick's revisionist pluralism and has proposed fresh grounds for a more fruitful dialogue to achieve peace among the followers of the three Abrahamic traditions. A balanced and more updated study regarding Islam and its relations with other monotheistic traditions is *Islam and Inter-Faith Relations: The Gerald Weisfeld Lectures 2006*, ed. Perry Schmidt-Leukel and Lloyd Ridgeon (London: SCM Press, 2007).

13. Whether Sunni or Shī'ite, the majority of religious leaders representing traditionalist scholarship reject the notion of relative truth claims in order to produce a theology of interreligious dialogue. Several articles and books that were published in the late 1990s, when pluralism was the catchword of the new world order in which the Declaration was asserting its moral authority to promote freedom of religion, prominent Muslim leaders, while rejecting a revisionist pluralism that denied exclusive truth claims to the faith communities, reasserted the Qur'anic notion of pluralism as a source of social coexistence. For details of this debate, see Abdulaziz Sachedina, *The Islamic Roots of Democratic Pluralism* (New York: Oxford University Press, 2000).

14. Marshall G. S. Hodgson, *The Venture of Islam: Conscience and History in a World Civilization* (Chicago: University of Chicago Press, 1977), 1:336.

15. The term *rite* or *legal school* is the translation of *madhhab*—a system of rules that covers all aspects of human spiritual and moral obligations (*taklīf*, plural of *takālīf*) that a Muslim must carry out as a member of the community. Four *madhhab*s, Mālikī, Ḥanafī, Shāfi'ī, and Ḥanbalī, were ultimately accepted as legitimate by the Sunnis, while the Shī'ites formulated and followed their own rite, known as Ja'farī.

16. I have treated the matter of freedom of conscience from the Qur'anic point of view in my earlier work: "Liberty of Conscience and Religion in the Qur'an," in *Human Rights and the Conflict of Cultures: Western and Islamic Perspectives on Religious Liberty*, coauthored with David Little and John Kelsay (Columbia: University of South Carolina Press, 1988), pp. 53–100.

17. Historically, Muslims, like other religious groups, have demonstrated far greater intolerance toward dissenters within their own ranks. Muslim history is replete with instances of intrareligious violence, not only between the majoritarian Sunni and the minority Shī'ite communities, but also among the Sunni adherents of different legal rites, such as the Ḥanafī and the Ḥanbalī schools. See Benjamin Braude and Bernard Lewis, eds., *Christians and Jews in the Ottoman Empire: The Functioning of a Plural Society* (New York: Holmes and Meier, 1982), pp. 1–34; G. R. Elton,

"Introduction," in *Persecution and Toleration*, vol. 21 of *Studies in Church History*, ed. W. J. Shields (Oxford: Basil Blackwell, 1984), pp. xiii–xv.

18. Jane Damien McAuliffe, *Qur'ānic Christians: An Analysis of Classical and Modern Exegesis* (Cambridge: Cambridge University Press, 1991), has done extensive work on the verses dealing with Muslims' perceptions of Christians through the exegetical works produced both by the Sunni and Shī'ite commentators, from the classical to the modern period. Her study concludes accurately that the issue of the prophethood of Muḥammad remained an important element in affording non-Qur'anic peoples of the Book a share in the salvation. However, in the midst of this exclusivist soteriology there have been Muslim commentators, more in the modern period of interfaith hermeneutics, who have regarded the promise in Q. 2:62 as still important in constructing inclusive theology founded upon belief in God, the Hereafter, and right action as overriding the criteria for attaining salvation.

19. Al-Sayyid Abū al-Qāsim al-Mūsawī al-Khu'ī, *The Prolegomena to the Qur'an*, trans. with an introduction by Abdulaziz A. Sachedina (New York: Oxford University Press, 1998), pp. 186–253; also, John Burton, "Introductory Essay: 'The Meaning of Naskh,'" in Abū 'Ubaid al-Qāsim b. Sallām, *K. al-nāsikh wa-l-mansūkh*, ed. with commentary by John Burton. E. J. W. Gibb Memorial Series, New Series, 30 (Suffolk: St. Edmundsbury Press, 1987).

20. For the classical exegetical formulations that dominate the intolerant and exclusivist attitude toward the peoples of the Book based on the notion of abrogation of the tolerant Q. 2:62 by Q. 3:85, see: Ṭabarī, *Jāmi' al-bayān*, 2:155–156, where he cites exclusivist opinions and then rejects the view that God will exclude those who had lived in faith and acted righteously because he finds it incongruent with the divine promises Ismā'īl ibn 'Umar Ibn Kathīr, *Tafsīr al-Qur'ān al-aẓīm* (Beirut: Dār al-Andalūs li al-Ṭibā'a wa-al-Nashr, 1385/1966), 1:103, limits salvation to the people of the Book before Muḥammad became the Prophet; Rashīd Riḍā, *Tafsīr al-qur'ān al-ḥakīm al-shahīr bi-tafsīr al-manār* (Beirut: Dār al Ma'rifa, 1970), 6:479, however, grudgingly, does concede the validity of salvation for the people of the Book.

21. Ṭabarī, *Jāmi' al-bayān*, 2:155–156.

22. Ibn Kathīr, *Tafsīr al-qur'an*, 1:103.

23. For the theological problems faced by early Christianity in declaring its originality and working out its relation to Judaism, see Marcel Simon, *Verus Israel: A Study of the Relations between Christians and Jews in the Roman Empire (AD 135–425)* (New York: Oxford University Press, 1986), in particular chapter 3.

24. Riḍā, *Tafsīr al-manār*, 1:339.

25. Ibid., 1:336.

26. Ṭabāṭabā'ī, *al-Mīzān*, 1:193.

Select Bibliography

'Abbās, 'Abd al-Hādī. *Huqūq al-insān*. Damascus: Dār al-Faḍl, 1995.

Abou El Fadl, Khaled. "A Distinctly Islamic View of Human Rights: Does It Exist and Is It Compatible with the Universal Declaration of Human Rights?" In *Islam and Human Rights: Advancing a US-Muslim Dialogue*. Ed. Shirin T. Hunter with Huma Malik. Washington, DC: CSIS Press, 2005.

———. "Islam and the Challenge of Democratic Commitment." In *Does Human Rights Need God?* Ed. Elizabeth M. Bucar and Barbara Barnett. Grand Rapids, MI: Eerdmans, 2005.

Abu Sa'īdī, Mahdī. *Mabānī-yi ḥuqūq-i bashar*. Tehran: Intishārāt-i Āsiya, 1964.

Abū Zayd, Naṣr Ḥāmid. *Al-Ittijāh al-'aqlī fī al-tafsīr: dirāsa fī qaḍīyāt al-majāz fī al-qur'ān 'inda al-mu'tazila*. Beirut: Dār al-Tanwīr li al-Ṭibā'a wa-al-Nashr, 1982.

———. *Al-Khiṭāb al-dīnī: ru'ya naqdīya: naḥwa intāj wa'y 'ilmī bi dalālat al-nuṣūṣ al-dīnīya*. Beirut: Dār al-Muntakhab al-'Arabī li al-Dirāsāt wa al-Nashr wa al-Tawzī' 1992.

———. *Al-Khiṭāb wa-al-ta'wīl*. Casablanca, Morocco: al-Markaz al-Thaqāfī al-'Arabī, 2000.

———. *Al-Mar'a fī khiṭāb al-'azma*. Cairo: Dār Nuṣūṣ, 1994.

———. *Al-Naṣṣ, al-ṣulṭa, al-ḥaqīqa: al-fikr al-dīnī bayna irādat al-ma'rifa wa-irādat al-ḥaymana*. Beirut: al-Markaz al-Thaqāfī al-'Arabī.

———. *Dawā'ir al-khawf: qirā'a fī khiṭāb al-mar'a*. Casablanca: al-Markaz al-Thaqāfī al-'Arabī, 1999.

———. *Mafhūm al-naṣṣ: dirāsa fī 'ulūm al-qur'ān*. Cairo: al-Hay'a al-Miṣriya al-'Āmma li al-Kitāb, 1990.

———. *Naqd al-khiṭāb al-dīnī*. Cairo: Sīnā li al-Nashr, 1994.

———. *Voice of an Exile: Reflections on Islam*. With Esther R. Nelson. Westport, CT: Praeger, 2004.

'Alawī, Hādī al-. *Shakhṣiyāt ghayr qaliqa fī al-islām*. Beirut: Dār al-Kunūz al-'Adabīya, 1995.

'Amāra, Muḥammad. *Al-Islām wa ḥuqūq al-insān: Ḍarūrāt... lā ḥuqūq* (Islam and Human Rights: Necessities... Not Rights). Kuwait: al-Majlis al-Waṭanī, 1405/1985.

Anas, Mālik b. *Al-Muwatta*. Vols. 1–2. Beirut: Mu'assasa al-Risāla, 1993.

An-Naim, Abdullahi A., Jerald D. Gort, Henry Jansen, and Hendrick M. Vroom, eds. *Human Rights and Religious Values: An Uneasy Relationship?* Grand Rapids: Eedermans, 2004.

Arberry, A. J. *The Koran Interpreted*. New York: Macmillan, 1955.

Ayatollah Bojnūrdī, "Ta'āmul wa ta'āruḍ bayn-i fiqh wa ḥuqūq-i bashar." *Farzane* 6, no. 3 (1997), 7–14.

Ayoub, Mahmoud. *The Qur'an and Its Interpreters*. Albany: State University of New York Press, 1984.

Badawī, 'Abd al-Raḥmān. *Al-Insān al-kāmil fī al-islām*. Beirut: Dār al-Qalam, 1976.

Bayḍāwī, 'Abdallah b. 'Umar, al-. *Anwār al-tanzīl wa asrār al-ta'wīl*. Cairo: al-Maṭba'a al-'Uthmānīya, 1939.

Bayyināt (Beirut: Maktab al-Thiqāfa wa al-I'lām, 2001), 22, no. 207 (January, 2001).

Bellah, Robert. "Islamic Tradition and the Problems of Modernization." In *Beyond Belief: Essays on Religion in the Post-Traditional World*. New York: Harper and Row, 1970.

Braude, Benjamin, and Bernard Lewis, eds. *Christians and Jews in the Ottoman Empire: The Functioning of a Plural Society*. New York: Holmes and Meier, 1982.

Bukhari, Muhammad b. Ismā'il al-. *Ṣaḥīḥ al-bukhārī*. Beirut: 'Ālam al-Kutub, 1986.

Buṭī, Muḥammad Sa'īd Ramaḍan al-. *'Alā ṭarīqat al-'awdā ilā al-islām: Rasm li-manāhij wa ḥall li-mushkilāt*. Beirut: Mu'assasa al-Risāla, 1992.

Cragg, Kenneth. "Islam and Other Faiths." In *Theology of Religions: Christianity and Other Religions*. Rome: Editrice Pontificia Universita Gregoriana, 1993.

Cuneo, Terence, ed. *Religion in the Liberal Polity*. Notre Dame, IN: University of Notre Dame Press, 2004.

Dalacoura, Katerina. *Islam, Liberalism, and Human Rights*, rev. ed. London: I. B. Tauris, 2003.

Dickens, W. T. "Frank Conversations: Promoting Peace among the Abrahamic Traditions through Interreligious Dialogue." *Journal of Religious Ethics* 34, no. 3 (2006), 397–420.

Donnelly, Jack. *Universal Human Rights in Theory and Practice*. Ithaca, NY: Cornell University Press, 2003.

Elton, G. R. "Introduction," in *Studies in Church History*, vol. 21: *Persecution and Toleration*. Ed. W. J. Shields. Oxford: Basil Blackwell, 1984.

Enayat, Hamid. *Modern Islamic Political Thought*. Austin: University of Texas Press, 1991.

Fanjarī, Muḥammad Shawqī al-. *al-Islām wa al-ḍimān al-ijtimā'ī*. Cairo: Al-Ḥay'a al-Miṣrīya al-'Āmma li al-Kitāb, 1980.

Gaus, Gerald F. *Justificatory Liberalism: An Essay on Epistemology and Political Theory.* New York: Oxford University Press, 1996.

Ghannūshī, Rashīd al-. *al-Ḥurriyāt al-'āmma fī dawlat al-islāmīya.* Beirut: Markaz Dirāsāt al-Waḥdat al-'Arabīya, 1993.

Ghazālī, Muḥammad b. Muḥammad al-. *Al-Iqtiṣād fī al-i'tiqād.* Beirut: Dār al-Amāna, 1969.

Ghazālī, Muḥammad al-. *Al-Ta'ālīm al-islāmīya wa i'lānāt al-umam al-muttaḥida.* Alexandria: Dār al-Da'wa, 1993.

———. *Qaḍāya al-mar'a bayna al-taqlid al-rākida wa al-wāfida.* Cairo: Dār al-Shurūq, 1992.

———. *Ḥuqūq al-insān: Bayn ta'ālīm al-islām wa i'lān al-umam al-muttaḥida* (Human Rights: Between the Teachings of Islam and the Declaration of the United Nations). Alexandria, Egypt: Dār al-Da'wa, 1422/2002.

Greenawalt, Kent. *Religious Convictions and Political Choice.* New York: Oxford University Press, 1988.

Gustafson, Carrie, and Peter Juviler, eds. *Religion and Human Rights: Competing Claims?* New York: M. E. Sharpe, 1984.

Habermas, Jürgen. "Struggles for Recognition in the Democratic Constitutional State." In *Multiculturalism: Examining the Politics of Recognition.* Ed. Amy Gutman. Princeton, NJ: Princeton University Press, 1994, pp. 107–148.

Hodgson, M. G. S. *The Venture of Islam: Conscience and History in a World Civilization.* 3 vols. Chicago: University of Chicago Press, 1974.

Hourani, George. *Islamic Rationalism: The Ethics of 'Abd al-Jabbar.* Oxford: Clarendon Press, 1971.

Ḥuqūq al-insān fī al-islām bayn al-khuṣūṣīya wa al-'ālamīya: Buḥūth wa munaqishāt al-Nadwā 'uqidat fī al-Ribāṭ. Amman, Jordan: al-Majma'a al-Malakī li Buḥūth al-Haḍara al-Islāmīya, Mu'assasa Āl al-Bayt (Rabat), UNESCO, 1998.

IbnḤanbal, Aḥmad b. Muḥammad. *Musnad ibn Ḥanbal.* Beirūt: Mu'assasa al-Risāla, 1993.

Ibn Kathīr, Ismā'īl ibn 'Umar. *Tafsīr al-qurān al-aẓīm.* 7 vols. Beirut: Dār al-Andalus lil-Ṭibā'a wa-al-Nashr, 1385/1966.

Ibn Manẓūr, Jamāl al-Dīn Muḥammad b. Mukarram. *Lisān al-'Arab.* 15 vols. Beirut: Dār Sādir, 1956.

Ibn Taymīya, Aḥmad b. 'Abd al-Ḥalīm. *Al-siyāsa al-shar'īya fī iṣlāḥ al-rā'ī wa al-ra'īya.* Cairo: Dār al-Kutub al-'Arabī, 1969.

———. *Al-ḥisba fī al-islām.* Cairo: al-Maṭba'a al-Salafīya, 1967–1968.

Ignatieff, Michael. *Human Rights as Politics and Idolatry.* Princeton, NJ: Princeton University Press, 2001.

'Ikhwa, Muḥammad b. Muḥammad b. 'Aḥmad b. al-. *Kitāb ma'ālim al-qirba fī aḥkām al-ḥisba.* Ed. Muḥammad Maḥmūd Sha'bān, et al. Cairo: al-Hay'a al-Miṣrīya al-'Āmma li- al-Kitāb, 1976.

Inglehart, Ronald. "Culture and Democracy." In *Culture Matters: How Values Shape Human Progress.* Ed. Lawrence E. Harrison and Samuel P. Huntington. New York: Basic Books, 2000, pp. 80–97.

Jābirī, Muḥammad ʻĀbid al-. *Al-ʻaql al-siyāsī al-ʻarabī: muḥaddadātuh wa tajlliyātuh.* Beirut: Markaz Dirāsāt al-Waḥda al-ʻArabīya, 1990.

———. *Al-dimuqratīya wa ḥuqūq al-insān.* Beirut: Markaz Dirāsat al-Waḥda al-ʻArabīya,1994.

———. "Mafāhīm al-ḥuqūq wa al-ʻadl fī nuṣūṣ al-ʻarabīya al-islāmiya." In *Ḥuqūq al-insān fī al-fikr al-ʻarabī.* Ed. Salmā Khaḍrā Jayyūsī. Beirut: Markaz Dirāsāt al-Waḥdat al-ʻArabīya, 2003, pp. 25–76.

Jadʻān, Fahmī. "Al-ṭāʻa wa al-ikhtilāf fī ḍawʻ ḥuqūq al-insān fī al-islām." In *Ḥuqūq al-insān fī al-fikr al-ʻarabi.* Ed. Salmā Khaḍrā Jayyūsī Beirut: Markaz Dirāsat al-Waḥdat al-ʻArabiya, 2003, pp. 201–220.

Jamīl, Ḥusayn. *Ḥuqūq al-insān fī al-waṭan al-ʻarabī.* Beirut: Markaz al-Waḥdat al-ʻArabīya, 1986.

Javādī Āmoli, ʻAbd Allāh, *Falsafe-yi ḥuqūq-i basher.* Ed. Sayyid Abū al-Qāsim Ḥusaynī. Qumm: Isrā', 1375/1996.

Jāwīsh, ʻAbd al-Azīz. *Al-Islām dīn al-fiṭra wa al-ḥurriya.* Cairo: n.d.

Kandiyoti, Deniz. "Reflections on the Politics of Gender in Muslim Societies: From Nairobi to Beijing." In *Faith and Freedom: Women's Human Rights in the Muslim World.* Ed. Mahnaz Afkhami. Syracuse: Syracuse University Press, 1995.

Kant, Immanuel. *Religion within the Limits of Reason Alone.* Trans. Theodore M. Greene and Hoyt H. Hudson. New York: Harper and Row, 1960.

Kashānī, Mullā Fatḥ Allāh. *Minhāj al-ṣādiqīn fī ilzām al-mukhālifīn.* 10 vols. Tehran: Kitābfurūshī-i Islāmīya, 1969.

Khalīl, Ḥāmid. "Al-farḍ wa sulṭa fī al-fikr al-ʻarabī al-ḥadīth." In *Ḥuqūq al-insān fī al-fikr al-ʻarabī.* Ed. Salmā Khaḍrā Jayyūsī. Beirut: Markaz Dirāsāt al-Waḥdat al-ʻArabīya, 2003, pp. 891–914.

Khaṭīb, ʻAdnān. *Ḥuqūq al-insān fī al-islām. Awwal taqnīn li-mabādī al-sharīʻa al-islāmīya.* Damascus: DārṬalās, 1992.

Khūʻī, Sayyid Abū al-Qāsim al-Mūsawī al-. *The Prolegomena to the Qur'an.* Trans. with an introduction by Abdulaziz A. Sachedina. New York: Oxford University Press, 1998.

Kymlicka, Will. "Two Models of Pluralism and Tolerance." In *Toleration: An Elusive Virtue.* Ed. David Heyd. Princeton, NJ: Princeton University Press, 1996.

Lambton, Ann K. S. *State and Government in Medieval Islam.* Oxford: Oxford University Press, 1981.

Lane, Edward W. *An Arabic-English Lexicon.* Beirut: Librairie du Liban, 1968.

Li, Xiaorong. "Tolerating the Intolerable: The Case of Female Genital Mutilation." *Philosophy & Public Policy Quarterly* 21 no. 1 (2001), 2–8.

———. "What's in a Headscarf?" *Philosophy & Public Policy Quarterly* 24 no. 1/2 (2004), 14–18.

Little, David. "Duties of Station vs. Duties of Conscience: Are There Two Moralities?" *Private and Public Ethics*: Tensions between Conscience and Institutional Responsibility. Ed. Donald G. Jones. New York: Edwin Mellon, 1978.

Mabīd, Muḥammad Saʻīd. *Ilā ghayr al-muḥajjabāt awwalan.* Doha, Qatar: Dār al-Thiqāfa, 1988.

MacIntyre, Alisdair. *After Virtue.* London: Duckworth, 1981.

———. "Community, Law, and the Idiom and Rhetoric of Rights," *Listening* 26 (1991), 96–110.

Mahmoud, Saba. *The Politics of Piety: The Islamic Revival and the Feminist Subject.* Princeton, NJ: Princeton University Press, 2004.

Maine, Sir Henry Sumner. *Ancient Law: Its Connection with the Early History of Society and Its Relation to Modern Ideas,* repr. ed. New York: Dorset Press, 1986.

Māwardī, 'Alī b. Muḥammad al-. *Al-aḥkām al-sulṭānīya wa al-wilāya al-dīnīya.* Kuwait: Maktabat Dār Ibn Quṭayba, 1989.

Mayer, Ann Elizabeth. "Citizenship and Human Rights in Some Muslim States." In *Islam, Modernism and the West: Cultural and Political Relations at the End of the Millennium.* Ed. Gema Martin Munoz. London: I. B. Tauris, 1999.

McAuliffe, Jane Damien. *Qur'anic Christians.* New York: Cambridge University Press, 1991.

McGoldrick, Dominic. *Human Rights and Religion: The Islamic Headscarf Debate in Europe.* Portland, OR: Hart Publishing, 2006.

Mīlād, Salwā 'Alī. *Wathā'iq ahl al-dhimma fī al-'aṣr al-'uthmānī wa ahamiyyataha al-tārikhīya.* Cairo: Dār al-Thiqāfa, 1983.

Mir-Hosseini, Ziba. "The Politics and Hermeneutics of Hijab in Iran: From Confinement to Choice." *Muslim World Journal of Human Rights,* 4, no. 1 (2007).

Moosa, Ebrahim. *Ghazali: The Poetics of Imagination.* Chapel Hill, NC: University of North Carolina Press, 2005.

Morsink, Johannes. *The Universal Declaration of Human Rights: Origins, Drafting, and Intent.* Philadelphia: University of Pennsylvania Press, 1999.

Muḥammad 'Abduh. *Al-islām wa al-naṣrānīya ma'a al-'ilm wa al-madanīya.* Beirut: Dār al-Ḥadātha, 1988.

Musaylih, Muḥammad al-Ḥusaynī al-. *Ḥuqūq al-insān bayna al-sharī'a al-islāmīya wa al-qānūn al-duwalī.* Cairo: Dār al-Nahḍa al-Miṣrīya, 1988.

Muslim b. al-Ḥajjāj al-Nisābūrī. *Ṣaḥīḥ.* Beirut: Dār Iḥyā' al-Turāth al-'Arabī, 1972.

Najm, Aḥmad Ḥāfiẓ. *Ḥuqūq al-insān bayna al-qur'ān wa al-i'lān.* Cairo: Dār al-Fikr al-'Arabī, 1979.

Novak, David. *Covenantal Rights: A Study in Jewish Political Theory.* Princeton, NJ: Princeton University Press, 2000.

Nussbaum, Martha C. "Religion and Women's Human Rights." In *Religion and Contemporary Liberalism.* Ed. Paul J. Weithman. Notre Dame, IN: University of Notre Dame Press, 1997.

Outka, Gene, and John P. Reeder Jr., eds. *Prospects for a Common Morality.* Princeton, NJ: Princeton University Press, 1993.

Pajūhish-hāye qur'ān: vije-ye zan dar qur'ān 7, no. 25–28 (1380/2001), 14–29.

Perry, Michael J. *The Idea of Human Rights: Four Inquiries.* New York: Oxford University Press, 1998.

Posner, Richard A. *The Problematics of Moral and Legal Theory.* Cambridge, MA: Harvard University Press, 1999.

Qāḍī 'Abd al-Jabbār al-Mu'tazilī. *Sharḥ al-uṣūl al-khamsa.* Ed. 'Abd al-Karīm 'Uthmān. Cairo: Maktaba Wahba, 1965.

Qaräḍāwī, Yusuf al-. *Fatāwā mu'āṣira li-al-mar'a wa al-'usra al-muslima.* Amman, Jordan: Dār al-Ḍiyā' 1988.

———. "Ḥuqūq al-aqalliyāt ghayr muslima." *al-Tawḥīd.* 84 (2006), 13–23; *al-Tawḥīd* 85 (2007), 15–28.

Qarāfī, Aḥmad b. Idrīs al-. *Tahdhīb al-furūq wa al-qawā'id al-sunnīya fī al-asrār al-fiqhīya.* Beirut: 'Ālam al-kutub, n.d.

Quṭb, Sayyid. *Fī ẓilāl al-qur'ān.* 8 vols. Beirut: Dār al-Shurūq, 1973.

Rawls, John. "The Idea of Public Reason Revisited." *University of Chicago Law Review* 64, no. 3 (1997), 765–807.

———. "The Priority of Right and Ideas of the Good." *Philosophy and Public Affairs* 17, no. 4, 251–76.

———. *Political Liberalism.* New York: Columbia University Press, 1993.

Rāzī, Muḥammad b. 'Umar Fakhr al-Dīn al-. *Al-Tafsīr al-kabīr.* 32 vols. Cairo: al-Maṭba'a al-Bahīya, 1938.

Riḍā, Rashīd. *Tafsīr al-qur'ān al-ḥakīm al-shahīr bi-tafsīr al-manār.* Beirut: Dār al Ma'rifa, 1970.

Ruston, Roger. *Human Rights and the Image of God.* London: SCM Press, 2004.

Sachedina, Abdulaziz. "The Clash of Universalisms: Religious and Secular in Human Rights." *The Hedgehog Review* 9, no. 3 (2007), 49–62. Charlottesville, VA: Institute for Advanced Studies in Culture.

———. *The Islamic Roots of Democratic Pluralism.* New York: Oxford University Press, 2000.

———. "Justifications for Violence in Islam." In *War and Its Discontents: Pacifism and Quietism in the Abrahamic Traditions.* Ed. J. Patout Burns. Washington, DC: Georgetown University Press, 1996.

———. "The Search for Islamic Bioethics Principles." In *Principles of Health Care Ethics.* Ed. Richard E. Ashcroft, et al. West Sussex, UK: John Wiley and Sons, 2007, pp. 117–125.

Sachedina, Abdulaziz, David Little, and John Kelsay. "Liberty of Conscience and Religion in the Qur'an." In *Human Rights and the Conflict of Cultures: Western and Islamic Perspectives on Religious Liberty.* Columbia: University of South Carolina Press, 1988.

Sa'īd, 'Alī Aḥmad. *Al-thābit wa al-mutaḥawwil: Baḥth fī al-atbā' wa al-ibda' inda al-'Arab.* Beirut: Dār al-'Awdā, 1974.

Sālim, Amīr, ed. *Ḥuqūq al-insān ma'ārik al-mustamirra bayna al-shimāl wa al-junūb.* Cairo: Markaz al-Dirāsat wa al-ma'lūmāt al-qānūnīya li- ḥuqūq al-insūn, 1994.

Schacht, Joseph. *An Introduction to Islamic Law.* Oxford: Clarendon Press, 1964.

Seligman, Adam B. *The Idea of Civil Society.* New York: Free Press, 1992.

———. *Modernity's Wager: Authority, the Self, and Transcendence.* Princeton, NJ: Princeton University Press, 2000.

Shabistarī, Muḥammad Mujtahid. *Naqdī bar qarā'at-i rasmī az dīn.* Tehran: Ṭarḥ-i Nov, 2002.

Shahrūr, Muḥammad. *al-Islām wa al-īmān: manẓūmat al-qiyam.* Damascus, Syria: al-Ahālī li al-Ṭibā'a wa al-Nashr wa al-Tawzī', 1996.

———. *al-Kitāb wa-al-qur'ān: qirā'a mu'āṣira*. Damascus, Syria: al-Ahālī li al-Ṭibā'a wa al-Nashr wa al-Tawzī', 1990.

———. *Dirāsāt islāmīya mu'āṣira fī al-dawla wa al-mujtama'* Damascus, Syria: al-Ahālīli al-Ṭibā'a wa al-Nashr wa al-Tawzī', 1994.

———. *Naḥwa uṣūl jadīda li al-fiqh al-Islāmī: fiqh al-mar'a : al-waṣīya, al-irth, al-qiwāma, al-ta'addudīya, al-libās*. Damascus, Syria: al-Ahālī li al-Ṭibā'a wa al-Nashr wa al-Tawzī', 2000.

Shelley, J. "Introduction." In Dorothee Solle, *Political Theology*. Philadelphia: Fortress Press, 1974.

Shīshānī, 'Abd al-Wahhāb 'Abd al-'Azīz al-. *Ḥuqūq al-insān wa ḥurriyatahu al-asāsīya fī al-niẓām al-islāmī wa al-niẓām al-mu'āṣira*. Saudi Arabia: Maṭ'ab al-Jam'īya al-'Ilmīya al-Malakīya, 1980.

Shriver, Donald W., Jr. "Foreword." In *Religion and Human Rights*. Ed. Carrie Gustafson and Peter Juviler. Armonk, NY: M.E. Sharpe, 1999.

Shweder, Richard A. "When Cultures Collide: Which Rights? Whose Tradition of Values? A Critique of the Global Anti-FGM Campaign." (forthcoming).

Shweder, Richard A., Martha Minow, and Hazel Markus. *Engaging Cultural Differences: The Multicultural Challenge in Liberal Democracies*. New York: Russell Sage Foundation, 2002.

Simon, Marcel. *Verus Israel: A Study of the Relations between Christians and Jews in the Roman Empire (AD 135–425)*. New York: Oxford University Press, 1986.

Soroush, Abdolkarim. *Reason, Freedom, and Democracy in Islam: Essential Writings of Abdolkarim Soroush*. Trans. and ed. M. Sadri and A. Sadri. New York: Oxford University Press, 2000.

Stackhouse, Max. *Creeds, Society, and Human Rights*. Grand Rapids, MI: Eerdmans, 1984.

———. "Human Rights and Public Theology: The Basic Validation of Human Rights." In *Religion and Human Rights: Competing Claims?* Ed. Carrie Gustafson and Peter Juviler. Armonk, NY: M. E. Sharpe, 1999.

Steiner, Henry J., Philip Alston, and Ryan Goodman. *International Human Rights in Context: Law Politics Morals*. New York: Oxford University Press, 2008.

Stout, Jeffrey. *Democracy and Tradition*. Princeton, NJ: Princeton University Press, 2004.

———. "What Is the Meaning of a Text?" *New Literary History: A Journal of Theory and Interpretation* 14, no. 1 (1982–1983), 1–12.

Suyūṭī, Jalāl al-Dīn 'Abd al-Raḥmān al-. *Al-durr al-manthūr fī tafsīr al-qur'ān bi al-ma'thūr* (Beirut: Dār al-Iḥyā' al-Turāth al-'Arabī, 2001.

Ṭabarī, Muḥammad b.Jarīr al-. *Jāmi' al-bayān fī tafsīr al-qur'ān*. 16 vols. Beirut: Dār al-Ma'ārif, 1972.

Ṭabarsī, Abū 'Alī al-Faḍl b. al-Ḥasan al-. *Majma' al-bayañ. fī tafsiř al-qur'ān*. 10 vols. Beirut: Dār Iḥyā' al-Turāth al-'Arabī, 1959.

Ṭabāṭabā'ī, Sayyid Muḥammad Ḥusayn al-. *Al-mīzān fī tafsīr al-qur'ān*. 20 vols. Beirut: Mu'assasa al-A'lamī, 1392/1972.

Tarmanīnī, 'Abd al-Salām al-. *Ḥuqūq al-insān fī naẓar al-sharī'a al-islāmīya*. Beirut: Dār al-Kitāb al-Jadīd, 1968.

Tierney, Brian. *The Idea of Natural Rights*. Grand Rapids, MI: Eedermans, 1997.

Tocqueville, Alexis de. *Democracy in America*. New York: Harper Collins, 1988.

Tuck, Richard. *Natural Rights Theories: Their Origin and Development*. New York: Cambridge University Press, 1979.

Ṭūsī, Muḥammad b. al-Ḥasan al-. *Al-tibyān fī tafsīr al-qur'ān*. Najaf: al-Maṭba'a al-'Ilmīya, 1957.

'Ūmlīl, 'Ali, *Fī shar'īya al-ikhtilāf*. Beirut: Dār al- Ṭībā'a, 1993.

United Nations. *Human Development Report 1995*. New York: UN Development Program, 1995.

'Uthmān, 'Alī 'Īsā. *Falsafat al-islām fī al-insān*. Beirut: Dār al-Adab, 1986.

'Uthmān, Muḥammad Raf'at. *Al-ḥuqūq wa al-wājibāt wa al-'alāqāt al-duwalīya fī al-fiqh al-islāmī*. Cairo: Dār al-Kitāb al-Jāmi'ī, 1983.

Wāfī, 'Alī 'Abd al-Waḥīd. *Ḥuqūq al-insān fī al-islām*. Cairo: Dār al-Nahḍa al-Miṣrīya, 1979.

Walzer, Michael. *Thick and Thin: Moral Argument at Home and Abroad*. Notre Dame, IN: University of Notre Dame Press, 1994.

Wolterstorff, Nicholas. "Why We Should Reject What Liberalism Tells Us about Speaking and Acting in Public for Religious Reasons." In *Religion and Contemporary Liberalism*. Ed. Paul J. Weithman. Notre Dame, IN: University of Notre Dame Press, 1997.

Yāsin al-Sayyid, et al, eds. *Al-Turāth wa tahddiyāt al-'aṣr fī al-waṭan al-'arabī: al-iṣāla wa al-mu'āṣara*. Beirut: Markaz al-Waḥdat al-'Arabīya, 1985.

Zabīdī, Muḥammad b. Muḥammad Murtaḍā al-. *Tāj al-'arūs min jawāhir al-qāmūs*. 29 vols. Kuwait: Maṭba'a Ḥukūmat al-Kuwayt, 1965–1997.

Zaydān, 'Abd al-Karīm. *Ḥuqūq al-afrād fī dār al-islām*. Beirut: Mu'assasa al-Risāla, 1988.

Index